Hollinghurst,
Camp and Closet

Hollinghurst, Camp and Closet

By

Serkan Ertin

Cambridge Scholars
Publishing

Hollinghurst, Camp and Closet

By Serkan Ertin

This book first published 2018

Taken from the dissertation *Perpetuation of the Gay Male Stereotype: A Study on Camping & Closeting the Gay Male Subculture in Hollinghurst's Fiction* by Serkan Ertin

Cambridge Scholars Publishing

Lady Stephenson Library, Newcastle upon Tyne, NE6 2PA, UK

British Library Cataloguing in Publication Data
A catalogue record for this book is available from the British Library

Copyright © 2018 by Serkan Ertin

All rights for this book reserved. No part of this book may be reproduced, stored in a retrieval system, or transmitted, in any form or by any means, electronic, mechanical, photocopying, recording or otherwise, without the prior permission of the copyright owner.

ISBN (10): 1-5275-0408-5
ISBN (13): 978-1-5275-0408-0

To love that dare not speak its name

TABLE OF CONTENTS

Acknowledgements ix

Chapter One 1
Introduction
    1.1 Scientia Homosexualis: Historical Background 4
    1.2 Genealogy and Deployment of Crimen Contra Naturam 15
    1.3 Heteronormativity and the Gay Male Subculture 17
    1.4 The Representation of the Gay Male in Anglo-American Fiction 21
    1.5 Camp and Closet in Gay Fiction 24
    1.6 Camp and Closet in Hollinghurst's Novels 30

Chapter Two 37
Camp
    2.1 Camp as Disenfranchisement: Homosexual / Heterosexual 42
    2.2 Camp as the Oversimplified Homosexual Stereotype 53
    2.3 Camp and Transgender Talk 76

Chapter Three 85
Closet
    3.1 Closeting the Gay Male: Modern Heterotopias 93
    3.2 Homo-phobia: Fear of the Same 123
    3.3 Closetedness in Polyandrous Happenings 142
    3.4 Closet and Occupation: Stereotyping the Gay Male Subject 147

Chapter Four 155
Conclusions

Bibliography 161

ACKNOWLEDGEMENTS

First and foremost I offer my sincerest gratitude to Assoc. Prof. Dr. Nurten Birlik, who supported me throughout my DPhil studies with her enthusiasm, great effort, patience and kindness, as well as her academic experience, which is invaluable to me. She always provided encouragement, good company, and good ideas. She is also the one who encouraged me to transform my dissertation into a book and get it published, and this book is the end product.

I would like to thank Prof. Dr. Nursel İçöz and Assoc. Prof. Dr. Nur Gökalp Akkerman for their kind assistance, positive attitude, and sound advice throughout the process of writing the dissertation which now has become a monograph.

I am also indebted to my colleagues, friends, and students for providing a stimulating and fun environment in which to learn and grow. I feel blessed to have met and to have you in my life.

I would like to include a special note of thanks to Barış Doruk Güngör, who has enriched my life since he broke into it and made my world a much better place to live in with his charm.

Lastly, and most importantly, I wish to thank my family for their unconditional love and support, even though from distance.

CHAPTER ONE

INTRODUCTION

Queer theory has been employed in the analyses of a great number of literary or non-literary texts in the last few decades. These analyses aspire to detach sexuality from the heterosexual gaze and re-establish its previously stolen fluid and indeterminate character by subverting heteronormative texts, movements, and genres. Queer studies are by their very nature contradictory and subversive; they lay bare the heteronormative oppression and its mechanisms behind the deployment of sexuality; and it is within these contradictory and fluid frames that "queer theory emerges to augment lesbian and gay studies of the recent past.... Similarly, theorizations of performativity and speech act theory, drag, camp, the carnivalesque, and masquerade point in the direction of a reconceptualisation of sexuality and identity" (Waugh 444). Indeed queer studies are anti-essentialist in nature which interpret and regard any and every cultural form, not only sexuality and identity but also gender, class, race, desire, norms, and so on, as discursive constructions which can be altered, subverted, repeated, or recreated. Likewise, queer fiction is supposed to question heteronormative ideology and subvert mainstream values by laying bare the power mechanisms which configure and maintain the perpetuation of stereotype identities.

This book intends to explore the terms camp and closet against the background of Alan Hollinghurst's fiction, since all four of his novels - *The Swimming-Pool Library* (1988), *The Folding Star* (1993), *The Spell* (1998), and *The Line of Beauty* (2004) – give a hearing to and reveal the gay male experience throughout the late-twentieth century, and falsely claim to employ a queer narrative style, which is supposed to be without any centralising or judgemental positions. Along with these terms, this book will also employ a genealogical approach to GLBT terminology in order to prepare the ground for a more comprehensive understanding of the gay male subjectivities in these novels.

Alan Hollinghurst's novels have been chosen for this monograph since in his novels he deals with gay issues, and in his interview in *The Guardian*, after receiving the Booker Prize, he underlines that he does employ gay narrative techniques. This is of great significance for the study: Some writers themselves are gay; some writers –gay or not- write on gay characters and themes; and some –gay or not- take up a subversive and queer approach in their works. Hollinghurst claims that he is all! In the interview, he explains his approach and authorial position: "From the start I've tried to write books which began from a presumption of the gayness of the narrative position. To write about gay life from a gay perspective unapologetically and as naturally as most novels are written from a heterosexual position" (2004). His remark shows that his approach aims to problematise dominant Western ideology, which is phallocentric, as his work is, allegedly, freed from the mainstream binaries. He does not intend to justify homosexual desire or apologise for being gay on behalf of all others. What he says he wants to achieve is the naturalisation of homosexuality just like that of heterosexuality. He does not mind being called a gay writer as long as people can see all the other vital issues going on in his novels. His work deals not only with sex but also with such significant issues as race, class distinction, history, culture, and so on. His so-called subversive attitude and playful approach could be seen in the epigraph to *The Line of Beauty*, which is an extract from *Alice's Adventures in Wonderland*:

> `What do you know about this business?' the King said to Alice.
> `Nothing,' said Alice.
> `Nothing *whatever*?' persisted the King.
> `Nothing whatever,' said Alice.
> `That's very important,' the King said, turning to the jury. They were just beginning to write this down on their slates, when the White Rabbit interrupted: `*Un*important, your Majesty means, of course,' he said in a very respectful tone, but frowning and making faces at him as he spoke.
> `*Un*important, of course, I meant,' the King hastily said, and went on to himself in an undertone, `important—unimportant—unimportant—important—' as if he were trying which word sounded best. (ii)

The extract, which is promising in terms of a queer approach, is a witty play on signifiers, and repeating the important/unimportant binary it blurs and erases the difference between the opposite poles. Thus, this short extract could be suggestive of the position and approach which the writer claims to possess. While exploring gay subjectivity and its fight for recognition in a non-gay world, Hollinghurst does not attempt to reach a single stable or universal truth: "I don't make moral judgments," Hollinghurst says, in the same interview, "I prefer to let things reverberate with their own ironies and implications" (2004).

However, a close look at Hollinghurst's fictional contexts reveals that while trying to naturalise homosexuality, he overemphasises the previously and traditionally shadowy leg of the binary, and as a result, in his work the non-gay world almost perishes, and the gender roles and the mainstream culture of the heteronormative discourse are kept alive and mimicked by gay individuals, ironically. Tim Edwards argues that the denial of the dominant culture and ideology culminates in a paradox, i.e., "in separating oneself from mainstream culture and asserting difference there is a tendency to assert sameness within that separate community whilst the opposite process operates in a politics of assimilation" (113-114). In Hollinghurst's novels, the assertion of sameness in the gay community not only re-establishes the campy gay male subculture but also closets them by depicting gay male characters as promiscuous and beastly figures that cannot distinguish between love and sex, often mistaking the latter for the former, and sooner or later come down with AIDS and die an *unnatural* death. As a gay writer he cannot escape the traps of the homophobic discourses within the dominant Western epistemology. In such a context, it would not be wrong to say that his authorial position falls short of meeting the expectations he verbally promises and that, in fact, he undermines with his novels what he claims in his interview given above.

The English context –under Thatcher's government—in which Hollinghurst wrote these novels has already changed and he is well aware of the fact: "When I began, there was an urgency about it which isn't there now. Things have changed so much over those 20 years; attitudes towards homosexuality are so different now." Gays' struggle for recognition or their own space and voice would be redundant in the contemporary English context. His approach to queer movement and his narrative style in these four novels sound repetitive and outdated considering the relatively emancipated space occupied by gay male subjectivities at present. Moreover, although he claims to maintain a queer and subversive approach in his work, he cannot go beyond producing mainstream gay novels which are inevitably in line with identity politics. This monograph is an attempt to analyse the first four novels of the writer since all four relate to one another in some way. Hollinghurst does not regard them as a tetralogy, yet admits the parallelism: "I do have a sense of having completed a quartet of books which, while not a tetralogy in any narrative sense, do cohere in a way" (2004). *The Stranger's Child*, his fifth novel published in June 2011, is not included in this study since it does not fit in the tetralogical frame –regarding camp and closet—of the first four novels. The first four novels are important for the gay canon because they point out an era in the historical deployment of homosexuality in England, which seems to be over by the twenty-first century. However, they fall short of the claim as queer texts since they are unable to reveal the ideological mechanisms at work in constructing subjectivity, gender and sexual identity, and the discursively-constructed nature of these epistemic categories.

1.1 Scientia Homosexualis: Historical Background

Although the [1]Stonewall riots, commencing in New York on 27 June 1969, are widely accepted and celebrated as the origin of gay liberation and queer movements in the Western world, the theoretical base feeding and enabling the awareness of gay subjectivity and the rejection of institutional oppression indeed dates back to the work of such significant theorists and philosophers as Freud, Althusser, Saussure, Lacan, and Foucault. Prior to these major thinkers, who led the way to the post-structuralist ambience which problematised the taken-for-grantedness of gender itself, there had already been quite a few abortive attempts to explore the reasons for and the nature of same-sex desire and subjectivity, though there had been none to seek the origin of heterosexual desire and identity. These attempts were extensions of modernity with its positivism, which had an unquestioning faith in knowledge and progress, and which took the innocence and naturalness of knowledge and language for granted. However, they could not see through the gender politics of the dominant discourse within which the meaning of *woman* is created "by excluding everything that is non-Woman, and vice versa for Man" and idealised templates are configured "for what is perfectly masculine or perfectly feminine by excluding whatever doesn't fit: the queer, the different, the mixed" (Wilchins 36). Their method was trapped in binarism and dichotomous thinking, and accordingly they could not see that in these binaries what one leg of the polarity refers to depends on the existence of the other, and thus, it cannot be reliable or stable.

Many theoreticians, even while trying to get out of the heteronormative system, failed to do so, since they could not go beyond binaries. In fact, they modelled themselves after the previously established models of

---

[1] The Stonewall riots, a series of spontaneous, violent demonstrations against a police raid that took place in the early morning hours of June 28, 1969 at the Stonewall Inn, New York, are frequently cited as the first instance in American history when gays and lesbians fought back against a government-sponsored system that persecuted homosexuals, and these reactions marked the start of the gay rights movement in the United States and around the world.

thinking. For instance, in the nineteenth century German lawyer and social commentator Karl Heinrich Ulrichs attempted to decriminalise homosexuality by defining and categorising it. He claimed that *urnings* and *uringins*, feminine male attracted to men and masculine female sexually drawn to women respectively, have the physical features of one sex and the instincts of the other (Sullivan 5). By relying on the mind / body binary, he ended up re-establishing the same old Cartesian dualism and excluded many other undefined minorities like masculine gays or feminine lesbians. Hirschfeld attempted to develop Karl Ulrich's model and claimed that homosexuality was "an intermediate condition, a 'third sex' that combined physiological aspects of both masculinity and femininity" (qtd. in Jagose 23). These attempts were, indeed, the results of homophile movements in the nineteenth century, which tried to increase tolerance for homosexuality and even rouse pity and sympathy for homosexuals, in order to decriminalise homosexuality. Homophile movements, thus, differ highly from gay liberation movements, which were mass movements aware of their presence as a socio-political minority imprisoned in a dominant heteronormative discourse. Whereas the former wanted to present an acceptable image of the homosexual –based on the principle of similarity— within the mainstream, the latter antagonised and shocked the society highlighting their difference, which is very similar to what Hollinghurst does in his novels. Edward Carpenter, British socialist pioneer of homosexual freedom and women's rights who had an enormous impact on the cultural and political life of the late nineteenth and early twentieth centuries, stated that homosexuals were superior to heterosexuals (qtd. in Sullivan 12). In this way, while trying to naturalise homosexuality, he reversed the heteronormative binary Heterosexual \ Homosexual and created a new one: Homosexual \ Heterosexual. These binary Western accounts fail to avoid being prescriptive and reductive, and none of them is convincing for Claude J. Summers, who states that "many individuals repeatedly participate in a wide range of homoerotic behaviour without defining themselves as homosexual" (13). The signifier 'same-sex sex', therefore, does not necessarily refer to the signified 'homosexuality'. Moreover, the binary relation of the 'homosexual' to the 'heterosexual' is not a real dichotomy; it is just one of the numerous reifications of Western thought. Peter Barry states that apparently elemental classes like heterosexual and homosexual do not refer to fixed essences at all; they are just like Saussurean signifiers flying in a structure of differences without fixed referents (145). However, being an end product of power relations and mainstream discourses on sexuality, the reified relation between 'heterosexuality' and 'homosexuality' persistently centralises and normalises the former, whereas it marginalises and stigmatises the latter as the 'other'.

The banishment and stigmatisation of the homosexual, though still a common phenomenon in the twenty-first century, is not a universal truth whose existence dates back to the earliest existence of mankind on earth. Sexuality, disregarding the heterosexual / homosexual binary, has been moulded and reconfigured in different forms by dominant ideologies and discourses in the course of history, which have employed simplistic binaries to create totalising hierarchies. Within the frames of totalising ideologies and discourses, many theorists and philosophers since Plato attempted to account for the construction of gender and sexuality; however, they failed in their attempts as they could not move beyond binarism. They were still moving on a Platonic discursive ground as they were looking for a single transcendental truth. None of these philosophers and thinkers accused these frames or grand narratives of being totalistic before Derrida, for whom all these frames were just myths to be demystified. Derrida's deconstructing Western thought led the way to the deconstruction of any and every grand narrative. Wilchins reveals how the former process paved the way for the latter: "If Derrida had deconstructed thought, it fell to another French philosopher, Michel Foucault, to deconstruct the thinker" (47). Foucault expanded the margins of deconstruction since it was him who critiqued the universalising and totalising aspect of Western thought creating Certainty, Knowledge, and Truth, and his groundbreaking work *History of Sexuality* was the first extensive analysis of the production, configuration, and deployment of sexuality. History and a diachronic approach to history were of great significance to Foucault in that they would reveal the constructed and variable nature of sexuality. Drawing on history, Foucault demystifies and deconstructs sexuality, by contrasting the practices in his own society with those in Ancient Greece and Rome. In Ancient Greece, for instance, there were not any rules or norms restricting sexuality. They never regarded same-sex sex as unacceptable and "never imagined that sexual pleasure was in itself an evil or that it could be counted among the natural stigmata of a transgression" (Foucault, *Sexuality* 2: 97). The space of sexuality, for Foucault, is a historically constructed apparatus; an elaborate system of morals, discourses, and procedures created in order to control and lead sexual practices to the desired political ends. Through the apparatus, Foucault argues, sexuality "was driven out of hiding and constrained to lead a discursive existence. From the singular imperialism that compels everyone to transform their sexuality into a perpetual discourse, to the manifold mechanisms which, in the areas of economy, pedagogy, medicine, and justice, incite, extract, distribute, and institutionalize the sexual discourse, an immense verbosity is what our civilization has required and organized" (1: 33). Science is one of the major sources of heteronormative discourses which deploy and control sexuality. Accordingly, science is not always reliable. Chrys Ingraham underlines the fact that it was science in the nineteenth century that claimed women should not be exposed to college education lest it would harm their reproductive organs (74). Science disregards relativity since there must be only one truth applicable in any context. Foucault exemplifies the medical discourses which stigmatise homosexuality by mentioning the science of perversion and the program of eugenics during the second half of the nineteenth century, culminating in the theory of degenerescence, which

> explained how a heredity that was burdened with various maladies (it made little difference whether these were organic, functional, or psychical) ended by producing a sexual pervert (look into the genealogy of an exhibitionist or a homosexual: you will find a hemiplegic ancestor, a phthisic parent, or an uncle afflicted with senile dementia); but it went on to explain how a sexual perversion resulted in the depletion of one's line of descent -rickets in the children, the sterility of future generations. The series composed of perversion-heredity-degenerescence formed the solid nucleus of the new technologies of sex. (*Sexuality* 1: 118)

These technologies attempt to reify the so-called correlation, or rather a cause-effect relationship, between perversion and other *illnesses*, and normalise heterosexuality. However, trying to set norms on sexualities is not always possible. In the case of intersexuality, for example, the individuals having both male and female sexual characteristics and organs are revered in some societies because they are able to inseminate and give birth, though not always in a literal sense. In many other cultures, however, the intersexual individual is regarded as a deformity and is forced to undergo surgery; s/he must choose male or female genitals. In patriarchal societies privileging masculinity, parents tend to prefer male genitalia. This extreme sense of discrimination stems from a misrecognition; the belief that the male is completely different from, even opposite and superior to, the female. According to Laqueur, since the first Greek anatomists, there had been one sex, the male. The female body was regarded as an inferior version "lacking in some vital essence that caused it to be smaller, more delicate, and come with an *inny* instead of an *outty*" (qtd. in Wilchins 90). Greeks, Foucault argues, believed that the desire for a boy or a girl was subject to the single condition that the motive was noble. However, he adds;

> they also thought that this desire called for a particular mode of behavior when it made a place for itself in a relationship between two male individuals. The Greeks could not imagine that a man might need a different nature—an 'other' nature—in order to love a man; but they were inclined to think that the pleasures one enjoyed in such a relationship ought to be given an ethical form different from the one that was required when it came to loving a woman. In this sort of relation, the pleasures did not reveal an alien nature in the person who experienced them; but their use demanded a special stylistics. (*Sexuality* 2: 192)

Misogynous and dualistic as this claim is, it reveals the fact that Ancient Greeks defined sexuality on the principle of similarity, not difference. Accordingly, for Foucault, human body is not sexed or gendered before it takes its place within a discourse. Only after that and through its positionality among power relations can the body have a meaning. Sexuality is a "historically specific organization of power, discourse, bodies, and affectivity. As such, sexuality is understood by Foucault to produce 'sex' as an artificial concept which effectively extends and disguises the power relations responsible for its genesis" (qtd. in Butler, *Gender* 117). He denaturalises the heterosexual / homosexual binary by contextualising and historicising it. In this way, he reveals the fact that since sexuality is discursively constructed and it is history-specific and culture-specific, there cannot be a fully reliable account of it. Thus, terms such as invert, faggot, dyke, sodomite, and so on, are cultural artefacts "tied to ways of understanding and of being that are specific to a particular cultural milieu" (Sullivan 2). This is the reason why Foucault constantly compares the modern cultural milieu to the others while denaturalising the dogma of sexuality and desire. For instance, in his diachronic analysis of desire, he refers to the Ancient Greeks again and states that they did not categorise desire into two; one for women and the other for men. They were not bisexuals, either, since they did not have the modern dualistic way of thinking. For them:

> what made it possible to desire a man or a woman was simply the appetite that nature had implanted in man's heart for 'beautiful' human beings, whatever their sex might be. True, one finds in Pausanias' speech a theory of two loves, the second of which—Urania, the heavenly love—is directed exclusively to boys. But the distinction that is made is not between a heterosexual love and a homosexual love; Pausanias draws the dividing line between 'the love which the baser sort of men feel'—its object is both women and boys, it only looks to the act itself (to diaprattesthai)—and the more ancient, nobler, and more reasonable love that is drawn to what has

the most vigor and intelligence, which obviously can only mean the male sex. (*Sexuality* 2: 188-189)

This does not mean they avoided categorising or naming desire, but they categorised desire on the basis of the faculties of the brain rather than the biological givens, which resulted in the conclusion that the desire for boys was more heavenly, as in Shakespeare's sonnets, than the one for women, which was seen as a procreative act and thus more nature-al, i.e., bestial.

The term 'homosexuality' is quite a recent phenomenon. The relation of the virile man to the effeminate one in Ancient Greece does not coincide with the modern hetero / homo binary opposition nor with the active / passive homosexual binarism. In the former, Foucault states, one's attitude to pleasures determined his femininity or masculinity. Provided that a man was able to control his pleasures and was active during the sexual intercourse, he was not charged with effeminacy; however, a man who became a slave to his desires was considered, disregarding his sexual object of desire, feminine (*Sexuality* 2: 85). Contemporary traditional signs of effeminacy, also signs of camp, such as too much preoccupation with looks, refusal to engage in the relatively rough activities like sports, fancy for perfumes and adornments, interest in visual arts, graceful use of gestures and so on, were not necessarily associated with men in Ancient Greece who would be called effeminate or homosexual in the nineteenth century and afterwards. Identifying individuals based on their object of desire is a recent phenomenon invented by dominant heteronormative discourses. Eve Kosofsky Sedgwick argues that it is "a rather amazing fact that, of the very many dimensions along which the genital activity of one person can be differentiated from that of another... precisely one, the gender of object choice, emerged from the turn of the century, and has remained, as *the* dimension denoted by the now ubiquitous category of 'sexual orientation'" (8).

Tracing the reasons for the sharp discrepancy between the past and his own time on a diachronic level, Foucault, in the first volume of *History of Sexuality*, puts the blame on the seventeenth century, the beginning of an age of repression by bourgeois discourses, in which censorship and silence controlled the free circulation of sex at the level of language. Ironically, for the last three centuries there has been a discursive explosion, and too many allusions and metaphors have been codified. Foucault's "objective is to analyse a certain form of knowledge regarding sex, not in terms of repression or law, but in terms of power" (*Sexuality* 1: 92). Power, which may be taken as the origin of closet, in his view, is not a concrete or visible institution; it is just a name attributed to complex strategies in a particular society. There has always been resistance to power, for sure, but it has developed inside the discourse power has created, since one is always inside power and there is no escaping it. As for the relation between camp and closet, accordingly, it would not be wrong to state that "[t]he closet has given us camp" (Case 189). Power is omnipresent, produced from one moment to the next, at every point. It is everywhere and it actually comes from below; there is no binary opposition between the ruler and the ruled at the root of power relations (*Sexuality* 2: 94). In this way, Foucault located the long-mistaken space of power and determined the way to fight it back.

Same-sex sexual activities, disregarding the extent to which they were accepted or rejected, have been documented in all primitive or civilised societies. Until the late nineteenth century, when Western civilisation condemned and stigmatised it, there was no categorical identification to refer to 'the class' of men having same-sex sex acts. Richardson & Seidman acknowledge that same-sex feelings, desires, or sexual acts may have always existed, but they deny the existence of 'homosexuals', since it would be an anachronistic use of the term for individuals (2). The term 'heterosexuality' actually appeared after the term 'homosexuality' was coined first. Thus, the heterosexual was able to define himself only against the homosexual, employing the homosexual as the suppressed leg of the binary. In such a context, it might be interesting to give a hearing to Jagose, who summarises the historical background and deployment of sexual categories in a rather humorous manner:

> First there was Sappho (the good old days). Then there was the acceptable homoeroticism of classical Greece, the excesses of Rome. Then, casually to skip two millennia, there was Oscar Wilde, sodomy, blackmail and imprisonment, Forster, Sackville-West, Radclyffe Hall, inversion, censorship; then pansies, butch and femme, poofs, queens, fag hags, more censorship and blackmail, and Orton. Then there was Stonewall (1969) and we all became gay. (75-76)

This short diachronic explanation mocks the configuration of sexual identities in the course of time based on one's sexual object of desire. It contrasts the freedom in Ancient Greece where there were no sexual categories defining the participants of same-sex sex acts to the Victorian Era when gay-banishing broke out and the clear-cut distinction between the heterosexual and the homosexual was created. Eve K. Sedgwick, being against defining sexual identity based on one's sexual object choice, mocks the formation of these two terms: "The word 'homosexuality' wasn't coined until 1869 — so everyone before then was heterosexual" (52). The term 'homosexuality' was coined in 1869 in Germany and preceded the invention of its so-called binary pole 'heterosexuality' by almost eleven years. However, the term, which originally intended to decriminalise and normalise homosexuality, turned out to be a medical and legal prescriptive term. This is the reason why critics like Sedgwick counterstrike the fictitious 'nature' and reified essentialism of the terms which tend to categorise sexual identities. Anti-essentialism regarding sexual identity is taken further by Judith Butler, too. Butler argues that terms like homosexual and heterosexual function as instruments of regulatory regimes. As a genealogical critic rereading Foucault, she does not look for the origins of gender or a genuine sexual identity. Instead, she states that "genealogy investigates the political stakes in designating as an *origin* and *cause* those identity categories that are in fact the *effects* of institutions, practices, discourses with multiple and diffuse points of origin. The task of this inquiry is to center on—and decenter—such defining institutions: phallogocentrism and compulsory heterosexuality" (*Gender* xxx). Even the discourse of homosexuality, as long as it is produced within the phallogocentric heteronormative discourse, cannot break away from the oppressive regimes. In other words, the concept and term of homosexuality is itself inevitably a tool employed by homophobic discourses.

In England, during the pretentious Victorian Era, where the 'other' Victorians were marginalised to the very end, homosexuality began to define "not simply what one does but who one is" (Summers 14). The marginal Victorian figures, the most famous of whom was Oscar Wilde, started to live as homosexuals, since homosexuality had transformed into an identity and "for the first time it was possible to be a homosexual" (Jagose 22). The radical change in the conception of homosexuality marked its transition from *doing* to *being*, which paved the way for the emergence of a distinct gay male subculture and identity seen in Hollinghurst's fiction. For Foucault, homosexuality as an identity "appeared as one of the forms of sexuality when it was transposed from the practice of sodomy onto a kind of interior androgyny, a hermaphrodism of the soul. The sodomite had been a temporary aberration; the homosexual was now a species" (*Sexuality* 1: 43). In terms of GLBT struggles for more rights or equality, this might imply recognition to some extent; however, this transition did not mean liberation in practice for the homosexual whose being was eventually recognised. Halperin argues that Foucault draws on homosexuality just in order to gain insight into power relations and their influence on the deployment of sexuality and that he did not regard homosexuality "as a newly liberated species of sexual being but as a strategically situated marginal position from which it might be possible to glimpse and to devise new ways of relating to oneself and to others" (68). In other words, it was not Foucault's main target to differentiate homosexual identity from same-sex sex acts, but his work yielded invaluable results and prepared the ground for his followers. His work led GLBT activists to form a counter-discourse to fight heteronormativity:

> There is no question that the appearance in nineteenth-century psychiatry, jurisprudence, and literature of a whole series of discourses on the species and subspecies of homosexuality, inversion, pederasty, and "psychic hermaphrodism" made possible a strong advance of social controls into this area of "perversity"; but it also made possible the formation of a "reverse" discourse: homosexuality began to speak in its own behalf, to demand that its legitimacy or "naturality" be acknowledged, often in the same vocabulary, using the same categories by which it was medically disqualified. (*Sexuality* 1: 101)

This counter-discourse, whose counterpart in gay liberation movements is camp, used the same weapons as the heteronormative discourses to fight homophobia, an agent and effect of closet, which is in accordance with Foucault's argument that discourses have their counter-discourses within their own domain. There is no discourse of power out there and another one opposite it; they are, instead, elements of power relations.

In the mid-twentieth century U.S, the American sexologist Alfred Kinsey amazed his readers when he published his famous reports demonstrating how common homosexuality was among Americans (Richardson and Seidman 1). His reports, starting with the publication of *Sexual Behavior in the Human Male* (1948) and followed by *Sexual Behavior in the Human Female* (1953), carried the discussions regarding homosexuality to a more radical ground and pushed it out of the closet. His publications, which led to a storm of controversy, became bestsellers catapulting Kinsey to an instant stardom and are still regarded by many as an enabler of the sexual revolution of the 1960s. The increasing visibility of homosexual subjectivity, however, did not lead to a higher recognition for the homosexual individual. On the contrary, in many Anglo-American and European nations, homosexuals were considered to be inverts until the mid-twentieth century and "the idea was well established that the homosexual was an abnormal or deviant and dangerous type of person" (Richardson and Seidman 1). In the 1950s homosexuals faced a severe form of discrimination, harassment, and repression. Furthermore, homosexuality was criminalised, psychologised, and psychiatrised institutionally. Particularly judicial formulations, Sedgwick states, codified "an excruciating system of double binds, systematically oppressing gay people, identities, and acts by undermining through contradictory constraints on discourse the grounds of their very being" (70).

In addition to legal discourses, religious doctrines closeted homosexuals, too. Dawne Moon argues that religions are inherently neither pro-gay nor anti-gay, yet "many religious thinkers assume that homosexuality is a sign of humanity's fall, that human beings were created heterosexual and that homosexuality is a part of society's degeneration" (314). However, sexualities and even same-sex sexual acts have received different treatments and reactions in different historical periods and different cultures. Therefore, legal or religious formulations have been incoherent and contradictory, raising the recognition of homosexuals on one hand, i.e., allowing them to camp, and denying their right to exist on the other, i.e., closeting them. Very suitably, Jagose states that "modern knowledges about the categories of sexual identification are far from coherent" (19).

After the 1950s, especially in the following two decades, gay individuals began to define and identify themselves as social and political entities to fight back the closet. They realised that they had to unite around a common purpose and, thus, began establishing activist liberation organisations to seek social and legal reforms and equality. Mattachine Society, for example, the earliest homophile organization in the United States, emphasised the fact that homosexuals did constitute a population unaware of its status as a social minority imprisoned within the heteronormative system and aimed to "foster a collective identity among homosexuals who, recognising the institutional and hegemonic investments in their continued marginalisation, might consequently be energised and enabled to fight against their oppression" (Jagose 25). In such a context, the initial objective was to achieve public acceptance of homosexuality. Nonetheless, especially in the 1960s, these movements turned out to be more revolutionary and aggressive. Especially after the Stonewall riots, which were actually "modelled on the black civil rights struggle, the anti-war movement of the day, and the new wave of feminism," gay liberation movements challenged the stereotypical ideas about homosexuality and foregrounded their shared social and cultural experience, instead of their identification based merely on their sexual activities (Summers 16). This was a sign of the transition from homosexuality to gay identities, which would be hard to destroy once established. In this period, the influence of religion on sexuality lost its earlier power, and it was replaced by medical, literary, psychological, legal, and scientific discourses. There was a sense of dissatisfaction with the earlier quietist methods and soon the activists began "to critique the structures and values of heterosexual dominance. Instead of representing themselves as being just like heterosexuals except in their sexual object choice, gay liberationists… challenged conventional knowledge about such matters as gendered behaviour" (Jagose 31). The discontent with the previous pacifistic policies paved the way for the increasing radical liberation movements. Adam states that, in addition to the factors mentioned above, increasing divorce, extra-marital births, children raised by a lone parent, and infertile women helped decentre heterosexual institutions. Marriage as an institutionalised practice lost its privileged status and the heterosexual couple married with children was no longer considered "the centre-ground of western societies and... the basic unit in society" (34). Today even gay marriage, once a dream, is a controversial topic and many activists are against the long waited and demanded right. For them, marriage is a product of heteronormativity and it could, on the one hand, sound like more freedom and recognition for gay couples, yet it is the reestablishment of heteronormativity on the other hand. There are different arguments about gay marriages; for some, gay marriage is a way of normalisation, it dismantles gender norms, and it is more equal, whereas for others marriage bond is less important in the twenty-first century, it is always-already transforming and not fixed. The institution itself is very complex and the future regarding same-sex marriage may be analysed referring to the term 'precarity', literally meaning 'precariousness', but now referring to existence without predictability, certainty, or security, which does bind the disenfranchised and criminalised GLBT individuals. In the past, Foucault says, precarity referred to the fleeting character in a man's erotic relationship with an adolescent, i.e., the beloved losing his charm and the lover turning away from the beloved. Foucault mentions this fear and makes some suggestions:

> these relations needed to rid themselves of their precariousness: a precariousness that was due to the inconstancy of the partners, and that was a consequence of the boy's growing older and thereby losing his charm; but it was also a precept, since it was not good to love a boy who was past a certain age, just as it was not good for him to allow himself to be loved. This precariousness could be avoided only if, in the fervor of love, philia—friendship—already began to develop: philia, i.e., an affinity of character and mode of life, a sharing of thoughts and existence, mutual benevolence. (*Sexuality* 2: 201)

It is obvious that while precarity in Ancient times meant faithlessness or volatility in same-sex relationships, in contemporary cultures it refers to the external threats and agents of power who police and criminalise GLBT individuals, finally ending up becoming criminals themselves.

1.2 Genealogy and Deployment of Crimen Contra Naturam

It was Henry VIII who accepted sodomy as a civil offence in 1533. The law was confirmed by Elizabeth I. At first the term 'buggery' was not defined. Later jurists attempted to define it and in 1642 it was defined as anal penetration of a man or a woman by a man. Regarding sexual acts between animals and men, only penetration by a man was considered sodomy, whereas between animals and women any sexual act was regarded as sodomy (Cocks 32). In the nineteenth-century Britain, sodomy referred not only to anal sex but also to all sexual practices without a procreative aim. Sullivan underlines the fact that the laws prohibiting *crimen contra naturam* were only against sexual acts; not against sexual identities. However, sodomy had already been gendered, due to a law in 1781. In order to convict someone of sodomy, penetration and emission of seed had to be proved (3). This law meant that sodomy was a crime attributed only to the male. There are still some countries in the world which criminalise and persecute male homosexuality, while totally ignoring the female one: "We have more words that insultingly describe men who are feminine for the same reason that we fear and hate a man in a dress more than a woman in a suit: His transgression is more of an affront to the politics of gender and therefore more threatening" (Wilchins 38). This misconception is a direct consequence of the patriarchal male \ female binary, which praises masculinity in a woman while condemning femininity in a man. That is why all the interviewees in Wilchins's experiment accepted their homosexuality but denied being bottoms in same-sex sexual intercourse.

In the 1950s homosexuality, regarded as the opposite of heterosexuality, was still seen as a deviation to be treated. Many organisations were trying to decriminalise homosexuality in the world and their work bore fruit with the emergence of liberation groups. However, Sullivan critiques their arguments and policies which were based on the principle of sameness as the objective of these groups "was (and still is) to be accepted into, and to become one with, mainstream culture" (23). In other words, they were trying to prove that homosexuals were just like other people and they never posed a threat to the heteronormative society, an argument which depoliticised the movements.

In the 60s, gay liberation movements came up with the word 'gay', the nineteenth century slang for immoral women, and redeployed it. Though the word 'gay' originally referred both to male and female homosexual individuals, later on it turned out to signify only the male, and the female gay employed the term 'lesbian'. Finally in the 1980s, they started forming gay and lesbian communities, clubs, and institutions. Ambiguity fascinated people in this era and the trend was to reject traditional forms of categorisation. Transsexuals and transgendered individuals blurred the rigid binaries like male / female or heterosexual / homosexual (Sullivan 99). In this process, the term 'homosexual', which came into circulation in the late Victorian period, was phased out since this term was originally associated with and created by pathologising medical and scientific discourses. It was insufficient because it just referred to the sexual-acts of its members and excluded their existences as individuals with subjectivity and agency. 'Gay' and 'Lesbian', popular terms in the 1960s and 1970s, were also challenged by such terms as 'bisexual, transsexual, transgender, and queer'. Joseph Bristow argues that "these labels emerge from dynamic mid- and late twentieth-century struggles to emancipate anti-normative sexual desires and gender identities from legal, medical and moral oppression" (217). In this way plurality and variety of sexual identities would be established in the dominant discourse, and thus, recognised. In addition to liberating anti-normative sexual desires from various tools of oppression, the use and deployment of such terms as 'homosexual, gay, lesbian, bisexual, transsexual, transgender, and queer' also highlight the change in how the mainstream culture saw the stigmatised individuals and how these individuals defined themselves.

Non-heterosexual subjectivity is characterised by plurality and multiplicity, as in the examples given above. 'Queer' is quite a recent term to signify this multiple conceptualisation of reality; however, it is sometimes incorrectly used instead of gay or lesbian. In fact the scope of the term 'queer' is not limited to homosexuality; it marks "a flexible space for the expression of all aspects of non- (anti- , contra-) straight cultural production and reception" (Doty 73). Queer is "by definition *whatever is at odds with the normal, the legitimate, the dominant. There is nothing in particular to which it necessarily refers*" (Halperin 62). During the last decades of the twentieth century, gay and lesbian studies emerged as an academic field, yet some activists and thinkers started to criticise their exclusionary politics. In 1990 Queer Nation arose from the campaigning of the AIDS Coalition to Unleash Power and they reclaimed the word 'queer', which had previously been used to insult and discriminate homosexuals: "They eagerly resignified the meaning of queerness in the face of what they saw as an inert lesbian and gay politics that commonly refused to admit anyone into its ranks who did not subscribe to an inflexible homosexual politics of identity" (Bristow 219). They accused GLBT studies and politics of being in Western identity politics and rejected their exclusive approaches. Queer Nation, instead, aimed to embrace all stigmatised and marginalised individuals who did not conform to the requirements of heteronormative ideologies. Posing a threat to all 'normalising' regimes, 'queer' is definitely "not the Other of straight; in fact, its deconstructive position outside the hetero/homosexual binary makes its relationship to concepts like straight and gay oblique" (Barnard 11). Queer is a slippery term and it is ungendered. It means and covers a lot more than 'homosexual' or 'gay' do; cross-dressing, drag queens, hermaphrodites, and even gender-corrective surgeries are all among the numerous signifiers of the 'Queer'. Jagose claims that the definitional indeterminacy and ambiguity of queer is its main characteristic as queer studies analyse mismatches between sex, gender and desire (3). Richardson and Seidman highlight the factors moulding sexual identities, such as gender, class, race, and nationality; they argue that there is no universal experience of being gay, and therefore, "queer approaches to identity emphasize the fluid, performative character of identities" (5).

Jagose agrees that a number of dynamics configure and pattern queer identity and an all-inclusive approach is essential to fight back the heterosexist oppression. For her, it is essential to achieve "the unity of all oppressed people –that is, there can be no freedom for gays in a society which enslaves others through male supremacy, racism and economic exploitation" (34). Some liberation movements fail since they represent only one site of oppression, such as issues concerning white gays and lesbians; therefore, these different forms of exploitation must be handled together. These movements, whose traces abound in Hollinghurst's novels, tend to regard their experience as singular, and thus "universalize their limited understanding by colonizing other subjects" (Barnard 3). Such exclusive attempts in the past have always been bound to fail.

1.3 Heteronormativity and the Gay Male Subculture

As this study focuses on how Hollinghurst fictionalises camp and closet in his novels against the background of queer theory, a brief genealogical look at the theory might prepare the ground for a thorough analysis of these terms in his novels. Queer theory adopted and, in fact, was based on the key points Foucault made in his *History of Sexuality*. Particularly his analysis of the relation of power to the formation and emergence of homosexual identity led to queer thought. Donald Morton states that "the return of the queer has to be understood as the result, in the domain of sexuality, of the (post)modern encounter with –and rejection of- Enlightenment views concerning the role of the conceptual, rational, systematic, structural, normative, progressive, liberatory, revolutionary, and so forth, in social change" (qtd. in Jagose 77). It was a reaction to clear-cut categories imposed by the Enlightenment and Western metaphysics. It was a continuation, of course, of gay liberation movements, yet a clear break with them. Queer theory focuses on heteronormativity, i.e., the institutionalised heterosexual hegemony, and questions the validity of all categories, even those of 'man' and 'woman', which have always been taken for granted, although they are reified and constructed. Just as one is not born a woman, but, rather, becomes one, in Simone de Beauvoir's famous quote, so does a gay man; one is not born 'a gay man' but becomes one.

Unlike gay liberation movements which sought equality and reforms, queer politics "aims to be transgressive of social norms, of heteronormativity. It is not about seeking social inclusion, but nor does it want to remain on the margins" (Richardson and Seidman 8). What it intends to achieve is decentralisation of heterosexuality and disruption of the principle of difference and, in this way, to reveal the artificial division between heterosexual and homosexual. Queer theory does not want to establish primary signifiers or organising principles, but its goal, as Turner summarises, is "to investigate the historical circumstances by which 'sexuality' —especially the charge of 'homosexuality'– can automatically render subjects the somewhat pitiable victims of a determinism that 'heterosexual' subjects supposedly remain free of" (38). Queer theory intends to denaturalise and deconstruct gender in such a way that it will not end up in another reconstruction of the heterosexist normative hegemony. This is why it intentionally avoids any specific definitions or becoming a fixed normative discipline.

Regarding the intentions and elements of queer politics, it is obvious that Hollinghurst deliberately sacrifices political aims for the sake of popularity. He employs heteronormative definitions and attributes in his representation of the gay male experience and he creates a new gay mainstream culture, which contradicts the goals of queer theory. "Traditional gay culture is neither necessarily produced by nor addressed to gay people: it is high straight culture or showbiz, and always an identification with the 'feminine'" (Finch 143). The subculture he represents is, in fact, a discursive product of heteronormativity which partly covers the white middle-class and male gay community. In other words, his work is in accordance with the mainstream identity politics which reifies and regards the gay male as a distinct identity.

With references to poststructuralist thinkers like Foucault, Derrida, and Lacan, Judith Butler studied the production and deployment of sexualities and gender in Western epistemology. Butler's "mainly philosophical exploration frequently integrated Foucauldian insights into her analysis of the ways in which modern culture tended to use sexual categories as if they were natural, rather than socially constructed" (Bristow 232). Integrating Foucault's study on power relations and sexuality into her own work, she states that sex is always-already normative and all gender is, in fact, nothing but drag, which suggests "imitation is at the heart of the *heterosexual* project and its gender binarisms, that drag is not a secondary imitation that presupposes a prior and original gender, but that hegemonic heterosexuality is itself a constant and repeated effort to imitate its own idealizations" (*Bodies* 125). For her, drag cannot be an imitation since there is no original man or woman to imitate. She claims that gender is performative, a metaphorical sort of theatrical performance, and her conceptualisation of performativity cannot be grasped disregarding the process of iterability, and a regularised and constrained repetition of norms. She intends to denaturalise heterosexuality by way of illustrating a displaced repetition –like womanliness reperformed on a male body— of its performance. However, the repetition she mentions "is not performed *by* a subject; this repetition is what enables a subject and constitutes the temporal condition for the subject. This iterability implies that 'performance' is not a singular 'act' or event, but a ritualized production" (*Bodies* 95). Jagose sees eye to eye with Butler on the constitution of the subject by performativity. For her, the subject does not deliberately assume; it is not something the subject does, but "a process through which that subject is constituted" (87). By enabling access into the formation of sexuality and gender, Butler denaturalises and lays bare the working mechanisms of heteronormative frameworks and compulsory heterosexuality.

For theorists of queer studies it is essential "to investigate the historical and cultural underpinnings of nouns such as 'woman,' 'homosexual,' 'gay,' and 'lesbian' in order to examine what sorts of generalizations and assumptions enable the referential functions, and determine the meanings, of those terms" (Turner 33). These investigations drained the social, cultural, and historical meanings attributed to the so-called categories and this new perspective has led the way to the conceptualisation of sexual identities as:

> a constant switching among a range of different roles and positions, drawn from a kind of limitless data bank of potentialities. Further, what is called into question here is the distinction between the naturally-given, normative 'self' of heterosexuality and the rejected 'Other' of homosexuality. The 'Other', in these formulations, is as much something within us as beyond us, and 'self' and 'Other' are always *implicated* in each other.... As basic

> psychology shows, what is identified as the external 'Other' is usually part of the self which is rejected and hence projected outwards. (Barry 145)

This notion, reconciliating self and Other, indicates one of the ways postmodernism approaches sexual identities; "identity as a series of masks, roles, and potentialities, a kind of amalgam of everything which is provisional, contingent, and improvisatory" (Barry 146). This approach is anti-essentialist as it focuses on the fluidity of identities, highlights the infinite nature of potentialities, and rejects any fixed or stale sexual identity. Moreover, it is claimed that homosexuality is stigmatised as it is the outward projection of heterosexuality. To put it differently, it is not possible to draw a clear-cut boundary between the two terms since both are discursively produced and there is no essential distinction at all.

In the heteronormative project of subordination, a drag, i.e., a man dressed as a woman, will always be a man, since the second term will always lack the so-called reality. Butler reveals the constructed nature of sexuality and denaturalises its apparent naturalness, by way of which she undermines and lays bare the imposed obligatory heterosexuality. What she tries to achieve is quite similar to what Foucault does; to indicate that sexuality and gender are discursive products constructed by cultures and ideologies. Developing her account of gender performativity, she draws on Foucault's work on subjectivity and sexuality, Simone de Beauvoir's account of gender as an acquired set of attributes and actions, Joan Rivière's notion of womanliness as masquerade, J. L. Austin's speech-act theory, and Derrida's deconstruction of speech-act theory. In deconstructing acquired gender stereotypes, however, Butler does not intend to subvert binaries lest it would culminate in new hierarchies: "Sexual practice has the power to destabilize gender" and thus, one is a man or a woman as long as one functions within the dominant heteronormative system, and questioning the system might end up in loss of place and identity (Butler, *Gender* xi). For Butler, gender is neither true nor false. The reason why she celebrates drag is that drag subverts the notion of a true and stable sexual identity. Drag is a female outside but has a male body inside; without woman's dress, drag is male outside but this time feminine inside. By giving this male drag example Butler aims to indicate that there is no nature; what we have, instead, is mere naturalisation or denaturalisation of things originally unnatural.

Although it has been nurtured and advocated by great philosophers and critics, queer theory has provoked quite a few reactions and criticisms, too. One of the defamations was the allegation that queer theory represents the values, desires, and expectations of particular people and groups, ignoring or silencing those of others. Accordingly, some theorists accused it of "repeating the same sort of exclusionary logic that is often associated with the Homophile Movement, with liberationist politics, and with second wave feminism" (Sullivan 48). Queer, for these critics, stood for what the heterosexual did not; thus, it led to new binaries such as Queer \ Gay, Queer \ Non-Queer, and so on. The solution to the conflict was suggested by Janet R. Jakobsen: Queer, she put forth, must be considered a verb, a set of actions, rather than a noun, an identity (qtd. in Sullivan 50). In other words, regarding queer as *doing* instead of *being* would solve the problem. However, it is an oversimplistic account of queer experience since it disregards and denies the existence of queer subjectivity. It sounds like a regression to the times when there were no homosexuals but only same-sex sex acts. Hence, it is vital to distinguish between queer theory and lesbian/gay criticism. Barry itemises lesbian/gay critics' tasks as follows:

> They identify and establish a canon of 'classic' lesbian/gay writers whose work forms a distinct tradition; identify lesbian/gay episodes in mainstream work; establish an extended sense of 'lesbian/gay' in order to signify a moment of crossing a boundary or blurring boundaries; expose the homophobia of mainstream literature and criticism; highlight homosexual aspects of mainstream literature which have been disregarded before; foreground previously overlooked literary genres influencing ideals of masculinity and/or femininity. (148-149)

Lesbian/gay criticism, therefore, was separationist in its attitude as its intention was to build up a gay canon which is essentially supposed to be different from the heteronormative mainstream canon. The notion based on the principle of difference instead of one on similarity helped broaden the polarisation between the binaries 'gay' and 'non-gay'. Re-establishing Western binaries as in Hollinghurst's novels, gay / lesbian criticism comes to have little in common with queer theory, which painstakingly avoids establishing new centres.

1.4 The Representation of the Gay Male in Anglo-American Fiction

Along with the liberation movements and the resulting theoretical framework, the popularity of the representation of the gay male in Anglo-American literature has boosted. Gay fiction consists of literary works written by gay writers, written about gay characters, or written with a queer vision of life. Modern gay fiction in English literature is generally believed to have begun with the work and life of Oscar Wilde, the first sensational homosexual martyr, whose life and career was ruined by the homophobic late-Victorian society. Summers mentions the highlights and background of homophobia in England as follows:

> Hatred of homosexuality has a long and ignoble history in England. As late as 1861, sodomy, frequently described as the crime not mentionable among Christians, remained a capital offense, and executions for sodomy were actually carried out as late as 1835, long after nearly all of Europe had abolished capital punishment for the offense and after France had decriminalized consensual homosexual activity altogether. When the death penalty was abolished in England in 1861, the penalty for sodomy was reduced to penal servitude for life or for any term not less than ten years. (33)

Wilde, though sodomy was no longer a capital offense when he was put in prison, was the sacrificed scapegoat of the Victorian homophobia. The time he spent in prison ruined his career and some critics like André Gide believe that his only masterpiece was his life. Despite the fact that his works have been met with modest acclaim, Wilde's *Dorian Gray*, in which Wilde depicts the rivalry of Lord Henry and Basil for the love of a beauteous youth—Dorian, and *De Profundis*, Wilde's letters addressed to his Bossie on his prosecution and imprisonment, have been rather influential on other gay fictions.

Gay fiction could not go beyond the bildungsroman structure in the second half of the twentieth century. Most gay male characters in this period were indeed male versions of Jane Eyre or Moll Flanders: The novels dealt with the spiritual, moral, psychological, or social development and growth of the protagonists from childhood to maturity, in both literal and metaphoric sense. Usually the protagonists suffered from heterosexual oppression and gay-banishing social norms, and had difficulty in coming to terms with their sexual identities. Melinda S. Miceli critiques the fiction on gay youth as it "focuses on the negative aspects of growing up gay, lesbian, or bisexual, giving the impression that homosexuality invariably leads to suffering and unhappiness.... What is missed by such a perspective is an understanding of g/l/b youth who have successfully avoided such negative experiences and outcomes, and the variables that contributed to such success" (203).

On a cultural level, heteronormativity is still the dominant sexual discourse in Western epistemology and determines what is right or wrong. Summers states that "[a]n overwhelming issue in gay fiction is the relationship of the individual to society. The incompatibility between the needs of the homosexual and the demands of a hostile and conformist society is the source of recurrent conflicts" (22). This is why the novels in this period were keen to analyse coming-out processes and how their protagonists managed or failed to realise their identities. E. M. Forster's *Maurice*, to illustrate, one of the earliest –first wave, perhaps— gay fictions, seems to be under the influence of the Wilde scandal of 1895 regarding both its paranoiac sense of being 'out' and its rejection of class barriers. Maurice, the protagonist, has the intense fear of coming out; however, he cannot help falling for men of lower classes.

While the first wave of gay fiction in English "is the outgrowth of the early homosexual emancipation movement and the Wilde scandal, the second wave is part of the post-World War II literary boom, and it is predominantly American rather than British" (Summers 23). James Baldwin's *Giovanni's Room* is an early example written in the context of the homophobic and turbulent 1950s. Baldwin uses David as an internally homophobic and unreliable narrator. What's more, he depicts the gay ambiance, places, individuals, and relationships as decadent and corrupt. Thus, Baldwin, intentionally or not, allows an anti-gay interpretation of gay experience. The repulsive depiction of the gay scene is a direct result of the homophobic reactions to the increasing gay visibility. This is why gay places, especially gay bars, are depicted in many novels as meat markets packed with lecherous wanton queens – another stigmatising misconception, misrecognition, and misrepresentation in gay fiction.

Many novels attempt to represent gay experience within heterosexual parameters, re-establishing compulsory heterosexuality since they end up depicting gay individuals based on the male \ female binary failing to give an insight into the authentic gay experience as it is lived. They fail to realise the fact that genders may be considered opposites but chromosomal sex XX is not the opposite of XY (Sedgwick 28). Sexual identities may be completely different from chromosomal sex or the socially-constructed gender stereotypes; however, some novels cannot break with the Western binary logic. For instance, during -the depiction of- sexual intercourse, one male character will "inevitably negotiate symbolic meanings usually associated with the other sex.... [and] one partner will employ the signs and symbolic language –acts, posture, stance, dress—of masculinity" (Wilchins 15). If a man is not *manly*, then he has to be *womanly*; there is no other choice in this frame. Gay men in these works, thus, must conform to the cultural stereotypes since, if they do not, they will claim to have the phallus, which is, for Butler, a challenge to the heterosexual matrix. The stigma of homosexuality is socially and culturally enforced, and people mostly see homosexuality in cultural stereotypes, media representations, or in religious metanarratives. These intentional misrepresentations indicate that "the process of normative heterosexuality is institutionalized and, therefore, produces a systematic negative impact on g/l/b youth's experiences and identities" (Miceli 209). As a consequence of these impacts, a misconception emerges: gay men must be what heterosexual men are not, for the heteronormative system works on the principle of difference. Peter Nardi calls this process of representing gay experience within the heterosexual frame of reference 'the mainstreaming of gay/lesbian issues'. He claims that it is important to discuss the everyday lives of gay men in order to counteract the stereotypes that still exist in many societies, yet he admits that this tendency might culminate in "depictions that often normalize and minimize the complexities of living as gay or lesbian in heterosexually-oriented social world" (45). Thus, when gay experience is depicted in heteronormative parameters, it cannot help being mainstreamed. However, gay novels, no matter how dichotomous, by repeating heterosexual constructs within gay culture, are actually supposed to denaturalise and mobilise gender categories: "The replication of heterosexual constructs in non-heterosexual frames brings into relief the utterly constructed status of the so-called heterosexual original. Thus, gay is to straight not as copy is to original, but, rather, as copy is to copy" (Butler, *Gender* 43). For this reason, the novels failing to represent queer perspective and apparently solidifying heteronormative system are expected to help deconstruct the dominant system.

1.5 Camp and Closet in Gay Fiction

For a better understanding of gay male representation in fiction, two concepts are of great significance; camp and closet. These terms are chosen in this study partly because they abound in Hollinghurst's novels and partly because they are indispensable elements and objects of gay studies and queer theory. The term 'camp' refers to a variety of concepts; aesthetic sensibility, irony, exaggeration, outrageousness, theatricality, effeminacy, and homosexual behaviour. Many critics believe that the word is derived from the French term 'se camper' (to flaunt), which implies that homosexuality is something one should indeed feel ashamed of. As a style, 'camp' dates back to the late seventeenth and early eighteenth centuries, when the rise of the homosexual identity was felt in Europe. Camp was a way of revealing a so-far-invisible identity then, as "gays and lesbians needed to remain hidden yet visible for so long that they developed ways of signalling their sexual orientation to like-minded people that would remain oblique to society as a whole. They also could choose to be so flamboyant that their sexuality could not be ignored" (Eadie 226). Emerging out of the need to be open in a hostile society, camp employed incongruity, witty dialogues, cross-dressing, gender-bending, and aestheticism. Later on these attributes began to signify homosexuality, particularly with the contributions of the work of Oscar Wilde. However, for some critics, camp actually signifies much more than homosexuality; it implies a political and revolutionary discourse challenging heteronormative discourses and parodying them. Moe Meyer associates camp with queer parody and believes that it is both political and critical. For him, camp "is not simply 'a style' or 'sensibility' as is conventionally accepted. Rather, what emerges is a suppressed and denied oppositional critique embodied in the signifying practices that processually constitute queer identities.... Camp is political; Camp is solely a queer (and/or sometimes gay and lesbian) discourse; and Camp embodies a specifically queer cultural critique" (1). Susan Sontag's 1964 essay *Notes on 'Camp'* was the first academic analysis and study on camp. However, Sontag's essay looks rather homophobic and prescriptive in the twenty-first century. Sontag, above all, does not identify camp with the gay male and she puts forth that camp cannot be in nature. It is, she claims, the love "of things-being-what-they-are-not," a homophobic utterance itself (56). She scorns and blames it for being duplicate, and thus, artificial. When she deals with the relation of camp to homosexuality, she states that the direct identification between the two is arbitrary. Though she admits that homosexuals constitute the majority of camp taste, she argues that "[c]amp taste is much more than homosexual taste," since –she suggests- camp emphasises the theatricality of life itself (64). Thus, Sontag not only detached camp from its gay male origin, moving queer politics back into a heterosexual context, but also exiled the gay male from the discourse.

Later critics have defined camp in various ways and today camp is still a slippery term. Piggford states that the ambiguity about the definition of camp is "also because camp functions within particular societies in particular periods in specific ways that no generic definition of camp will ultimately suffice" (289). David M. Halperin, for instance, defines it as a distinctively gay male practice and "a form of cultural resistance that is entirely predicated on a shared consciousness of being inescapably situated within a powerful system of social and sexual meanings. Camp resists the power of that system from within by means of parody, exaggeration, amplification, theatricalization, and literalization of normally tacit codes of conduct" (29). In his definition, camp is a deconstruction and subversion of the mainstream culture; and it is a form of resistance within power. Moe Meyer takes the term camp a step further and identifies it with queer. He underlines the critical and political significance of the term and adds that camp subverts and deconstructs the artificial homosexual/heterosexual dichotomy imposed and reinforced by dominant ideologies. He critiques Sontag's facile approach to camp and re-establishes the relation between queer and camp. For Meyer, "there are not different kinds of Camp. There is only one. And it is queer" (5). He states that camp is queer, not only homosexual, because queer implies and indicates the rejection of definition. Queer avoids the stigma of medical sciences labelled on the term 'homosexual'. Camp is always-already queer and its *raison d'être* is to look for the loopholes in the dominant systems and to decentre them by offering alternatives.

Cynthia Morrill, another critic disapproving of Sontag's approach, accuses Sontag of being restrictive without any clear or reasonable explanations. As for the relation of camp to sexuality, she argues that camp "has become appreciated as an eminently postmodern form. Indeed, Camp has become recognized as an example par excellence of a postmodern denaturalization of gender categories" (110). Andy Medhurst defines camp as a political and pleasurable survival strategy which highlights the performative nature of gender, sexuality, class, and so on, and denaturalises and queers heteronormative conceptions of identity (qtd. in Sullivan 193). Thus, camp, in his definition, turns into a gay practice employed as a weapon against heteronormative patriarchy. Camp is even regarded as an effect of homophobia, which brings it closer to closet, as it "disrupts the dominant order by serving as a marker for the queer subject's uncanny experience of the impossibility of representing his/her desire within the parameters of the essentialized ontology of the un-queer" (Morrill 19). Therefore, it poses a threat and a challenge to the heterosexist oppression and becomes a target for the homophobic encounters.

Closet is an effect of homophobia and in a sense it is in sharp contrast to camp. Whereas camp implies and requires visibility, closet implies and requires invisibility or privacy. Michael P. Brown refers to the genealogy and deployment of the term: It "appeared in Middle English sometime between 1150 and 1500, and originally referred to a small private room used for prayer or study. By the early seventeenth century it referred specifically to a small room or cupboard, while later that century it was resignified to connote 'private' or 'secluded'" (5). Closet is a place to store or hide things; thus, the word signifies lying, hiding, invisibility, secrecy, silence, and pretending to be what one is not. It is a result and agent of the Panopticon prison—which symbolises the surveillance of the dominant ideology. This prison was a type of building designed by Jeremy Bentham in the late eighteenth century. The aim was to observe the prisoners, while they would never know if they were being observed or not. It had a circular structure with an observing point in the middle. Bentham designed this building not only for prisons but also for hospitals, schools, poorhouses and mental asylums; however, later Michel Foucault, in his *Discipline and Punish*, employed the term as a metaphor to designate the normative modern Western society and its institutions like the army, schools and hospitals. Closet is an agent and effect of the Panopticon project; it is the space where the nonconformist queer is supposed to hide without knowing whether he / she is being observed or not. Since it is impossible to be totally closeted, the sense of being closeted culminates in the paranoiac anxiety of being under constant surveillance.

Closet is also the inevitable traumatic process by which a queer individual may actualise himself / herself, achieve his/her self-realisation and come to terms with his/her sexual orientation thanks to the sense of community and belonging it provides. The process is inevitable because even modern societies are based on heteronormativity and homosexaulity is not tolerated by their patriarchal systems. Many gay teenagers have little support and insufficient information when they become aware of their emerging feelings and desire. Seeing that heterosexuality is the only way accepted by the society, they feel anxious and scared because of the probability of being rejected by their families and friends. As a result, many of them prefer to conceal, deny, or even repress their authentic subjectivity, which is considered perversion or sin by social, medical, religious, or legal discourses. Due to the oppression these discourses inflict, gay adolescents generally regard especially their school life as "isolating, uncomfortable, and unsafe. Many g/l/b students endure the effects of this heteronormative institution alone and in silence" (Miceli 209). They are either considered nonexistent or invisible, because homosexaulity "indicates merely the failure to fit precisely within a category, and surely all persons at some time or other find themselves discomfited by the bounds of the categories that ostensibly contain their identities" (Turner 8). Miceli states that while trying to deny it, particularly to themselves, they act out, both for others and themselves, heterosexual norms (202). Heteronormative sexuality inevitably leads to homophobia, which originally and ironically means 'the fear of the same', discriminates, oppresses, terrorises, judges, criminalises, and psychologises queer individuals; thus, there is no way out of the closet. Even if one does come out of the closet, there will always be new barriers faced. Eve Kosofsky Sedgwick agrees that 'closetedness' is a never-ending process and adds;

> [A]t an individual level, there are remarkably few of even the most openly gay people who are not deliberately in the closet with someone personally or economically or institutionally important to them. Furthermore, the deadly elasticity of heterosexist presumption means that, like Wendy in

Peter Pan, people find new walls springing up around them even as they drowse: every encounter with a new classful of students, to say nothing of a new boss, social worker, loan officer, landlord, doctor, erects new closets whose fraught and characteristic laws of optics and physics exact from at least gay people new surveys, new calculations, new draughts and requisitions of secrecy or disclosure. (67-68)

In addition to 'closetedness', coming-out is another never-ending process. Each time a gay individual forms new social relationships, s/he encounters a dilemma: to stay in or get out of the closet. One can never be openly and fully out.

Homophobia was quite common even in the late 1990s. Valerie Jenness and Kimberly D. Richman announce the bias-motivated offenses, committed between 1991-1998, reported by the U.S. Department of Justice. According to the reports, the type of bias-motivation and the number of cases are as follows: Race, 5360 cases; religion, 1475 cases; sexual orientation, 1439 cases; ethnicity, 919 cases (406). As seen clearly, anti-gay violence is almost the second most common crime after the racial one towards the twenty-first century. Even today homophobia exists to a large extent in the very discourse science creates and circulates. For example, the homosexual is "regarded (especially in psychoanalytic theory) as one who fears the difference of the 'other' or opposite sex, and, in flight from it, narcissistically embraces the same sex instead.... In some instances 'sameness' comes to signify the tyranny of Western patriarchal metaphysics, and homosexuality its practice or, more vaguely, its metaphor" (Dollimore 249). The analogy drawn between homosexuality and tyranny is far-fetched and it is not a satisfactory explanation for readers aware of the heteronormativity underlying the Western patriarchy. The intentional misconception is a product of the system which created the closet as a ghetto for the gay. Indeed closeting itself is a form of tyranny, since the term refers to "the denial, concealment, erasure, or ignorance of lesbians and gay men. It describes their absence –and alludes to their ironic presence nonetheless—in a society that, in countless interlocking ways, subtly and blatantly dictates that heterosexuality is the only way to be" (Brown 1). A gay individual who demands "a job, custody or visiting rights, insurance, protection from violence.... could deliberately choose to remain in or to reenter the closet in some or all segments of their life" (Sedgwick 68). The closet is not peculiar to individuals facing sexual discrimination, yet it is still a fundamental and shaping element in their life.

Foucault was right to claim that power comes from below; not from the ruler to the ruled. He argues that "there is no binary and all-encompassing opposition between rulers and ruled at the root of power relations.... One must suppose rather that the manifold relationships of force that take shape and come into play in the machinery of production, in families, limited groups, and institutions, are the basis for wide-ranging effects of cleavage that run through the social body as a whole" (*Sexuality* 1: 94). Likewise, homophobia or the stigmatisation of so-called unnatural actions or identities is not directly imposed on individuals by the ruler. Sullivan highlights the fact that even when people see one naked, they tend to disdain or criticise, for individuals are "all both agents and effects of disciplinary regimes" (84). Homophobia, as a device of identity politics and policing of identity, circulates in order to reaffirm heterosexuality, i.e. the self, denying the existence of the other. Heteronormativity, being the dominant ideology, rules in all domains of culture such as language, education, and religion. As for homophobia, it does exist even in queer contexts. Most gay individuals cannot escape gender norms as they still tend to model themselves on straight couples; the manly one and the feminine other. Wilchins claims that this tendency "left the gay community with its share of internalized genderphobia. It is not uncommon to see gay personals that read 'straight looking and acting only' or 'no butches need reply.'.... For many gay men, gender is yet another closet to come out of" (18).

Discussing how power operated in the nineteenth-century society, Foucault reveals that power was not always and only a suppressive or constraining element; on the contrary, "it acted by multiplication of singular sexualities. It did not set boundaries for sexuality; it extended the various forms of sexuality.... It did not set up a barrier; it provided places of maximum saturation" (*Sexuality* 1: 47). For this reason, the places or rights offering queer individuals comfort and security, which make them feel 'normal', are nothing more than make-believe. These pretentious and illusory applications peculiar to queer people are intended to lock the ones who came out back into the closet. Outside the closet, the gay will never be considered 'normal'. Halperin agrees that coming out of the closet does not bring one satisfaction or freedom, and clarifies the function of the closet: "The only reason to be *in* the closet is to protect oneself from the many and virulent sorts of social disqualification that one would suffer were the discreditable fact of one's sexual orientation more widely known. To 'closet' one's homosexuality is also to submit oneself to the social imperative imposed on gay people by non-gay-identified people" (29). One can never be totally *in* or *out* of the closet; it is full of contradictions and not a single absolute act. Individuals just alternately get in and out of the closet in the course of their lives. Sedgwick puts forth that being in or out is not a simple dichotomy as "[d]egrees of concealment and openness coexist in the same lives" (qtd. in Barry 145).

Sedgwick, following Foucault's concept of 'many silences' in discourses, likens 'closetedness' to silence. For her, 'closetedness' is "a performance initiated as such by the speech act of a silence—not a particular silence, but a silence" (3). Silence in both theorists' conceptions refers to the artificial dichotomy between what is said and what is not. In this respect, one's coming out of the closet and airing his gayness and one's remaining in the closet and concealing his gayness are not binaries indeed. Nevertheless, the hetero/homo binary will always survive despite the so-called liberation movements, as will silences underlying and existing in discourses. Thus, queer studies focus on the "analysis not only of the overtly homosexual, but also a reading between the lines for patterns of absences and silences through which texts deny same-sex desire" (Adam 19). Employing a deconstructive approach, they look for loopholes in binary oppositions in the mainstream canon and decentre these binaries.

1.6 Camp and Closet in Hollinghurst's Novels

The crucial point in analysing the terms *camp* and *closet* in Hollinghurst's fiction is to find out whether the author writes from the margin or from the centre to recreate the 'origin'. Gay male subjectivities are of great concern to this book and it means that the book will not be a product of identity politics, but in fact it will question the operating principles of Hollinghurst's representation of gay male identity. Identity politics is another agent of essentialism, and it does regard gender, race, or ethnicities, which are nothing but social constructions, as fixed or biologically determined traits. Thus, identity politics, while trying to recentre the decentred and marginalised identities, re-establishes the binary structure of the Western epistemology. This monograph, in contrast, takes up a poststructuralist approach to identities and favours multiplicity. Poststructuralism criticises the liberationist ideal of the freedom of the true self as it finds identity politics inherently problematic. In poststructuralist mode of thinking there are different accounts of subjectivity (Sullivan 41). As this monograph problematises the deployment of camp and closet in Hollinghurst's first four novels, it inevitably lays bare the decentred position of the marginalised gay male subjectivity and its alienation from the mainstream culture with the reification of a distinct gay male subculture.

Analysing camp and closet in Hollinghurst's work also sheds light on the social, political and economic atmosphere the author lived in while writing his four novels. Hollinghurst started writing during Thatcher's administration and his work is a mirror held to the mainstream course of things in England in the 1980s. Hugh David states that in those years the image of the simpering stereotype homosexual man was being replaced with a masculine macho image—which he calls 'the clone'— in England, and with the new government's neo-liberal policies homosexual identity became a part of consumerism:

> There was an overt sexuality about the clone which was at once uniform — the tight T-shirt or vest; the button-fly Levi 501 jeans; the cropped hair and clipped moustache—and individual. His Clone Zone shops (a chain established in 1981) stocked all the costumes as well as a range of props — variously coloured handkerchiefs, fetish gear, American magazines, specialist reading matter, bottles of 'poppers' (Amyland Butyl Nitrate stimulants), a connoisseur range of condoms — which, for those in the know, differentiated and deliciously delineated the pleasures in store. (254)

These changes strengthened the campy image of the homosexual as a distinct identity and rendered him more visible. The gay community was financially important for the new government and its new policies. That is why, for many, Thatcher's government gave the homosexual their golden age. Especially the year 1983, when Thatcher's party won a second term in office,

> acquired mythic status —but only because - as Alan Hollinghurst recognized when he chose to set his 1988 novel *The Swimming Pool Library* in that *annus mirabilis* —parties, by their very nature, cannot run for ever. Had they but eyes to see, all the revellers should have noticed, like Hollinghurst's hero William Beckwith, that midnight was fast approaching: "My life was in a strange way that summer, the last summer of its kind there was ever to be. I was riding high on sex and self-esteem – it was my time, my belle époque— but all the while with a faint flicker of calamity, like flames around a photograph, something seen out of the corner of the eye." (David 255)

Hollinghurst's first novel, *The Swimming-Pool Library*, was published in 1988, the year in which the notorious Section 28 –the item criminalising any promotion of homosexuality or any teaching of homosexuality as a family relationship— passed into law as a substantial part of the 1988 Local Government Act. This act revealed the fact that the apparently pro-gay government was in fact trying to closet homosexuality, and it resulted in another disillusionment for the homosexual individuals in England. The homosexual in England experienced both camp and closet due to the ambiguious and inconsistent attitude toward homosexuality. On the one hand, Thatcher was one of the few MPs to support Leo Abse's bill decriminalising male homosexuality, she never showed any personal homophobic reactions or attitudes, and she even appointed gay ministers. However, on the other hand, her speech in 1987 and the Section 28 addition, which prohibited any form of funding or promoting homosexuality, showed that the underlying ethos of Thatcherism was homophobic. In his article, Brian Coleman, a Conservative Party politician, refers to the irony of the period and states that although the Thatcher government had an anti-gay aura, particularly due to the notorious Section 28, in fact no one was prosecuted under Section 28, and many of the gay Politicians in the Tory party joined the Conservative party and became active during the Thatcher years, and she even appointed gay ministers including the tragic Earl of Avon.

Alan Hollinghurst's acclaimed first novel, *The Swimming-Pool Library* (1988), gives a vivid account of London gay life in the early 1980s through the story of a young aristocrat, William Beckwith, and his involvement with the elderly Lord Nantwich, Charles, whose life he saves in public lavatories. *The Swimming-Pool Library* is a sensational work as it holds a mirror to the double lives gay male individuals lead in London. It was followed by *The Folding Star* in 1993, which was shortlisted for the Booker Prize for Fiction and awarded the James Tait Black Memorial Prize for Fiction. The novel is set in London and Bruges. The narrator, Edward Manners, 33, travels to Belgium to teach English to two pupils. Soon he finds himself in love with one of them; the cute and mischievous 17-year-old Luc, as a result of which his life rotates around gay bars and passionate obsessions. Paul Echevin –father to Edward's other pupil, Marcel– is the director of a museum and he is devoted to the work of fin-de-siècle Belgian painter Edgard Orst. Edward soon finds out that he feels drawn to the strange, twilight world of the painter. *The Spell*, Hollinghurst's third novel, portrays the complex and confusing relationships between Robin Woodfield, an architect in his 40s, his alcoholic lover Justin, and Justin's ex-boyfriend Alex, who falls in love with Robin's son Danny. The setting of the novel is alternately the English countryside and London, where Danny introduces Alex to drugs. *The Spell* is a conventional representation of the modern camp life. *The Line of Beauty* (2004), traces a decade of change and tragedy. It won the 2004 Man Booker Prize for Fiction and was adapted for BBC Television in 2006. In the summer of 1983, twenty-year-old Nick Guest moves into the Notting Hill home of the Feddens as a friend of their son Toby, though

Toby does not live there any longer, and he becomes a friend to their daughter Cathy. The novel is about the attempts of Nick to get rid of his own social class and to live a campy life like the Feddens, representing the upper class, do.

The second chapter of this monograph deals with the term camp and analyses Hollinghurst's deployment and depiction of camp in his novels. It discusses whether Hollinghurst portrays camp as the parody and theatricalisation of heteronormativity with a political purpose or as the apolitical imitation, i.e., a sensibility and taste in the Sontagesque sense, which is secondary to the heterosexual origin. Camp's "derivative nature, and its dependence upon an already existing text in order to fulfil itself are the reasons for its traditional denigration, a denigration articulated within a dominant discourse that finds value only in an 'original'" (Meyer 9-10). This sense of denigration has got political, social and cultural implications which are studied in Hollinghurst's work, since his gay male characters, with their life styles, affirm the existence of a 'merely gay' subculture and identity. For Sontag, Camp involves a wide variety of things: "Not only is there a Camp vision, a Camp way of looking at things. Camp is as well a quality discoverable in objects and the behaviour of persons. There are 'campy' movies, clothes, furniture, popular songs, novels, people, buildings" (54). Accordingly, *The Swimming-Pool Library* is camp, particularly in the Sontagesque sense, because main events take place in or around such camp ghettos as The Corinthian Club; the homosocial club providing its members with aphrodisiac air. It offers an alternative lifestyle which does not problematise or question dominant ideology which marginalises and stigmatises gay male subjectivity. The camp depicted in the novel as a sensibility is in fact the representation of a reified gay male identity, "a male community, delighting in men, but always respectful and fraternal" (SP^2 10). There is class-consciousness as camp involves only the white, middle-class and well-educated gay male characters, and there is a clear-cut boundary between the heterosexual and the homosexual world. Moreover, the gay male is depicted as a stereotype; vulgar, indecent and hedonistic gay male characters with no depth but with an exaggerated sexual identity. With this oversimplified and exaggerated stereotype and the transgender talk which is used by some characters as if it were peculiar to the stereotype, the gay male is disenfranchised from the straight male and given an apparently stable identity. *The Folding Star* is camp as it creates a non-realistic gay world isolated from the heteronormative world

---

[2] The novels *The Swimming-Pool Library*, *The Folding Star*, *The Spell*, and *The Line of Beauty* will be referred to as *SP,FS,TS,LB* hereafter.

where the gay male stereotype ghettoises himself in the gay scene, sleeps around, and finally comes down with AIDS. The author's representation of the gay male seems to be under the influence of ancient Greek stylistics of the love of boys and it is directly identified with hedonism, foregrounding sexual characteristics in male-to-male intimacy. This identity full of extravagance and extremities, however, is portrayed with a playful tone without any judgments or questioning, which makes it Sontagesque camp. *The Spell* is camp because even in the country gay male individuals, who are white middle-class men as usual, make themselves visible and lead a campy lifestyle full of extremities. The novel ignores the existence of heteronormativity to such an extent that in London heterosexuality is marginalised; for instance, the restaurant Alex takes Danny to is the one place among gay blocks, a haven for heterosexuals (*TS* 75). This representation, ignoring the existence of the traditionally privileged leg of the binary, only affirms the existence of a distinct and gay male subculture and a stable identity. The characters are prurient, dandy, parasitical and nymphomaniac men who constantly cruise for sexual gratification. Besides the representation of this reductive and prescriptive stereotype, the use of a transgender talk, in which obsession with sex is revealed, adds to the disenfranchisement of the gay male. *The Line of Beauty* is camp because, just like the other novels, it depicts a white affluent gay world with class solidarity excluding the non-gay and the non-campy gay where gay male characters are just after sex and drugs, as a result of which they sooner or later suffer from AIDS and die. This depiction of gay life is camp because it is based on extremities and extravagance, which is the hallmark of camp according to Sontag, who likens camp to "a woman walking around in a dress made of three million feathers" (59). Hollinghurst's deployment of camp strengthens the conventional notion of gay male subculture and identity without intending to subvert or criticise heteronormativity and power relations which establish and reinforce these reified constructs.

 The third chapter of the book focuses on the closetedness of gay male subjectivities and, to some extent, it juxtaposes closet, the invisible, to camp, the visible. This chapter is an attempt to find out the extent to which Hollinghurst closets or discharges gay male identity. *The Swimming-Pool Library* is closet with its depiction of the gay scene closeted in modern heterotopias such as gay cinemas, bars, clubs, parks and bushes. The characters encounter physical and psychological violence and they use a transgender jargon to avoid the homophobic attitude. In their ghettos designated by the heteronormative system, they form polyandrous relationship chains, which is another indicant of the closet in the novel.

Finally, they are attributed clichéd jobs, which are traditionally identified with women, or they are unemployed parasitic creatures living off other men. *The Folding Star* lends itself for an analysis of the closet as seen at the beginning of the novel when Edward describes the room he rents: "The room I chose was so hidden away that it gave me the sensation of having entered, with dreamlike suddenness, into the secret inner life of the city" (*FS* 13). Just like this room, the gay male is closeted in various other heterotopias of deviation such as bars, public conveniences, hotel rooms and even in their own hometowns or homelands. Moreover, even when in their closets, they face homophobia as there is no tolerance for visibility, and thus, they are obliged to lead double lives. Last but not least, the depiction of the gay male in polyandrous sex chains is another indicant of the closet in the novel. In *The Spell*, despite being visible, gay male characters are still imprisoned in the closet. They seem to be enjoying their sexual freedom to pick up new men for sex whenever they feel like it; however, their apparent liberty is a vicious circle indeed, and the gay bars they go cruising in turn out to be their heterotopias of deviation. Besides bars, the other major heterotopias in the novel are public conveniences, the characters' houses, bushes and parks. In addition to the ghettos, the characters are portrayed in an exaggerated sense of promiscuity and they sleep around. Finally, they are identified with style jobs, attributed to the homosexual, which brings the representation of camp closer to the Sontagesuqe camp. The last novel, *The Line of Beauty*, is also closet because the characters are ghettoised in cinemas, bars, a nudist yard, parks, and gardens. Outside these heterotopias, they are not allowed to become visible and they are supposed to conceal their sexual orientation, which is an indicant of homophobia. The characters are again depicted as promiscuous men in same-sex sex chains. Lastly, they are identified with style jobs, illegal jobs, or parasitic lives without any job at all. This representation regards and portrays the gay male as a type with a distinct identity and subculture of its own; that is why it is camp in the Sontagesque sense, too.

CHAPTER TWO

CAMP

CATHY. L'homosexualité est un délit!
NICK.   Délit is a crime unfortunately.
CATHY. Oh, is it?
NICK.   Delight is délice, délit is misdemeanour.
CATHY. Well, it's bloody close.
NICK.   Well, they often are! (*LB* 308)

The extract above, a dialogue between Cathy and Nick, illustrates how queer texts should question and blur Western binaries such as Law/Desire, and it gives the reader a hint about the desired camp structure in the twenty-first century novels. Today camp colloquially refers to gay or non-gay individuals, usually male, acting effeminately or flamboyantly, as if mimicking the other gender. When used within a gay context, camp denotes overt homosexuality, through verbal and/or non-verbal means. However, in the late twentieth and early twenty-first centuries the gay male nature and origin of camp have been reclaimed and redeployed by critics. Fabio Cleto underlines the queer origin of camp, which underlies the difficulty of reducing it to a single definition: "Tentatively approached as *sensibility, taste,* or *style*, reconceptualised as *aesthetic* or *cultural economy*, and later asserted/reclaimed as (*queer*) *discourse*, camp hasn't lost its relentless power to frustrate all efforts to pinpoint it down to stability" (2). In accordance with its ambiguous origin and nature, the term has got multiple forms: it is used as an adjective: camp, campy, campish; it has got noun forms: camp, campness, campiness; an adverb form: campily; and verb forms: to camp and to camp (sth) up. Cleto states that Sontag had degayified and depoliticised camp before Esther Newton described it as an exercise in homosexual taste and a mode of existence. Jack Babuscio also equalled camp with the gay sensibility a few years later and defined gay sensibility as:

> [A] creative energy reflecting a consciousness that is different from the mainstream; a heightened awareness of certain human complications of feeling that spring from the fact of social oppression…. Such a perception

of the world varies with time and place according to the nature of the specific set of circumstances in which, historically, we have found ourselves. Present-day society defines people as falling into distinct types. Such a method of labelling ensures that individual types become polarised. (118)

What he suggests is that the notion of camp is in fact relative, for it is time and culture-bound. A campy object may not be considered campy in a different culture or in a different era. This notion of camp as taste and sensibility, which was common in the late 60s, changed with the contribution of gender studies and queer theory especially in the late 80s and camp gained importance thanks to the parodic mode of gender deconstruction (Cleto 202). For example, Meyer states that camp encompasses the oppositional critique within power and it is an ontological challenge to the system. It is the political, critical and discursive voice of the queer. As stated above, previously camp was regarded as an aesthetic experience which was essentially apolitical. Moreover, Susan Sontag had accused camp of being anti-serious and related it to comedy, denying its identification with the homosexual. Differentiating camp from its incorrectly-attributed non-gay and apolitical tags, Meyer establishes that camp is only and always queer, and states that:

> [A]ll un-queer activities that have been previously accepted as "camp," such as Pop culture expressions, have been redefined as examples of the appropriation of queer praxis. Because un-queer appropriations interpret Camp within the context of compulsory reproductive heterosexuality, they no longer qualify as Camp as it is defined here. In other words, the un-queer do not have access to the discourse of Camp. (Meyer 1)

Camp is the theatrical, the parodic, the oppositional, the ironic, the outrageous and the revolutionary; it cannot be expected to fit in the heteronormative system because it cannot be defined and assessed within mainstream parameters. It is the queering parody of the non-queer.

Jonathan Dollimore refers to the ambiguous nature of camp and agrees that its definition "is as elusive as the sensibility itself, one reason being simply that there are different kinds of camp" (224). In accordance with Dollimore, Meyer points out various perceptions of camp, such as camp and pop camp: the former being naïve and pure, while the latter is deliberate and corresponds to Sontag's definition of camp. However, Meyer argues that this is a misconception as there are not kinds of camp; there is only one and it is queer (4). He considers camp and pop camp as two halves of a single phenomenon. By eliminating the queer from the camp discourse, Sontag superficially created the so-called pop camp.

Otherwise, nothing within the popular culture could become camp. Cleto too agrees that queer is the key to camp discourse and shows how Sontag unintentionally led to the appearance of pop camp: "In order to restore camp to its original, and *true*, mode of existence, one would need to restore its critical and political value, and its foundational element, the one corresponding to its intimate essence –the *queer*—without which we have the fundamentally 'else' of Pop camp" (17). As a result, writers and critiques following Sontag simply deny camp as a queer discourse, and gay writers seeking to reclaim the discourse of camp through a restoration of its homosexual origins fail to address issues of non-queer and pop culture appropriations (Meyer 6). In fact, Meyer's classification is one of the latest among different definitions and categorisations of camp, which were all triggered by Christopher Isherwood's definition of camp in his novel *The World in the Evening*. In the novel, Charles, the elderly man whose life William saves in the public lavatories, asks his friend Stephen—a minor character in the novel, whether he has ever heard the word 'camp', and later interrupting his friend, explains it himself: "You thought it meant a swishy little boy with peroxided hair, dressed in a picture hat and a feather boa, pretending to be Marlene Dietrich? Yes, in queer circles, they call *that* camping. It's all very well in its place, but it's an utterly debased form." Charles adds that it is called Low Camp, and then gets to the main point:

> High Camp is the whole emotional basis of the Ballet, for example, and of course of Baroque art. You see, true High Camp always has an underlying seriousness. You can't camp about something you don't take seriously. You're not making fun of it; you're making fun out of it. You're expressing what's basically serious to you in terms of fun and artifice and elegance. (125)

It could be argued that there are at least two kinds of camp, both of which are queer: The first one is naïve, natural, feminine and apolitical. It is the one usually identified with sensibility, taste, dandyism, and flamboyance. The second form of camp is intentional, political, but still not masculine. There is no agreement on how many types of camp there are, but the claim that camp is originally gay seems to be well-accepted. Jeffrey Escoffier refers to how it emerged and restores camp back to its gay context:

> Camp originated among homosexuals many decades ago. Gay men widely appreciated it as a form of ironic commentary and broad humor that plays with the situation of a man's being sexually attracted to another man. ("Is a man attracted to another really a woman?") A man would adopt feminine

mannerisms and sometimes dress as a woman to comment ironically on male homosexual life. (147-148)

There are some disagreements about the gay origin of camp and some claim that women can be camp, too. Pamela Robertson strongly disagrees and argues that the denial of camp's affiliation with gay male subculture would be foolish, adding that women may be objects of or subjects to camp but definitely not camp subjects (267-269).

As for the deployment and use of camp, it may be used against gay individuals as well as being used in favour of them. Andrew Ross explains why camp may turn out to be harmful for queer movements:

> Because of its zeal for artifice, theatricality, spectacle, and parody, camp has often been seen as pre-political, even reactionary. In its commitment to the mimicry of existing cultural forms, and its refusal to advocate wholesale breaks with these same forms, the politics of camp fell out of step and even into disrepute (as a kind of blackface) with the dominant ethos of the women's and gay liberation movements. (325)

Camp is conventionally associated with extravagance and this extravagance results in the invention of gay male stereotypes. For instance, in the media campy characters are employed to arouse laughter. These characters, real as in a reality show or fictional as in a TV show, use exaggerated mimicry and gestures, wear lots of make-up, and change their pitches of voice to sound more feminine. This artifice may seem to be stemming from a gay friendly attitude; however, it sooner or later culminates in homophobia and re-establishment and affirmation of cultural archetypes, such as the misbelief that all gays are feminine, flamboyant and bottom. This is the representation of the psychologised and parodied 'homosexual' in the mainstream culture. Similar to the notion of sexuality which was most rigorously subjugated by the dominant discourse and which was strengthened by various discourses producing the truth about sex, misrecognition or misrepresentation of camp in the mainstream is in line with bourgeois values and it reaffirms them.

Hollinghurst, as an allegedly queer writer, depicts male gay characters who have established their own campy world and who, in that world, imitate the fictional heteronormative society. However, the author's representation of relationships in this alternative world—from which the non-gay is almost totally banished— does not intend to pose a challenge to the mainstream culture by revealing the performative nature of gender. Camp as queer parody and critique has its own voice and space only when uttered or employed by the queer with a queer approach; however, as Meyer suggests, it would be wrong to subvert the binary and banish the non-queer from the discourse (10). Therefore, Hollinghurst's fiction fails to meet queer expectations and cannot go beyond the earlier gay novels. He claims and, perhaps, intends to have a queer vision in his writing, yet he ends up portraying gay men fascinated by a life of sex and drugs in the gay scene which, at times, culminates in a tragic death from AIDS, the syndrome often attributed to same-sex sexual intercourse by heterosexist discourses. This gay male subculture is directly related to the conventional affinity between camp and homosexual as type:

> Given the stereotypical merging of theatricality, male homosexuality, and the aesthetic sense whose discursive origins can be traced in Oscar Wilde's martyrdom, we can draw an hypothesis in which the origins of camp and those, by way of the Wilde trials of 1895, of the homosexual as 'type', identifiable because articulated on the effeminate Wildean theatricality, are inextricable. (Cleto 21)

Camp, in the political sense, aims to critique and decentre the mainstream by parodying, exaggerating, showing loopholes in the system, and it proposes alternatives. Hollinghurst, however, depicts an alternative lifestyle, which is actualised in an unrealistic, even in a utopian context, and his apolitical depiction does not critique or problematise the life outside of his work. His male gay characters' fascination with sex and drugs, in addition to other conventional attributes like cruising in parks and cottaging, ends up in the reinforcement of the stereotype male gay image and this image, which is based on the performative, acquired and theatrical gay role, is camp, yet in the Sontagesque sense.

Camp affords some advantages for gay individuals. It enables intersubjectivity and the feeling of solidarity and a sense of community. It is entertaining and full of witty remarks, which critique and parody the loopholes in heteronormative systems. However, the hindrances of camp might outweigh its benefits. First of all, camp is discriminatory; it leaves the non-camp out. Richard Dyer argues that not every one is camp and a "bunch of queens screaming together can be exclusive for someone who isn't a queen or feels unable to camp" (111). Such queens denigrate the non-queenly or the straight-looking/acting gays, and in return activists scorn campy gays and queens since they do reinforce the public image of gays as marginal, decadent, degenerate, frivolous and dandy. In this way, the queer subjects are divided into discriminatory subcategories and conflict with one another, replicating the stigmatising and binary nature of heteronormative discourses they are supposed to challenge and subvert. Secondly, the campy image of the gay male as dandy, nymphomaniac, flighty, and hedonistic is, in addition to the discriminatory aspect of camp, another issue to be tackled as it reinforces the stigmatised identity of the gay male which is reduced to and based on only same-sex sex acts by heteronormativity. This misconception gives the impression that gay identity is all about sexuality and the gay is equal to the Homo-sexual. The repetition of the same image of the gay male in the novels affirms the reified identity of the gay as a stable and fixed group of individuals. Thirdly, camp shows itself in the use of language, i.e., the coarse gay jargon employed by gay characters. Dyer refers to the use of fun, humour, and self-mockery in language and states that when overused, they would result in the impression that campy people cannot take anything seriously and act as if they had to turn everything into a joke or a witty remark (111). Furthermore, he argues that self mockery may have a corrosive effect on individuals in that they could keep mocking themselves to the point where they will really be convinced that they are pathetic and inferior. He puts the blame on the situation, not individuals, and states that camp sometimes prevents people from seeing that (111). These features abound in Hollinghurst's novels, which lends the quality of Sontagesque camp to his work and adds to the always-already high notoriety of homosexuality.

Piggford states that camp, without dividing identity into subcategories, undermines the gender assumptions of particular societies and it celebrates alienation and distance since it moves beyond the boundaries outlined by mainstream notions of identity, gender, and sexuality (297). Hollinghurst's use of camp is far from going beyond heteronormative values and definitions; moreover, he homosexualises even non-homosexual elements, such as drugs, promiscuity, and AIDS, whereby his portrayal of the gay male becomes nothing but a traditional stereotype who is imprisoned in a distinctly depicted gay male subculture. For this reason, whether it is called low or pop, it would not be wrong to claim that his use of camp is Sontagesque.

2.1 Camp as Disenfranchisement: Homosexual / Heterosexual

Susan Sontag argues that camp, which is a taste for her, "is by its nature possible only in affluent societies, in societies or circles capable of experiencing the psychopathology of affluence" (63). Accordingly, in Hollinghurst's four novels protagonists and many major characters are white upper class élite gay men, which makes his fiction restrictive and reveals that his representation of the gay male bears traces of the social milieu in which he was raised. The author himself was born to an upper-middle class family—the only child of a bank manager father, got his bachelor's and master's degrees at Oxford, and then worked as a lecturer and editor. Sontag claims that "as the dandy is the nineteenth century's surrogate for the aristocrat in matters of culture, so Camp is the modern dandyism" (63). Similarly, the author's representation of camp excludes the non-camp, reinforces the dandy libidinous performative image and role of the homosexual, and culminates in the impression that it is anti-serious. Sontag agrees that camp is anti-serious, for it just proposes a comic vision of the world without offering a bitter or polemical comedy (63). By rejecting the political facet of camp, Hollinghurst, in line with Sontagesque camp, fails to subvert or queer heteronormative values of the dominant discourse and represents the sensibility of a certain class of gay men. This seems to be a consequence of the fact that from the 1970s on, monogamy, a construct of heteronormativity, lost its meaning among gay communities and their drift away from stable long-term relationships led them "into the trap of creating stereotypes, particularly white, middle-class, well-educated stereotypes of emotional inadequacy. It was, and is, primarily a heterosexual stereotype to which gay men in general found it difficult to relate and felt excluded from and therefore effectively remained disinterested" (Edwards 115).

The Swimming-Pool Library, to start with, depicts a campy heaven designed for the homosexual and it leaves out not only the non-homosexual but also the non-campy homosexual. In this way, the representation of gay life is reduced to campy queens, who constitute a white gay male class with internalised bourgeois values. Sontagesque camp "sees everything in quotation marks. It's not a lamp, but a 'lamp'; not a woman, but a 'woman'" (56). Hollinghurst's gay characters, likewise, are not simply gay, yet they are 'gay', or rather 'Gay' representing a class of individuals. For instance, the narrator and protagonist of the novel, William Beckwith is the idle son of an aristocratic family who devotes almost all his time and energy to his hectic sex life cruising men here and there. Brookes likens him to a vampire as he leads a loitering, leisure-class way of life which may be seen as parasitic (132). At the age of thirteen, he gets his first recognition and status in the society when he is appointed "Swimming-Pool Librarian," a title given to prefects according to their aptitude for particular tasks or interests at his school. The incongruous use of 'swimming-pool' and 'library' together implies the binary relation of nature to culture, sexuality to taboos, homosexuality to heterosexuality, and so on. It also refers to the campy lives they lead, which William regards as "a notion fitting to the double lives we [lead]" (*SPL* 141). The Library, which has got nothing to do with books, in fact, turns out to supply the private campy space for the randy gays to alleviate their insatiable libidinal energy. Duff claims that "Thatcher's shift away from socialism changed not only the industries and spaces that had been state run but also suggested a shift toward a British identity that was becoming increasingly privatized" (185). This process of privatisation allowed for the emergence of gay space, while, at the same time, it clarified the boundary between the gay and heterosexual space. The relation of gay space to the outside world, during Thatcher's government in England, where heteronormativity reigned, would fall into the category of closet; however, the space itself is camp, though not political but Sontagesque camp only, which strengthens the reified homosexual / heterosexual binary.

Booth, referring to how Versailles became a paradigm of *high* camp society with Louis XIV, who pulled the nobles into margins, and his brother, who held camp fantasy parties where people dressed as shepherds and shepherdesses, highlights the extravagant nature and class-solidarity of camp: "All camp people are to be found in the margins of society, and the richest vein of camp is generally to be found in the margins of the margins" (76). William's involvement and advance in Sontagesque camp, a life led in the margins of the margins, accelerate as soon as he gets into university life. There he meets James at one of the little parties organised by his tutor. The parties were "genially queeny occasions where gay chaplains (chaplains, that is to say) and the more enlightened dons mingled with undergraduates chosen for their charm or connections.... I was feeling particularly full of myself: I had been fucking a French boy from Brasenose" (*SPL* 16). The idea of tutors having posh fantasy parties with their undergraduate students, clergymen, and noblemen sounds like a campish fantasy of the gay male libido and these events bear similarities to the aforementioned Versailles parties. These parties also function as carnivalesque because no matter what one's social or economic status is they strip off all their roles and act as they feel like at those parties. These parties are some of the rare occasions where gay individuals can liberate their sexual urges and desires. However, in the absence of the other leg of the binary, and in the absence of the castrating power of the patriarchal metaphor, the characters are driven by and suffer from the lack of *jouissance* and they can never experience total satisfaction but always yearn for more.

Class-consciousness is a must in the representation of camp. Brookes states that the kinds of sexual relations William enjoys are determined by the reactionary, sexist, and racist attitudes of his class and that he is attracted to power, to the exercise of it, and to men who wield it (30).

Arthur is in William's life only because he is an attractive black bottom boy; otherwise, shouldering the weight of a monandrous relationship is not possible for William. He explains how he abided those hard times:

> If I had not been so fiercely and sexually in love with him, these days would have been utterly intolerable. And even so there were spells of repugnance, both at him and at my own susceptibility. Sex took on an almost purgative quality, as if after hours of inertia and evasion we could burn off our unspoken fears in vehement, wordless activity. Sex came to justify his presence there, to confirm that we were not just two strangers trapped together by a fateful mistake. (*SPL* 29)

The depiction of his relationship with Arthur, owing to the exaggerated significance attached to sexuality, is camp. Without sex, he claims, they would be two incompatible strangers in the same place, which would be a mistake regarding their social, economic and cultural status. The portrayal is again exclusive in that it reduces the base of relationships to sex as if there would be no compatibility between two individuals of different classes.

Sontagesque camp as taste and sensibility of a certain class of people, which can also be seen in furniture and buildings, reveals itself in the houses and neighbourhoods gay characters live in. The over-fondness of luxury, comfort, wealth, élitism, and the inevitable boasting that accompanies all confirm Sontagian definition of camp. Booth distinguishes camp from kitsch as "camp does not even have honourable intentions. Yet, although kitsch is never intrinsically camp, it has a certain toe-curling quality that appeals to the camp sense of humour. Kitsch is one of camp's favourite fads and fancies" (70). Kitsch is generally identified with coarseness and vulgarity, which brings it closer to camp. In the novel, the day William waits for the Arab boy in Kensington Gardens lavatory, an old man has a heart attack and falls down in front of him. William helps him thanks to his experience of swimming-pool librarianship. After a while, William comes across the old man in the showers at the Corry and introduces himself. The old man, Charles, eighty-three years old and known as Lord Nantwich, invites William to his place for a luncheon. The depiction of Charles's house consolidates the features of both kitsch and camp. Among the first details William notices are the classical figures on the library walls; "it was almost with embarrassment that I noticed that exaggerated phalluses protruded in each case from toga and tunic" (72). Classical figures represent the campy ancient Greeks, who, Foucault claims, were bisexual since they did not have a dual notion of gender or desire; desire was one and it was for beautiful human beings. Thus, there was no binary division of heterosexual / homosexual love in their society (*Sexuality* 2: 188). The use of 'exotic' classical images in a house in England might also represent their yearning for liberation from heteronormative stigmatising categories. The use of these figures, homo-erotic or rather pornographic, in an English library is not heteronormative or conventional. The books in the library, a place representing the dominant heteronormative culture which colonised the gay—its Other, conflict with the obscene drawings and figures on the walls, which represent the repudiated homosexual nature, i.e., camp. Then Charles takes William to a section in his house which he is proud of and which he claims is unique. There is a Roman pavement in the room with many figures from Roman London. Charles fantasises about naked legionaries, though he does not need to, since the figures are so obscene that they leave no room for one's imagination. There is a gleaming slave who "was towelling down his master's buttocks. In front of them two mighty warriors were wrestling, with legs apart, and bull-like genitals swinging between" (80). Charles finds this scene amusing, which brings to mind Sontag's "ultimate Camp statement: it's good because it's awful" (65). Camp, in other words, is not only a fondness for vulgarity, kitsch or bad art, but it is the appreciation of the vulgar and kitsch. That is why Charles's taste of decoration, architecture, and amusement is definitely camp. Brookes notices not only the promiscuous way of life Will leads but also the long history of homosexuality in this scene, and he underlines the link and continuity between the idealised male-centred pagan Roman world and the contemporary gay scene in Will's everyday life (138).

There is a popular assumption that camp exists only "in the eye of the beholder" (Cleto 89). Charles's requesting William to write his biography and offering to pay in return, thus, reveal how campy –at least he, being the beholder, finds- his life is and how narcissistic he is. He regards his life as a work of art, his masterpiece, which must definitely be transmitted to younger generations, which is another campy notion. The depiction of his house, furniture, ornaments, mind, of camp in brief, solidifies the boundary between the straight world and the queer one, distancing, alienating, and banishing the gay male from the non-gay world, or vice versa, the non-gay from the gay space. Les Brookes agrees that *The Swimming-Pool Library* is exclusive and argues that it is a ghetto novel with its focus on the gay male subculture. He also states that if Hollinghurst is ambivalent in his attitude to this culture, he, nonetheless, shows "a strong sense of identification with it, as well as an urge to record its particularity, its distinctive 'feel'. [He writes] primarily for a gay readership, and [he makes] the sexuality of [his] characters central, as if to lay stress on this as the core feature of their identity" (15).

The Folding Star is a novel depicting Belgium as the embodiment of camp in contrast to the closeting England; however, this portrayal is also exclusive and it functions as an empty signifier without the presence of the heterosexual or the non-campy homosexual. The narrator of the novel, Edward Manners, is a white well-educated middle-aged English teacher who moves to Belgium for a while and starts teaching two pupils there. However, very soon Edward loses his control and gets lost in the constant search for sex, gay bars, and young lads, which culminates in the representation of gay men as a distinct category clashing with the mainstream culture. The stylistics in the depiction of a middle-aged man falling for young lads seems to reflect the influence of the texts from Socratic and Platonic tradition. Foucault states that ancient Greeks did not believe that the nature of a man who loved men was different from the one who loved women; however, loving a man, for the Greeks, required a special stylistics and it was different from loving a woman: The first requirement was an age difference between lovers. Such a relationship was possible only "between an older male who had finished his education— and who was expected to play the socially, morally, and sexually active role—and a younger one, who had not yet achieved his definitive status and who was in need of assistance, advice, and support. This disparity was at the heart of the relationship" (*Sexuality* 2: 195). Edward's obsession with Luc and passion for many other lads in the novel does nothing more than reproduce the ancient tradition and stylistics, which reveals that in this novel class-consciousness is not only of social and economic parameters but rather of a life style dedicated to pursuit of pleasure.

There is a close relationship between camp and hedonism in the Sontagesque sense: "The man who insists on high and serious pleasures is depriving himself of pleasure; he continually restricts what he can enjoy.... Camp taste supervenes upon good taste as a daring and witty hedonism" (65). As for the hedonistic and campy nature of the novel, the opening scene is more than foreshadowing; Edward sees a man at a tram stop and just because he is charmed by his eyes and smile, he decides to follow him (*FS* 3). Unlike *The Swimming-Pool Library*, this novel gives voice and room to the non-gay and the non-campy at least in this scene, whereby Edward cannot have the man, who gets off at the next stop and hugs a woman waiting there for him. Just like William in *The Swimming-Pool Library*, Edward is one of the campy kind; a stereotype falsely representing all the individuals in a reified class, the emergence of which dates back to the emergence of capitalism and bourgeois discourse, when labour capacity had to be utilised to the greatest extent. The primary aim of sex and sexuality had to be reproduction to maintain the survival of the system, and other purposes like pleasure pursuits were out of question. Eventually, population became an important concern in the eighteenth century and "it was necessary to analyze the birthrate, the age of marriage, the legitimate and illegitimate births, the precocity and frequency of sexual relations, the ways of making them fertile and sterile, the effects of unmarried life or of the prohibitions, the impact of contraceptive practices—of those notorious 'deadly secrets" (Foucault, *Sexuality* 1: 25-26). The gay male, in this way, became a personage and was regarded as a threat to the system since he did not conform to the needs of the capitalist society. Donald Hall emphasises the significance of class theories for lesbian and gay history and politics referring to John D'Emilio's groundbreaking essay "Capitalism and Gay Identity," which

> explores how previously unknown patterns of social organization arising from capitalism...allowed for new opportunities for homosexual behavior and a new consciousness of specifically homosexual identity during and after the latter part of the nineteenth century.... Thus capitalism both enables contemporary notions of lesbian and gay identity and, inevitably, helps determine its least laudable aspects (consumerism, blindness to class inequities, etc.). (88)

Capitalism not only commodifies gay identity but also takes part in the configuration of it. However, by not marrying and refusing to reproduce, gay individuals pose a challenge to the system and this is why the dominant ideology stigmatises them as dandy, nymphomaniac and hedonistic. Hollinghurst's repetitive use of these attributes affirms the conventional deployment of homosexuality and, in the novel, it leaves no room for the non-dandy, non-nymphomaniac or the non-hedonistic.

The identification of hedonism with homosexuality may also be seen in relation to narcissism in the novel. When Edward first visits the Altidores, Luc is away on a trip, but Mrs. Altidore tells him that Luc used to be a student at a very old and exclusive Jesuit college, St. Narcissus; however, because of an obscure event, he was expelled (*FS* 18). The name of the college is significant since it implies the hypocritical attitude of the heteronormative society. On the one hand, Narcissus, the young man in Greek mythology falling in love with his own image in a pond, connotes same-sex affection. Steven Bruhm refers to man's deployment in the Symbolic and likens it to Narcissus's pool, which can be taken as a signifier of man's presence, while at the same time it displaces man and he suggests that "Narcissus's presence destroys the illusion of self-presence yet inscribes queer desire where presence might be" (17). This is the conventional identification of Narcissus with homosexuality, which is also employed by positivist psychology. On the other hand, St. Narcissus, an early patriarch of Jerusalem, is a symbol of religious and heteronormative doctrines. Moreover, the name of the college has wider implications in psychoanalysis as in both Freudian and Lacanian psychology narcissistic phase is the cognitive phase in which the infant has a symbiotic tie with the mother in the pre-castrated register. Narcissism has close affinities with the infant's formation of its ideal ego. Lacan, rereading Freud, argues that before the ego develops, an infant first identifies with his / her mirror image and perceives the image as totality of its own being. This imaginary function, he suggests, is narcissistic (696). In other words, the ego –which emerges during this fascination—is based on misrecognition as it is based on an illusory narcissistic image of wholeness and perfection. Consequently, whereas a subject is constituted in the symbolic order, the ego functions in the imaginary register. Butler likens heteronormativity to the primary narcissism and claims that "heterosexual matrix proves to be an *imaginary* logic that insistently issues forth its own unmanageability" (*Bodies* 239). To gain access to the symbolic and to be defined as a Man, the initial step is to repress same-sex desire and leave it in the imaginary realm. Since the identification with the specular image helps the formation of the ego, an individual finds himself / herself in the deceptive realm of surface appearances. Taken-for-grantedness of heteronormativity, thus, is exposed and undermined through the author's choice of the name 'St. Narcissus,' and through the context and the connotations of the name, it becomes clear that heteronormativity is also transient, deceptive and imaginary.

The Spell, too, depicts a magical heterotopic world belonging to the white affluent and well-educated homosexual, and it excludes all that do not fit in. The novel opens with a retrospective narrative depicting the first visit of a twenty-three-year old British man, Robin, in the United States for research towards a dissertation. Robin's first portrayal is given within the frame of a homoerotic trip with a local Indian pick-up driver who gives him a lift. He is the Englishman in America and his identity is constructed in opposition to the Other. In terms of ethnicity, the local Indian boy is the Other to an Englishman, so both are positioned in the margin of the mainstream discourse. However, regarding sexual orientation, the well-educated gay Englishman is the Other to the straight Indian, and the situation, which involves repressed feelings which are seen as threats to the ego, results in feelings of discomfort or repulsion. Thus, when individuals resort to projection as a defense mechanism in case of failure to differentiate themselves—for sexual identity, ethnicity, and race are a priori truths constructed by dominant ideologies—they regard the one they cannot distinguish as the Other. This is exactly what Robin tries to do when he meets the local man. When they part, Robin "smiled his clean seducer's smile, though it was a mask to his confusion, his fleeting apprehension not of the honoured quaintness of being British, but of the class sense which tinted or tainted all his dealings with the world" (*TS* 7). The beginning of the novel gives the reader an insight into how exclusive camp could be, not only in terms of sexual orientation and ethnicity but also class distinction.

In the novel, the main characters, as are many others in Hollinghurst's work, are of white upper class élite gay community. To illustrate, Robin, a PhD candidate at the beginning of the novel, goes to a bar, The Blue Coyote, where he meets Sylvan, a rough, beautiful, and available man as soon as he gets off the pick-up. During their conversation, he leaves the man for a while and calls Jane, whom he left two days ago, only to learn that she is pregnant and he is going to be a father. The only information about Jane is that she is not married to Robin; however, there is still a new life awaiting both of them and Robin, unlike a father-to-be who has just been told he is going to be a father, is indifferent:

> He would go back into the bar as if he hadn't just had a conversation that changed his life. He saw perhaps he could forget the conversation, and put off his new life till the morning. A beautiful man was waiting for him and Robin glowed in the urgency and the lovely complacency of their wanting each other. He wanted nothing in his mind, in his sight, in his hands but Sylvan. (*TS* 13)

Robin's indifference is obviously an example for the aforementioned exclusive stereotype gay male of emotional inadequacy. Terry Boggis, analysing gay parenthood, states that GLBT individuals face a vast variety of considerations when they plan their families. These considerations are those which heterosexual families do not have to deal with: "surrogacy or adoption? adoption or alternative insemination? alternative insemination with a known donor, or with an anonymous donor? Will a known donor be a father to the child, an involved parent, or will he be defined and identified as an uncle, a friend, or merely a donor to his biological child?" (175). These concerns may be the reasons behind Robin's apparently indifferent parenthood. Another interpretation is that *sylva*, in Latin, means *forest* and the choice of this name highlights the libidinal and bestial energy which this man creates and which makes Robin desire him desperately. Forest, in mainstream psychology, may refer to the unconscious, primitive instincts and the mysterious, which, in this encounter, implies Robin's released life instinct and libido. He does not even get excited about the baby he is going to have. The only feeling he has is the fear that he might have to marry Jane when the baby is born. This attitude is exclusively camp because a male individual is supposed to repress his latent homosexual inclination in order to be configured in the symbolic register; nevertheless, Robin refuses to be deployed in the mainstream and remains campy, a decision which challenges the dominant patriarchal discourse, yet excludes the non-campy.

Sontagesque camp taste "has an affinity for certain arts rather than others. Clothes, furniture, all the elements of visual decor, for instance, make up a large part of Camp. For Camp art is often decorative art, emphasizing texture, sensuous surface, and style at the expense of content" (55). Robin is a good example to illustrate camp's affinity for decorative art as well as for promiscuity since, in the main story line, when he is in his late forties and his son Danny is a grown-up young man in his early twenties, he is a campy architect working mainly on houses which belong to old queens.

The Line of Beauty is the last ring of Hollinghurst's chain of deploying the gay male within the stigmatising and degrading heterosexual frame, excluding him from the heteronormative world, and representing a distinct category of gay men. The 'line' in the title of the novel refers to a line of cocaine, which supplies the gay individuals in Hollinghurst's work with 'beauty' and renders them disoriented in the heteronormative world. As in the other three novels, the world in which the queer characters are depicted is exclusive.

Gerald and Rachel Feddens are the affluent couple in the novel hosting Nick in their mansion as a friend of their son's. Nick and Toby are Oxford graduates—typically white, at-least-middle class, and well-educated characters, and although Toby does not live with his parents any longer, Nick stays there and accompanies Catherine as a surrogate brother, and a surrogate son for the couple. Gerald is an MP working for Thatcher's Tory government. Nick, with a humble background and parents in Barwick, does not, indeed, fit in or belong with these upper class people; however, he aspires for the campy life they lead and this is one of the reasons why he lives with the Feddens for more than four years until he is forced out. His moving in and staying there also has to do with subjectivity formation; Nick desperately seeks to regain the lost narcissistic perfection of the imaginary register and re-build his imago, ideal ego, in the Symbolic register. He unconsciously wants to do it by identifying with the Feddens, who, in fact, function as the Other in this identification.

Camp's supportiveness of class solidarity, and thus of exclusiveness, finds embodiment in the portrayal of the Feddens' house, which is a big white Notting Hill building in Kensington Park Gardens. Sontag's camp is "either completely naïve or else wholly conscious" (59). In Nick's case, he definitely plays at being, or rather becoming, campy. As a result of his fondness for extravagance, Nick is carried away with the house and the neighbourhood:

> He loved coming home to Kensington Park Gardens in the early evening, when the wide treeless street was raked by the sun, and the two white terraces stared at each other with the glazed tolerance of rich neighbours. He loved letting himself in at the three-locked green front door, and locking it again behind him, and feeling the still security of the house. (*LB* 5)

Nick is fascinated with the living standards and prosperity of the residents in the neighbourhood. When he gets into the Feddens' house, he feels as if the house belonged to him as he wants to re-home himself. He even poses as the owner of the house to impress outsiders and to feel the lower-class heterosexual gaze. By doing so, he reveals his desire to be discursively positioned in the mainstream discourse. For instance, wandering on the balcony and watching the scenery, he notices a girl walking a white dog and wonders "how he might appear to her, if she glanced up, as an enviable figure, poised against the shining accomplished background of the lamplit room" (*LB* 17). He poses as if he were a motif in an elaborate landscape painting using the girl as a mirror reflecting his superiority to the other. He looks at himself from the position of the gaze or the girl can also be taken as the Lacanian gaze. James Mellard states that the gaze "cuts in many directions, as it links the subject to the object and by that linkage turns each into the other whenever one reverses (by a shift in point of view) the scopic field" (84-85). In other words, the girl is the object since it is Nick who spots the other and narrates the moment, yet Nick's narration reveals that in fact he desires to be the object of the public gaze. Nick's desperate efforts to fit in the upper-class life are essential to demonstrate and comprehend how Hollinghurst's portrayal of the camp excludes the non-camp in the novel. There are characters of lower classes, of course, but the main plot takes place around the upper class campy figures living in ivory towers.

Core is among the numerous writers who defined camp: "Camp is laughing at *The Importance of Being Earnest* without knowing why. Camp is laughing at *The Importance of Being Earnest and* knowing why" (81). Camp is, in other words, a comedy of manners with or without political ends—the latter is the case in Hollinghurst's fiction, though. Toby's birthday party held at his uncle's house reveals the extent to which camp could go, particularly in terms of mannerisms. His uncle Lord Kessler lives at Hawkeswood, built in the 1880s for the first Baron Kessler. Nick's birthday is eight days later and the party is first planned to be a joint celebration, yet Gerald and Rachel never mention it again. Hawkeswood, a product of Victorian monstrosity, impresses and charms Nick at first sight: "On the ceiling, in a flowered ellipse, two naked females held a wreath of roses. Nick saw at once that the landscape over the fireplace was a Cézanne. It gave him a hilarious sense of his own social displacement. It was one of those moments that only the rich could create" (*LB* 45). Feeling ashamed, Nick denies both his upbringing and family, yet even he, as a wannabe aristocrat yearning for upper-class life standards, feels alienated in Lord Kessler's chateau-like campy house. The extravagant settings both there and at Kensington Park Gardens are exclusively camp in social and economic terms, shutting out all that do not fit in.

2.2 Camp as the Oversimplified Homosexual Stereotype

Sontagesque camp is "esoteric –something of a private code, a badge of identity" (53). It is, after all, a style or sensibility which is attributed to a heterogenous group of individuals. Hollinghurst's depiction of camp, therefore, is exclusive in many respects and it also shuts out the gay male individuals who do not fit in this homophobic depiction: the Gay as prurient, unable to distinguish between love and sex, junkie, and sooner or later afflicted with AIDS. The campy image of the homosexual is a constructed performative role and identity, and Hollinghurst's repetitive use of it re-establishes conventional notions and attributes related to the gay male. Claire Colebrook claims that "stereotypical representations of certain groups in the media reinforce rigid norms, preclude self-constitution and do not allow for subjects outside those norms to be recognised. On the other hand, there can be no creation of oneself *ex nihilo*" (14). Accordingly, Hollinghurst's male gay characters are extensions of cliché representations of homosexuality dating back to the ancient world and earliest civilisations, and they are also embodiments of Sontagesque camp. Camp adores cliché, surface, and image (Flinn 440). These clichés can be analysed in Hollinghurst's novels under four main categories: polyandrous relationships and obsession with sex, confusion between or interchangeable use of love and sex, drug addiction, and AIDS.

The exaggeration of sexual characteristics is an element of Sontagesque camp. In accordance with this feature, in *The Swimming-Pool Library*, Hollinghurst's gay male characters demonstrate how far obsession with sex could go and how far sexuality could be exaggerated in fiction.

Edwards questions why gay men are apparently so obsessed with sex and asks if they really practise a lot of sexual activities with a lot of sexual partners and if this promiscuity is really more significant for them than for their heterosexual counterparts. He refers to some sex studies of the late 1970s which reveal significant, but not extraordinarily high, degrees of sexual activity in some cities, and states that:

> More insight is perhaps developed in more personal or literary studies including the American work of acclaimed writer Edmund White (1986) and the ethnography of John Rechy (1977) and John Alan Lee (1978) or the UK comparisons of Quentin Crisp (1968) and Alan Hollinghurst (1988). All of these are fairly or even very positive pro-promiscuity pieces of work. (105)

The novel is seen as a pro-promiscuity fiction as sex does make characters feel satisfied for a short while, yet soon they get hungry and start looking for more. The characters glance at one another in the showers, or sometimes just a smile would be more than enough to have casual sex. William admits that he sometimes ends up in a bedroom of the hotel above the Corry with a man he smiles at in the showers, which, for him, proves the benefit of smiling in general (*SPL* 10). However, sexual gratification does not mean satisfying desire; desire is insatiable for Lacan and individuals are bound to feel disappointment as a result of knowing that there must be something beyond pleasure—*jouissance*—to be experienced but that they will never be able to get it (Homer 90). The permanent lack of *jouissance* is the reason lying beneath the prurient nature and continuous undersatisfaction of the gay characters in Hollinghurst's fiction. Another explanation, offered by Edwards, is that easy access to cruising places and the availability of many gay ghettos create the sexual activity: "A second explanation is that the stigmatisation of sexuality leads to an explosion of sexuality when presented with plenty of opportunity to practise it. This domino theory of sexuality also rests on a series of essentialist assumptions and the problem, at least partly, seems to be one of maintaining an identity" (105).

Sontagesque camp has affinities with the vulgar, coarse, indecent and exaggeratedly sexual: "The connoisseur of Camp has found more ingenious pleasures. Not in Latin poetry and rare wines and velvet jackets, but in the coarsest, commonest pleasures, in the arts of the masses" (63). In the novel, the relentless yearning for sex and consummation of this desire comprises most of the storyline and the narrative stars William with his endless libido and desire. The exaggeration of homo-sexuality and the coarse nature of gay male intimacies correspond to Sontag's definition of camp. For example, the scene depicting William's coming across Colin, the tanned boy from the Corry, shows Hollinghurst's narrative position: Colin and William hold each other's gaze for a moment and in this way "the sudden precipitation of sex" begins, despite all the efforts of William's other suitor on the train; Colin gets off the train with William and when asked if he lives there he just says he does not but he thinks he might go and check Will's place, after which they go to Will's place and have "some efficient sex" (*SPL* 94). Gay sex is very easy to find and loses its meaning as soon as partners get sexual gratification in the novel.

Polyandrous happenings do not ever slow down in the novel, in accordance with the promiscuous nature of camp, and gay male characters make use of public conveniences for sex. Edwards argues that after cruising, the next step is to find "nooks and crannies for sexual activity to take place, privately. This process of simultaneous exhibitionism and voyeurism is central to all public sexual activity" (93). This makes cottaging an integral part of the depiction of camp. William is the butterfly man perching on different male flowers for a short while and soon flying away, and so does he when he comes across Arthur long time after they break up. He realises that he misses him and even doubts whether he is alive. As soon as he sees him in a gay bar, he leaves his friends Phil and Archie and gives him a hug kissing him. He immediately takes him to the lav, pushes him into a lock-up, pulls his trousers down his knees, and feels in 'love' again—'love' consummated right there in the lock-up. Nonetheless, even after this casual sex in the lav, William feels "abjectly unhappy" (*SPL* 203). He might be regretting for losing his control and acting like a beast, but he already has a bestial nature regarding sex.

Casual sex is literally casual; it is deprived of all the rituals in the mainstream practice. It has become an object of consumption and it might emerge anywhere anytime and with anyone in the campy world Hollinghurst describes. The gay male characters' obsession with sex, Edwards suggests, may also be a consequence of their;

> sense of distance or difference that can potentially create a psyche so convinced of its isolation that relationships are put under particular stress and intensity. This sense of otherness, outsider identity, or simply difference, is partly the outcome of the definition of gay sexuality itself as other and different and partly the result of the practical and social parameters put around potential same-sex relationships. (112-113)

In other words, the representation of this obsession is a direct influence of the stereotype gay male identity and the subculture camp leads to. The approach to sex is also directly related to the increasing consumerism during the 1980s in England under the Thatcher government. With the growing emphasis on neo-liberalism and free market economy, same-sex desire and sex were commodified and were launched as consumption goods. William's sexual intercourse with Abdul illustrates the spontaneous and instant notion of sex: William, writing his biography, needs to ask Charles whether he has been in prison. Hoping to find him at the Club, William goes there, but sees Abdul closing the gate as he is about to lock and leave the place. Abdul affirms that Charles has been in prison and that everyone knows it. Then Abdul invites him into the kitchen, undresses him, turns him round and meanwhile Will waits greedily. William narrates the intercourse enthusiastically and describes how Abdul took him giving him both pleasure and pain. He adds that "[i]t was quickly finished, and he slurped out of me, and slapped me again. 'Hmm,' he said noncommittally; then, 'Fuck off out of here, man'" (*SPL* 262). It starts like an assault, but William seems to have been looking forward to the occasion. His consent, or desire— to be more precise, to get laid is camp; this is the camp fantasy, like the Versailles fancy dress parties, to get raped by a macho man, a voluntary rape in other words. As soon as the act is over, Abdul is very rude to him and dismisses him, which gives an insight into the author's notion of campy relationships; a masculinised macho man, straight if possible, and a feminised gay male, younger if possible. The narration in this scene reveals how Hollinghurst's attitude gets phallocentric as he employs the straight macho figures as object of Desire. Moreover, in this scene, homosexual sex acts are described in masculine terms of orgasm; there is an emphasis on silence and verbal communication does not exist. "The point is: it won't work including talking. Talking leads to distraction and more importantly personal communication and emotional attachment. Its excitement comes from its lack of contact: its minimalism" (Edwards 106). The anti-serious, irresponsible, carefree, prurient, and hypocritical image of the Homosexual confirms the gay male stereotype defined by homophobic dominant ideologies and renders Hollinghurst's depiction of camp Sontagesque.

Sexuality is on top of the list of priorities as a result of the male homosexual's social, economic, and political definition of identity through his sexuality (Edwards 105-106). In accordance with this identity in addition to the heteronormative biases and clichés regarding homosexuality, sex is always in the limelight in *The Swimming-Pool Library*. In the novel there is even a long paragraph dedicated to kinds of penis, which is like a mock-epic catalogue of the male organ:

> I was amazed and enlightened by the variety of the male organ. In the rank and file of men showering the cocks and balls took on the air almost of an

independent species, exhibited in instructive contrasts. Here was the long, listless penis, there the curt, athletic knob or innocent rosebud of someone scarcely out of school. Carlos's Amerindian giant swung alongside the compact form of a Chinese youth whose tiny brown willy was almost concealed in his wet pubic hair, like an exotic mushroom in a dish of seaweed. (*SPL* 164)

The catalogue is written with a tone of scientific seriousness and everything is calculated in detail; size, colour, shape and circumcision all are mentioned in a highly poetic language. However, the weird theme is in contrast to the tone, which is solved at the end of the paragraph with the two characters ejaculating in the lav. The obsession made clear with the long detailed description of penises also reveals the gay characters' desire to *be* the phallus, whereas heteronormative systems requires them to *have* the phallus instead, which, for Lacan means being the signifier of the Other's desire. For women, it involves rejecting the attributes of femininity and in Hollinghurst's fiction gay characters feminise themselves as a result of their obsession with the phallus. Lacan suggests that "male homosexuality, in accordance with the phallic mark that constitutes desire, is constituted along the axis of desire, while female homosexuality, on the contrary, as observation shows, is oriented by a disappointment that strengthens the axis of the demand for love" (583). The configuration of male homosexuality, therefore, which is based on same-sex desire only, is the underlying reason for the gay characters' preoccupation with penis, i.e., the incarnation of the phallus. As for the use of public conveniences for sexual purposes in this scene, which is, for Edwards, probably the most established and oldest male homosexual informal institution, there are two reasons: accessibility and its maleness (100).

The Folding Star is another novel quite rich in the sexual extremities ascribed to gay characters and the depiction of Sontagesque camp as meat market. This representation harms the struggles of queer movements, culminating in the re-production of dominant ideologies and clichés. For example, Edward's obsession with Luc does not constitute an impediment; he has random sex with anyone he finds. Restuccia refers to Lacan's transcendence and explains that in non-narcissistic love, i.e., second-order love, there is transcendence to the object, but in the narcissistic love, i.e., first-order love, there is not (373). Therefore, in the former, love is more than the love object and the love object is a person who is, in fact, not there. Edward's love, likewise, goes beyond Luc and he is permanently deprived of Luc as the love object. That is why he is after many other male gay characters in the novel even when he thinks he is in love with Luc. To illustrate, the second most important man in the novel for Edward is

Cherif, a Moroccan born in Paris. Edward meets him in the Town Museum, where Cherif had cruised men before although he was not interested in paintings at all. The invention of cruising is a modern phenomenon centred on the separation of sex from procreation; thus, it is not surprising that it should originate with gay men whose sexual activity is already regarded as separate from procreation (Edwards 93). As soon as the cruising stage is successfully completed, consummation comes as the next step. Accordingly, as soon as Edward and Cherif meet, they go to Edward's hotel, called 'the Mykonos', for sex. Mykonos, the famous holiday destination for queer people, symbolises the Englishman's longing for the liberty in ancient Greece. In *The Swimming-Pool Library* parks and public lavatories were cruising places, but in this novel characters lead a life of higher standards and they are campier, at least in terms of cruising places. Meanwhile, Edward writes a letter to his old friend Edie and tells her about his rapid start with Cherif; however, the same day he goes to the Bar Biff and starts looking for new preys:

> I leant against a mirrored pillar and kept my eye on a bunch of kids who hung around mocking and caressing each other, sipping quickly and shiftily at Cokes.... I found myself wondering as I watched a muscly little lad in a string vest and baggy hitched-up jeans licking blond froth from the black down on his upper lip and holding forth hoarsely like a schoolyard gangster. He couldn't be more than sixteen, surely? But that was okay here, unlike at home. (*FS* 22)

Gay bars in Hollinghurst's novels are often characterised through their isolation from the heteronormative world outside and one needs to know the place somehow to gain access. These gay bars, called "Formal Public Sex Contexts" by Edwards, which are defined as formal, institutional, intentional and manifest functional places,"reflect the temporal and spatial segregation of the homosexual subculture which ultimately becomes a complete counter-cultural separation: ghettoisation" (99-103). The ghettoisation of this stigmatised minority inevitably reinforces a distinct gay male subculture and identity primarily based on sexuality.

Sontag's camp relishes the little triumphs and awkward intensities of character and this taste identifies with whatever it is enjoying (65). Since camp is directly associated with hedonism and extremities, the use of polyandrous relationships and promiscuity in the representation of the campy gay male stereotype is not unpredictable in Hollinghurst's novels. Edward gets wild with the joy and freedom he finds in Belgium; he does not even mind seducing a sixteen-year-old boy in a gay bar. When he sees that the boy is indifferent to him, he finds another guy, Ty, a model who thinks Edward could help him go to London and have a successful career there. Cherif is also in the bar, but Ty apparently knows and dislikes him. Surprisingly, going home with the young lad, Ty, or Cherif does not make much difference to Edward: "I was already warming to Cherif's hand moving gently on the small of my back and could see and feel the pleasure of going home with him just as certainly as I could envisage the meaningless and unarousing performance I might have gone through with Ty" (*FS* 25). Edward, like many other gay characters in Hollinghurst's work, has sex for sex's sake; he is not selective and any guy will do. Sex loses all its ritualistic connotations and is far from giving any form of satisfaction. The characters' constant search for sex can be analysed with reference to Lacan, too. For him, desire is for a lack, something missing, and even when the need is met, the desire cannot be satisfied. Gay characters in the novel desperately try to fill in that lack, which seems to be love, or try to replace it with sex; however, the result is frustration and dissatisfaction. Likewise, Edward takes Cherif home and sleeps with him, yet he is of no special importance. He straightforwardly tells Cherif he is in love with his pupil Luc, though he knows Cherif loves him. Edward is definitely not in love with Luc; Luc is the only one he cannot gain access to and this is the only thing rendering him unique. The longer he fails to have him, the more valuable Luc gets. For the time being he enjoys sleeping with Cherif and exploits his feelings for himself. If Cherif functions as *satisfaction* for Edward, Luc is *jouissance* for a while. Pleasure gives Edward a limited form of satisfaction and it is temporary; however, he constantly tries to go beyond it in his attempts to have Luc and suffers as a result of his futile attempts from pain, which turns out to be the embodiment of *jouissance*.

Male homosexual activity, Edwards puts forth, is defined in masculine terms of orgasm as it is completely separated from procreation and partly separated from some forms of affection and emotional bonding. It is also limited to non-demonstrative gestures, few kisses, few cuddles and definitely no tears (106). Edward, accordingly, likes and sleeps with anybody without emotional bonding or a sense of attachment; he even finds Luc's father Martin hot and he admits he would love to have sex with him (*FS* 185). Matt is second only to Edward regarding random sex. Once two guys attempt to steal Edward's wallet in the showers and Edward decides not to complain only when the darker of the boys, whom he really falls for, offers to do anything Edward wants. Upon hearing of the incident Matt tells Edward that he should have brought the guy to his place so that they both could have taken turns with him (*FS* 85). Matt is into any kind of sex, including orgies, and he does not want to miss any opportunity regarding sex. The idea of orgy is still camp in the world and it is usually associated with porn pictures—particularly gay or bisexual ones; it is regarded only as a camp fantasy by many. As well as being Edward's partner, Matt has casual sex with many others and wants to have sex with even more boys. He is the embodiment of camp features and that of heteronormative representations of camp in Hollinghurst's work. One day his trick does not show up and instead he goes with Cherif: "I ended up with your friend, the Frenchman, the Moroccan.... He told me that he loves you, and he is *wild*" (*FS* 74). Matt tells him the details just in order to hurt his feelings or to find out about his feelings for Cherif. Matt even has Luc, which Edward learns from the barman in the gay bar. The barman says Matt picked the seventeen-year-old boy one night, and the next night he came and told the barman "he had him *seven times*—and that was just the first night" (*FS* 435). On the sexual freedom these characters enjoy, Edwards states that the first level of liberation is the individual one; the idea is that public sex liberates personal hang-ups and inhibitions about sexuality. Second, there is a collective level of liberation as "every fuck is a fuck for freedom," like a challenge to the heteronormative monogamy (94). However, the repetitive identification of camp and homosexuality with promiscuity makes the novel a pro-promiscuity novel and the gay male subjectivity a stable identity.

The Spell, just like the other novels analysed, renders the homosexual prurient and even nymphomaniac. Alongside with queer movements, camp is restored back into its queer origins; nevertheless, Cleto suggests that "the 'appropriate' queerness of camp can't be tamed into a homosexual property—on the contrary, such property should be refused as an effect of the bourgeois cognitive ordering" (33). Nevertheless, Hollinghurst depicts camp as gay sensibility and reduces it to sexual acts and desire, which is the image of the homosexual in heteronormative discourses since dominant ideologies do not recognise love or marriage between two men. It is the uncanny for the oppressive traditional patriarch. Truman Capote contrasts earlier homosexuals, who thought camp freed them from social exclusion and persecution, to the militants of the 1970s, who defined it as "a form of ghettoisation, which is complicit with mainstream culture in the reinforcement of the sexual binaries of gay and straight" (54). *The Spell*, just like the definition of camp in the 70s, isolates the homosexual from the heterosexual and in this way reinforces the dominant heteronormative values. This separation can be seen in the gay male characters's relationships and conceptions of sexuality. For instance, knowing that Justin had a boyfriend, Robin wanted to find out more about his rival, drove to the street they lived in, and began watching their house. He aspires to scrutinise his rival to compare him to himself; he wants to make sure that he is better than his rival. When he saw Alex, the boyfriend, Robin found him much more handsome than he had expected. "At the same time he thought brutishly of the sex-life he had with Justin and couldn't imagine how this man could ever have satisfied him" (*TS* 41). Robin's desire for his rival, even when Justin was still living with Alex, showed how shallow his feelings for Justin were. For Lacan, love "requires that the subject be prepared to give nothing of him or herself to the other and is also willing to accept in return the nothingness in the other.... Lacan calls for a mutual narcissistic divestment in both partners, which leaves each person being a lacking object for the other but who is loved anyway despite and with its lack" (Bernstein 720). This is the narcissistic nature of the gay characters in the novel; they give nothing and receive nothing in return, for they already do not possess it. If this 'love' triangle were to be put into the heterosexual frame, the oddity of the triangle would become more visible: the feeling upon seeing the same-sex person with whom a man or a woman is cheated on by their partners would probably not be desire for the stranger, even if same-sex desire itself were considered acceptable.

In this novel, too, Sontagesque camp appears in the form of promiscuity, hedonism, and exaggeration. Edwards refers to the mainstream pressures to couple up and the gay community's reactional resistance to long-term relationships, and states that it is only natural that "the outcome in the gay community is slightly contradictory as they do and they don't, it seems, succeed at personal relationships. The situation is worsened through...a whole series of heterosexist stereotypes" (120). Justin is one of these stereotypes; when he is in a relationship with Robin and living in his house, he looks for satisfaction somewhere else. To their country house, they invite Alex and Danny for dinner. Justin does not know exactly why he has invited Alex but he is obviously delighted to see the two men in his life who still desire him. He is also restless and desperately in need of trouble. Right after the dinner, he watches the night, the sky, and the stars, thinking of his life, and he realises:

> He longed for crowds and the purposeful confusion of the city; he wanted shops where you could get what you wanted, and deafening bars so full of men seeking pleasure and oblivion that you could hardly move through them.... He thought there were the great high times, the moments of initiation, new men, new excitements; and then there was all the rest. He turned back towards the lighted door. Only candlelight, but a subtle glare across grass and path. He thought resentfully of how this wasn't his house; it had been patched and roofed and furnished to please or tame another partner. (*TS* 43-44)

Sontagesque camp is "a mode of enjoyment, of appreciation –not judgement…. What it does is to find the success in certain passionate failures" (65). Likewise, the characters fail to achieve long-term and monandrous relationships or settle down, yet the narrative is like a celebration of such failures. Justin knows very well that he does not fit in a settled life. He aspires to be the flamboyant queen of crazy parties and he wants to lead a polyandrous life. A campy life is the only thing that can give him satisfaction, but not *jouissance*. In their country house, he is bored to death and develops a new desire for Robin's son Danny now and desperately desires him. Just as he lived in Alex's house for some time and left him to start a new life with Robin, he might start a new affair and move into someone else's house anytime. This is why he does not feel it is his home and states that it was decorated for another partner, not for him.

The Line of Beauty is also a novel portraying the gay male as obsessed with sex and polyamorous. Edwards considers the gay male obsession with sex as a reaction to dominant heterosexist ideology: "In the 1970s, monogamy in the gay community was in many ways perceived of as profoundly untrendy, and an ideology developed around the idea of the negativity of monogamy and the positivity of promiscuity" (114). Although this promiscuous image of the gay male characters seems to be apolitical in Sontag's sense of camp, since it does not serve queer politics, it does serve heteronormativity by way of reifying and solidifying a stable homo-sexual identity, and thus, it is highly political. Nick is an example to illustrate this promiscuous stereotype; after the first meeting, he finds himself in a relationship with Leo which he cannot name. The couple decide to keep seeing each other; however, a monandrous life is not satisfactory for Nick, as is typical in Hollinghurst's works. Thus, he manages to harness his lust only until the birthday party at the Hawkeswood and there he sets his libido free. At the party, he first feels attracted to one of the waiters, Tristão, and observes him from top to toe: "His hands were huge and beautiful, the hands of a virtuoso. His dressy trouser-front curved forwards with telling asymmetry. When he saw that Nick was looking his way he gave him the vaguest smile and inclined his head, as if waiting for a murmured order. Nick thought, he doesn't even realize I like him" (*LB* 63). The waiter charms Nick and staring at him fantasising Nick completely forgets about Leo. Among the party guests is Wani Ouradi, another obsession for Nick from university years. He attends the party with his intended Martine:

> Nick sometimes greeted Wani with a friendly grope between the legs, or a long breathless snog, and he'd once had him tied up naked in his college room for a whole night; he had sodomized him tirelessly more often than

he could remember. Wani himself, glancing back to see if his girlfriend, his intended, was following, had no idea of all this, of course; indeed, they hardly knew each other. (*LB* 65-66)

Nick has had a crush on Wani for years apparently and now and again he indulges in sexual fantasies about him. Wani, whose real name is Antoine, is of a prosperous Lebanese family and he uses his intended as a paid front to conceal his homosexuality. Martine functions as the mirrored image of Balzac's character Sarrasine in his novella called *Sarrasine*—the story of a French sculptor, Sarrasine, who goes to Rome and, not knowing that there are no female singers on stage and all soprano roles are performed by castrati, falls in love with a soprano named La Zambinella. Sarrasine's "e" at the end is a feminine linguistic property and its masculine form Sarrazin also exists in French; the play with the word highlights the castration of the male protagonist by a castrato, like "the discarded men of the story, all castrated, cut off from pleasure" (Barthes, *S/Z* 38). Likewise, Martine's 'e' at the end emphasises femininity, whereas Wani would love a Martin. In the process of his subjectification, Wani is castrated by the heteronormative society, which is represented by his cover intended Martine, and he is cut off from pleasure.

Foucault, contrasting the frankness of the seventeenth century to the normative prudence of Victorian bourgeoisie, analyses how power silenced behaviour or acts it considered abnormal. If any form of unacceptable trait or act "insisted on making itself too visible, it would be designated accordingly and would have to pay the penalty.... Not only did it not exist, it had no right to exist and would be made to disappear upon its least manifestation—whether in acts or in words" (*Sexuality* 1: 4). As Wani lives within the closet, Nick does not know the fact that Wani is gay yet and thus he keeps dreaming of him. Thinking of Tristão and dreaming of a future with Wani, Nick has enough room both in his mind and heart for Toby. Toby, just like Wani, "remained in the far pure reach of fantasy, which grew all the keener and more inventive to meet the challenge of his unavailability" (*LB* 59). The more unattainable a man looks, the more tantalising he is likely to become for Nick. Tristão, Wani, and Toby are straight, at least Nick thinks so, and this makes them, along with many others, a lot more desirable for a homosexual—in Hollinghurst's point of view. Flaunting is associated with camp and by portraying the protagonist in a constant search for random sex, Hollinghurst carries on and builds up the ongoing homophobic discourses; the only thing the Homosexual cares for is same-sex sex, whether with another homosexual or heterosexual man.

Hollinghurst's persistent emphasis on the bestial nature of gay relationships and their insatiableness might be an intentional attempt to naturalise same-sex sex acts in the Platonic-Socratic sense. Love of women, in ancient Greece, was seen as 'natural' simply because it was based on pleasure principle. Pleasure being the only concern for Hollinghurst's gay characters, the characters heterosexualise themselves by seeking sexual gratification in their partners. The obsession with pleasure and the search for *jouissance* which underlies it come out in the author's depiction of the party at the Feddens' house to which the Prime Minister is invited. Nick sees Jasper and Wani coming out of the same bedroom. Later on they go to Nick's bathroom, but this time with Tristão. There it comes out that at Toby's birthday party the waiter did not meet Nick because Wani gave him coke and money in return for sex. Now the couple rent the waiter, give him Charlie, and have orgy. Nick discovers that Wani time and again has the waiter to show him his tricks. The deal is very simple, explains Tristão: "He give me coke and I fuck him in the hass.... He always pay the best" (*LB* 339). The rich campy queen renting masculine straight guys to entertain him and to get laid is one of the numerous homophobic myths circulating in many cultures, yet it is not realistic. Also the scene involving the waiter's stripping and seducing the two is weird, for Tristão acts like a professional stripper or a character in gay porn, as if confirming all heteronormative clichés.

Hollinghurst's gay male characters reject the imposed ethical or moral values of the dominant ideology. Apparently they challenge the possession of their bodies and subvert the notions of pairing and monogamy. On the surface, this presentation queers the accepted values and norms which are traditionally attributed to married couples and it renders a queer approach to the author's work. However, in fact it does not go beyond reproducing and re-establishing the traditional image of the gay male in the heteronormative world. The characters, conforming to all clichés attributed to themselves, do not hesitate to make advances even at their friends' lovers. To illustrate, when Nick goes to France to stay at Toby's place with Wani, Catherine is there with her new boyfriend Jasper. Nick is so bold that he can imagine having Jasper and regards his acts as signals of flirting and seduction. For instance, once Cathy and Jasper were in the swimming-pool making love and kissing, and Nick "felt Jasper might try to involve him too if he went in.... He thought he could probably have him if he wanted, but he didn't want to give him that satisfaction. A minute later they got out, intently casual, Jasper's stocky hard-on sticking up at an angle" (*LB* 273-274). Nick obviously feels sexually attracted to Jasper and desires him, just as he does many other men. Stephen Mitchell suggests that it is safer to have romance and excitement with someone you cannot spend much time with or one you will not see again: "What is far more hazardous to explore than the unknown in a passionate romance is the unknown in the familiar, the 'heimliche' in the other" (Bernstein 713). The precarious nature of love underlies the fear of falling in love because love means risking all narcissistic illusions and misrecognitions.

In addition to promiscuity, the gay male in Hollinghurst's novels is also associated with the confusion between love and sex. In *The Swimming-Pool Library*, Sontagesque camp is employed to depict a lascivious and insatiable stereotype of gays who prioritise sex over love, or rather who fail to tell the two concepts apart. Priority of pleasure and sexuality is an indispensable element in Sontag's definition of camp: "Allied to the Camp taste for the androgynous is something that seems quite different but isn't: a relish for the exaggeration of sexual characteristics and personality mannerisms" (56). Since Hollinghurst follows the established patterns in his representation of the gay male subculture and identity, it is not surprising that his male gay characters fail to tell love and sex apart, mistaking the latter for the former. Frances Restuccia suggests that since love is the basis of the striving of the sexual, it is affiliated with the drive, and seems to be interchangeable with desire (372). Similarly, the characters in the novel experience only pleasure, but they cannot experience a narcissistic identification which would lead to an encounter with their desire. In other words, they use one another as objects of pleasure, which gives them only temporary satisfaction, yet their sexual gratification does not result in *jouissance*. For example, William's love for Arthur is not love but pleasure only, which is revealed in his being proud of his relationship the first week of which was all spent in bed. Actually this fact is revealing about the true nature of their relationship. Telling James about Arthur in detail, William cannot find any words to describe him but "total bliss, endless fuck, suck, schmuck" (*SPL* 19). Moreover, he admits that one day the conversation with Arthur during dinner at a restaurant was so tedious that he had (to have) Massimo, a waiter, in the back yard while Arthur was waiting for him at the table. Indeed Massimo wanted to have Arthur, too, but, funnily enough, William states that he knew where to draw the line. William tries to justify his insatiable libidinal energy and unfaithfulness by accusing Arthur of being dull.

The Line of Beauty is another novel portraying a male homosexual space where love and sex are confused, and there is no room for the love of women, which is a reflection of the traditional camp stylistics. The superiority of the love of boys to the love of women goes back to ancient Greece. Foucault explains why the love of boys was favoured over that of women. First, female beauty was considered artificial because of adornments and perfumes, which sharply contrasts with the natural beauty of boys. However, the main reason was that having sex with women was considered a natural inclination, which was "a behaviour found everywhere in the animal world, a behaviour whose reason for being is basic necessity.... The other difference is marked by the role of pleasure. The fondness for women cannot be detached from pleasure. The love for boys, on the contrary, does not truly accord with its own essence unless it frees itself of pleasure" (*Sexuality* 3: 200). However, in the novel it is hard to distinguish between the love of boys and pleasure; the two terms, love and pleasure, constantly overlap. In this respect, the depiction of homosexual love / sex act is similar to the portrayal of heterosexual love / sex in ancient Greece. Whether it is with a friend, a friend's father, or a servant in the household, sexual satisfaction always overweighs in the novel and has privilege over anything and everything else. For instance, the protagonist Nick had a crush on his friend Toby at college and this is the beginning of the entire story:

> He had only come out fully in his last year at Oxford, and had used his new licence mainly to flirt with straight boys. His heart was given to Toby, with whom flirting would have been inappropriate, almost sacrilegious. He wasn't quite ready to accept the fact that if he was going to have a lover it wouldn't be Toby. (*LB* 24)

His crush on Toby was a typical one that a young gay individual, usually not out yet, experiences. His feelings for Toby were much more than friendship, yet either he was unaware of or did not voice them. Thus, somehow they became close friends but what triggered their relationship was not only friendship, at least it was not so for Nick. Toby took Nick to their house on summer holidays when they were at Oxford and after graduating all of a sudden Nick becomes the family's lodger, though Toby has already started phasing out his existence at home. Not having Toby around, his lack, fuels Nick's desire further. Now he is apparently in love with Toby but cannot gain access to him; he is straight. Having lived with the Feddens for about a year, he thinks back; "sliding on to the seat beside Toby, taking in the soap and coffee smell of him, pressing briefly against his bare knee as he reached for the sugar, he felt what a success he had had,... he picked up the notebook, which had barely been looked at, and stroked the soft pile of its cover, to make up for Toby's lack of appreciation and remotely, too, as if he were thumbing some warm and hairy part of Toby himself" (*LB* 22). Nick just cannot express his feelings to Toby, for it would be futile and unacceptable to a straight man who considers him a close friend.

For Sontag, in fact for many other critics and writers too, camp is feminine, or at least not masculine. As "[t]he separation of sex and love is a deeply masculine construction," the gay male stereotype who cannot distinguish between the two is camp (Edwards 115). In the novel same-sex desire, which can never be satisfied and which leads to the overlap between love and sexual gratification, is seen even between Nick and Gerald. Nick's 'love of boys' cannot rid itself of pleasure and in this respect resembles the love of women in ancient Greece, which was regarded as natural and bestial. In other words, Hollinghurst puts gay relations into a heterosexual context by gendering gay male individuals. When the Feddens came back from France, Nick had already seen Leo's ad –"Black guy, late 20s, v.good-looking, interests cinema, music, politics, seeks intelligent like-minded guy 18-40"— in a newspaper and started corresponding with him, but they had not met yet (*LB* 8). Since Nick was a lonely and desperately horny young gay man having no other man nearby, he felt sexually attracted even to Gerald: "He couldn't help noticing the almost annoying firmness of the MP's backside, pumped up no doubt by daily tennis and swimming in France. The suntanned legs were a further hint of sexual potential that Nick would normally have thought impossible in a man of forty-five—he thought perhaps he was so excited by the prospect of Leo that he was reacting to other men with indiscriminate alertness" (*LB* 21). Nick thinks it might be his lust for Leo that makes him desire Gerald; however, Hollinghurst's choice of words reveals that Nick's desire for men is indiscriminate and any man will do for him. This is 'sex for sex's sake' attitude in the homosexual world depicted in Hollinghurst's interpretation of camp.

Besides polyandry and the confusion between love and sex, drug addiction is another essential element in Hollinghurst's deployment of Sontagesque camp in order to re-produce the gay male stereotype. *The Spell* is one of the novels representing gay characters who cannot live without drugs. For example, while Danny and George were planning Danny's birthday party and talking about the guests to be invited, George warned Danny about one of the most important issues: "[The Guests] may not be able to breathe country air. You'll need respirators of poppers and CK One" (*TS* 100). Drug addiction even causes Danny's losing his job and this representation in the novel shows that the characters can risk anything and everything for drugs.

Drug addiction is a major theme in *The Line of Beauty*, too, and it is associated with a certain class of people and a life style, which makes it camp. Satoshi Kanazawa, evolutionary psychologist, refers to the scientific fact that there is a correlation between the level of intelligence and consumption of psychoactive drugs. In the studies and research carried out in the United Kingdom it was discovered that more intelligent individuals used various types of drugs because drug is a recent and evolutionarily novel addictive substance, compared to more traditional examples like tobacco or alcohol. This correlation does not mean that drug addicts are more intelligent than people who do not use drugs; it just compares drug addiction to the traditional addictive substances like tobacco. This comparison also highlights the fact that drug use is attributed to a certain class, which makes it camp, and it, thus, excludes those who do not fit in. This is significant because Hollinghurts's gay characters are not alcoholic, but they prefer psychoactive drugs, which is campy and shows their social status. Likewise, the characters in *The Line of Beauty* cannot breathe without drugs, especially cocaine. At the nudist yard, Leslie talks across Wani—who was stoned—to Nick: "KY not good enough any more, apparently. We have to have some other substance called Melisma. Then Melisma's not good enough, apparently, either. We're moving on to Crest" (*LB* 164). He talks as if homosexual identity were such a heavy unbearable burden that the only way to cope with it and lessen the pain was using drugs. These characters have their own space, though they cannot be fully out, and they lead campy lives. None of them suffers from unemployment or loneliness or gay bashing apparently. They are not living in the 1960s either, yet they still break ties off with the world outside and take refuge in the affectionate warmth of drugs, living in illusions. Quite frequently in the novel, the reader comes across gays—mostly Wani and Nick—chopping a spill of coke, drawing the powder into lines and snorting it. The novel itself is named after the line of coke, the sense and sensibility of campy beauty. Nick is Wani's intermediary responsible for drug dealing, in addition to rent boy dealing. Ronnie is the drug dealer Nick has to get in touch with; however, he is reluctant to call him: "He wished Wani could have done this, as usual, in the car, with the Talkman. Having given Nick the money, Wani liked to set him challenges" (*LB* 204). Wani employs Nick as a puppet and uses his financial power to reinforce his control over him. Because of Wani, Nick takes drugs into the house where he lives as a guest and does not mind risking neither his own life nor Gerald's career and seat. Moreover, Nick finds the dealer Ronnie hot and dreams having sex with him, while Ronnie is giving him a lift home. This is exactly where and how gay characters mingle sex and drugs, two vital and indispensable things in their life and it looks as if one triggers the need for the other and having only one of them does not satisfy. For instance, when the Prime Minister is at the Feddens', Nick catches Wani coming out of Gerald and Rachel's bedroom, but Nick himself "was too drunk and high himself to take the danger at all seriously.... Nick loved the way the coke took off the blur of champagne. It totted up the points and carried them over as credit in a new account of pleasure. It brought clarity, like a cure—almost, at first, like sobriety" (*LB* 330). Nick has become an addict and he cannot do without coke; cocaine is his sense of sobriety. Wani and Nick often appear in the novel taking drugs, getting high, getting aroused and then getting laid. For example, during the same party, Nick and Wani give some coke to Tristão in the bathroom and have sex after getting stoned:

> Wani had got his wallet out, and was crushing and chopping a generous spill of coke on the wide rim of the washbasin. 'A lot of funny old stuff in there,' he said. 'I know,' said Nick.... He loved the etiquette of the thing, the chopping with a credit card, the passing of the tightly rolled note, the procedure courteous and dry, 'all done with money,' as Wani said—it was part of the larger beguilement, and once it had begun it squeezed him with its charm and promise. Being careful not to nudge him as he worked, he hugged Wani lightly from behind and slid a hand into his left trouser pocket. 'Oh fuck,' said Wani distantly. In about three seconds he was hard, and Nick too, pressing against him.... Nick didn't know how long it could go on –he didn't dream of it stopping, but it was silly and degrading at twenty-three to be sneaking sex like this, like a pickpocket as Wani said. (*LB* 190)

The campy aspect of using coke is revealed here; using credit cards and banknotes to chop coke and draw lines makes it exclusive and stylish. The author uses the word 'sneak sex' describing Nick's desire, yet the word, which connotes quiet, caution, and secrecy, is not appropriate for Nick or Wani, who do not hesitate to take any risk in order to have fun. They meet strangers, enjoy orgies, take their tricks home, reveal their own names and jobs, and they are in touch with drug dealers. However, sex acts must be problematised here because they are depicted as if they were something one cannot bear when sober. Drug use may be an escape from the heteronormative world which functions as the symbolic register for the gay characters where they cannot position themselves. Drugs offer people an escape from the self and/or the real life. Sometimes it is an escape from an undesirable or unacceptable situation or even from individuals' own identities when they have difficulty in coming to terms with their reality. Drugs provide temporary relief from such experiences and help re-establish the imaginary within the symbolic. Lacan's mirror stage is a drama whose internal pressure pushes precipitously from insufficiency to anticipation—and, for the subject caught up in the lure of spatial identification, turns out fantasies that proceed from a fragmented image of the body to what I will call an "orthopedic" form of its totality—and to the finally donned armor of an alienating identity that will mark his entire mental development with its rigid structure. (78)

The gay characters taking refuge in the soothing arms of drugs temporarily see their fragmented and insufficient images as complete and flawless; however, in the heteronormative system, functioning as the Symbolic in this respect, they fail to see that their temporary vision is nothing but an illusion and a misrecognition. Hollinghurst's overemphasis on and the frequency of his use of drug addiction falsely identifies drug use with homosexuality. The repetitive theme of drug use is the same with the conventional gay porn industry; many gay male porn stars use poppers before and during the intercourse, while there is not any or much less drug used in straight porn. This heteronormative image and the representation of the homosexual as a nymphomaniac, dandy and junkie point out a sensibility, a gay sensibility, which is Sontagesque camp.

In Hollinghurst's representation of the gay male stereotype, AIDS is the last major attribute ascribed to the characters. AIDS is associated with camp as it traditionally implies a particularly sexual lifestyle, i.e., a homosexual lifestyle in particular. Edwards claims that even the shift from a focus upon risk categories to risk activities, a change from *being* to *doing*, has not changed much mainly because of the association of these activities with particular groups or lifestyles such as homosexuality and anal sex, or drug use and sexual permissiveness (123). Butler criticises the presentation of the syndrome as one peculiar to the homosexual and argues that "throughout the media's hysterical and homophobic response to the illness there is a tactical construction of a continuity between the polluted status of the homosexual by virtue of the boundary-trespass that is homosexuality and the disease as a specific modality of homosexual pollution" (*Gender* 168). Hollinghurst took up the theme because as a gay writer he felt he was obliged to deal with the issue. Actually he was not; for AIDS, the horrible 'disaster' appearing in the late twentieth century, was attributed to homosexuals, drug users, and prostitutes for a long time, yet it is interesting that in the twenty-first century, a gay writer reproduces the old identification between the disease and homosexuality. In the 1980s AIDS became a fact of life and the gay community in England looked desperate since "the new Thatcher government appeared to be doing little or nothing to support them.... Against this background, large numbers of homosexuals – in common with many youth, ethnic and minority groups — lost faith in

Thatcherism" (David 256). Hollinghurst was inevitably influenced by the social and political atmosphere and, as a result, he uses the theme of AIDS to a great extent especially in this novel. Nonetheless, now it is an established view that AIDS is not peculiar to homosexual men or any group of people and HIV may be transmitted through various ways such as unprotected anal or vaginal intercourse, transfer of contaminated blood, using contaminated needles, or from a mother to the baby during pregnancy, or breastfeeding.

Despite the medical improvements and discourse at present, Hollinghurst's male gay characters in general and in *The Folding Star*, as a result of their campy lives of lust, lechery, and vanity, sooner or later end up coming down with the syndrome. One of the examples is Dawn, whom Edward liked at school. They were in a sort of relationship for a while, but later Edward left England and Dawn had a new boyfriend, Colin. The couple die in a car crash, Edward explains to Luc: Dawn "was killed in a car-crash. It was very sad. He was very ill anyway, he had AIDS; but he probably had a few more months to live" (*FS* 276). Orst dies of syphilis, another venereal disease, yet he is the heterosexual artist in the novel and whereas the stigma of the homosexual is known by everyone, that of the straight is concealed. Paul, despite his own queer background, does not want to make this information public in the guide they prepare: "I'm afraid I'm of the school that rather disapproves of publicising artists' private lives" (*FS* 289). This special care for the privacy is not the same as the treatment of the homosexual, who must be visible and flamboyant, a must of camp.

A recent and controversial employment of camp is in the representations of AIDS and camp AIDS texts used for this purpose "exploit the ability of camp to unsettle the rigidity of identity, thus healthily destabilizing the association between AIDS and homosexuality camp AIDS narratives call into question the stereotypical image of the depressed, lonely and promiscuous dying homosexual so firmly established by mainstream media" (Truman 55). The traditional identification of the syndrome with the gay male, on the other hand, dates back to the nineteenth century, when, Foucault explains, medical discourse produced 'truths' and named a dynasty of evils to be passed on to future generations. It built upon the old fears of venereal diseases and "claimed to ensure the physical vigor and the moral cleanliness of the social body; it promised to eliminate defective individuals, degenerate and bastardized populations" (*Sexuality* 1: 54). In the nineteenth century, when medical discourse claimed to be the supreme power and authority in health issues, there was no distinction between venereal diseases and homosexuality, which was considered a form of perversion. Both belonged to the same group of anomalies which, according to the dominant ideologies of the time, required treatment or elimination.

In *The Spell*, in accordance with the mainstream medical discourse, Hollinghurst directly identifies the syndrome with the gay male stereotype. This is one of the reasons why his use of camp is anti-serious and apolitical, just as in the Sontagesque sense. When Hollinghurst portrays the hospital scenes in which Simon is in bed suffering from a fatal illness and Robin the faithful lover is depressed and doing his best for his lover, he does not reveal what illness Simon is inflicted with. Later on, when Alex asks Danny about Robin's boyfriend, Danny says that he had died the previous year:

> Alex raised his eyebrows and nodded, taking in the fact and with it a sense that he might have been unfair to Robin, whom he'd thought of up to now as a mere loose libido, a lordly saboteur of other people's happiness. 'AIDS?'
> Danny paused and said 'Yeah', as if it was unnecessary or even bad to mention it. (*TS* 76)

Even a gay man hesitates to mention the word AIDS and feels it is not necessary to say what killed a gay man; it is always AIDS in Hollinghurst's four novels. AIDS is the fatal venereal 'disease' circulating and spreading among male gay individuals only and in this novel, as in the others, there is no gay dying a natural death. Leo Bersani argues that non-gay individuals;

> may think of themselves as watching us disappear. The heightened visibility conferred on gay men by AIDS is the visibility of imminent death, of a promised invisibility.... In February 1993 the National research Council made public a study asserting that the AIDS epidemic will have little impact on the life of most Americans. Since AIDS is concentrated among homosexuals, drug users, the poor, and the undereducated—what the council calls "socially marginalized groups" with "little economic, political, and social power" –the epidemic will have minimal effect on "the structures and directions of [American] social institutions." (21)

AIDS, the 'devastating plague' which became widespread and visible in the 1980s, was attributed to marginalised minority groups and the homosexual was standing out among all since it is the only group defined on the basis of sexual orientation. With the increasing visibility of the homosexual thanks to the Gay Liberation movements in the same decade, the identification of one stigma with another was inevitable. Visibility is not always good; in fact it "marks the beginning of a complex process. The emergence into public view can aid in the process of liberation; surely liberation cannot be won from the space of the crowded closet. Yet the glare of commercial culture can often produce a new kind of invisibility, itself supported by a relentless march toward assimilation" (Walters 340). Hollinghurst had the first-hand experience of the 1980s, the Thatcherite period in England, and this is why he is under the influence of the medical discourses of the period. However, by repeating the same stigma, i.e., the identification of the syndrome with homosexuality, he affirms the performative identity tailored for the gay male by the heteronormative society.

AIDS is a major concern and a stigma identified with the gay male in *The Line of Beauty*, too. Hollinghurst, in this novel, re-stigmatises the homosexual with the syndrome and rejuvenates the homophobic myth. HIV weakens the immune system and renders it vulnerable to many other infections. However, not every person with HIV suffers from the AIDS symptoms and with treatment it is possible to slow the course of the disease. However, in *The Line of Beauty* many gay characters become older and weaker in a very short time and die at a young age. Edwards lays bare the misconceptions and overstatements about AIDS, which is exaggerated and depicted as a well-deserved disaster ascribed to the stigmatised gay male in the novel:

> AIDS was barely conceived of in Britain before 1983 or 1984.... AIDS was, and is, defined as a deadly disease, and as an epidemic of unparalleled scope when it is neither of these things. It is a syndrome not a disease, it is not necessarily deadly, and compared with other similar epidemics in the past such as cholera or syphilis, it is not particularly contagious or rapid in its spread through the population overall. The number of AIDS cases in Britain remains relatively small compared with other infections or causes of death such as heart attacks, cancer, or accidents. (123)

Despite the relatively small cases of AIDS in Britain, the novel is rich in gay male characters suffering from the syndrome. One of the deaths from AIDS is that of Leo. Nick does not see him for a long time while he is with Wani. One day he goes to a bar when Wani is abroad. He notices a little black guy talking to a middle-aged white man, with his back to him. The guy's beltless jeans, the muscular bottom, and the glimpse of his blue underwear suddenly and unexpectedly remind him of Leo; however, compared to Leo, thought Nick, this guy "was much too skinny, really, to excite him, and too odd: he had a beard that was so bushy you could see it from behind, the black touched with grey beside the ears.... The greying beard hid the gauntness of his features, and the hat was rolled down to his eyebrows" (*LB* 368-369). It is only when Nick sees the guy in profile does he realise that it is Leo. Frightened, he walks into another room, then into the Gents, where he comes across a guy he has seen before and decides to go to his place. Nick does not know that Leo is HIV-infected and acts like a coward, but how he describes the little black guy in the bar gives the reader the author's view of the disease, which reflects commonplace prejudices of the Thatcherite period:

> AIDS rapidly and inevitably became the issue uppermost in the mind of this new generation of agitators and, selfishly, as some saw it, they began trying to keep it for themselves, even positively embracing once-gibed-at references to a 'gay disease'. Gay men were, after all, inescapably the 'victims' of a brutal blend of prejudice and medical over-reaction. (David 257)

Leo becomes the embodiment of this mixture of biases and over-reaction; his weight loss is one of the most striking changes he has gone through, and his greying beard at a very young age is horrifying. Hollinghurst's dealing with the theme reactivates all misconceptions and fears of the 'disease'. After the incident, Leo's sister, Rosemary Charles, visits Nick with her girlfriend. She tells Nick that her brother died about a month ago and that they cremated his body. She shows him some photos of Leo and the last one horrifies Nick:

> [A] Leo with his life behind him. Nick remembered making jokes, early on, in the first unguarded liberty of a first affair, about their shared old age, Leo being sixty when Nick was fifty. And there he was already; or he'd been sixty for a week before died. He was in bed, in a sky-blue hospital gown; his face was hard to read, since AIDS had taken it and written its message of terror and exhaustion on it; against which Leo seemed frailly to assert his own character in a doubtful half smile. His vanity had become a kind of fear, that he would frighten the people he smiled at. It was the loneliest thing Nick had ever seen. (*LB* 357-358)

It seems that this is not what Nick sees in the photo but how Hollinghurst himself sees and feels about AIDS, i.e., his own castration. Another HIV-infected character, Pete, Leo's ex-boyfriend, had been ill for some time, but no detail was given about what his illness was. On their second date, Leo had taken Nick to visit Pete's antique shop and they had visited him, yet Leo did not tell Nick about Pete's illness. Rosemary and Nick mention Pete's death and then Rosemary's girlfriend Gemma asks whether Nick is all right. Nick says he is fine and adds that he was "lucky" and then "careful" (*LB* 350). The prurient polyandrous characters in the novel apparently do not use condoms and it is just by chance whether they get infected or not. Nick does not know whether he got infected or not, either.

He has an HIV test at the end of the novel, but it is not known whether the result is positive or not; these characters' lives hang by a thread.

Wani is another camp character who gets infected and dies. However, his health decays unrealistically fast and in a year's time after Leo's death, it is hard to recognise him. He appears in the business lunch scene, where Nick meets Brad and Treat to talk about the film they are making since he has written the script for it. Talking to the film-makers, Nick notices Wani entering the restaurant. Wani, at the age of twenty-five, who once aroused the feelings of charm and beauty, now arouses pity and fear:

> [Nick] raised a hand as Wani appeared at the desk by the door, and as he got up he heard both Americans murmuring, "Oh my god…." He went over to him, smiling and capable but in a fluster of emotions—pity, defiance, a desire to support him, and a dread of people seeing him. The girl held his stick for him as she helped him off with his coat.… He still wasn't quite convincing with the stick; he was like a student actor playing an old man. (*LB* 374)

The tragic discrepancy between his age and his appearance shows the author's attitude towards HIV patients. Hollinghurst, by depicting a young boy who is addicted to bareback sex and drugs and who finally comes down with HIV getting old in a few years, affirms the heteronormative misconception that having bareback sex with gay men will almost certainly infect you with AIDS, and you will soon lose many bodily functions and perish.

Pat Grayson is another character stigmatised with AIDS and given the end a gay character –in Hollinghurst's work—deserves. Pat was regarded as an old silly campy queen people made fun of and laughed at, and thus, he proved to be the unwelcome future to Nick. He was a friend of Rachel's at Oxford and godfather to Catherine. Rachel gives the household the bad news, yet does not say it was AIDS he dies of. Catherine reacts: "Mum, for Christ's sake…. He had AIDS!"—with a phlegmy catch in her voice, which her anger fought with. "He was gay…he liked anonymous sex" (*LB* 292). Catherine is Nick's close friend and she is not homophobic indeed; nevertheless, her attributing Pat's fondness for casual anonymous sex to his being gay indicates how established the heteronormative myths marginalising the homosexual are. Besides Pat, George is another minor gay character dying of AIDS. At the nudist yard, an old man talks to Nick and Wani, apprising them of a man's death. The man, whom Nick and Wani do not remember but the old man insists they do, was called George. He was one of the regulars of the place and he died at the age of thirty-one. This is another depressing depiction of camp sensibility. Many young gay men seem to have wasted their life because of too much involvement in anonymous sex and drugs, and the author's repetitive portrayal of such scenes is camp as a distinct gay male sensibility.

2.3 Camp and Transgender Talk

Camp excludes anything non-camp, and when misused it triggers homophobia by misrepresenting the homosexual. In addition, the self mockery, humour, and wit could have a negative effect on queer politics and subjectivities since when overused humour will give the impression that there is no seriousness, which paves the way for Sontagesque camp. Camp might prevent gay individuals from seeing that there is something wrong with the heteronormative system; instead, they may put the blame on themselves or degrade themselves to the point where the dominant ideology wants to deploy and keep them. The language Hollinghurst's gay male characters employ reveals how they further marginalise and stigmatise themselves, creating a world of their own. Capote explains the function of camp and transgender talk as an element of camp:

> [C]amp was a coded form for many gays and lesbians in the first half of the twentieth century to signal their queerness. It was central to a discourse through which homosexuals could come out to other homosexuals and thus form larger groups of individuals who shared the same sexual orientation. Camp strategies such as the substitution of female pronouns for male ones, and the reliance on double-entendres and on covert meanings were ways of claiming an insider's status in gay culture. (53)

Transgender talk, therefore, is a camp strategy and it is definitely a discursive practice. However, the use of a jargon peculiar to the gay male helps the reification of the gay male subculture and identity. Booth states that "the traditionally feminine" is the primary type of the marginal and camp parodies it in a stylised effeminacy (69). Therefore, the stylistic effeminacy in the jargon does feminise and further marginalise the gay male.

In *The Swimming-Pool Library*, the transsexual talk at the Corry shows the corrosive influences of camp. Transsexual talk is the jargon used by and among GLBT individuals to avoid intelligibility and oppression. Butler explains the emergence of this oppression referring to the sexualisation of speech. For her, speech incites action and the utterance of homosexuality itself is regarded as an offensive conduct only because it makes people think of the act (*Excitable* 74). As a consequence, any statement of being gay implies same-sex sexual acts and it brings the reactional oppression, persecution, and prosecution. This is why, using a jargon of their own, these people intend to speak of sex and sexuality without other people understanding them, and thus they want to create a space for themselves. For instance, it is common in the novel to hear gay characters referring to their gay friends as an auntie, sister, mommy, and so on—depending on the relationship and age. Thus, their language takes on a transgenderist feature and blurs the binaries. However, relegating a gay male who is insulted and discriminated by heteronormativity to womanhood, always-already insulted and discriminated by patriarchy, is nothing but the reaffirmation of the existence of so-called intrinsic genders Man and Woman. Bernstein refers to Freud's 'Fort/Da game' in his 1923 paper "Beyond the Pleasure Principle" and puts forth that the mother's absence is the reason for the child's substituting words and attaching meanings for and to the loss. However, she adds, the meanings constructed around the loss produce a remainder which reminds the becoming-subject that there is something wrong and permanently lost in this moment of symbolisation (715). Transsexual talk is the remainder and the reminder of the long-lost liberty the homosexual enjoyed in ancient times. Its absence motivates the emergence of this jargon, yet the subjects, just like the child, are aware of the fact that linguistic substitution will never give them the primal lost object, which is their freedom, and they are bound to live among empty signifiers.

In *The Swimming-Pool Library*, the language used by the members at the club is gender-bending, i.e., using a non-traditional and androgynous language to subvert gender roles. Foucault argues that power itself urges individuals to speak about sex rather than keep silent. However, this apparent freedom is misleading because power, on the other hand, aims to create and control discourses. Foucault refers to the way power operates giving examples from the evolution of the Catholic pastoral and the confession culture. Whereas many authors like Tamburini and Sanchez believed that a confession would be incomplete without the "description of the respective positions of the partners, the postures assumed, gestures, places touched, caresses, the precise moment of pleasure," according to the new pastoral discretion was essential and it gained increasing emphasis (*Sexuality* 1: 19). Power, in other words, wants everything to be told, but it also stigmatises anything that does not conform to the dominant ideologies and their discourses. In the course of time, this contradictory attitude to the mention of sex and sexuality obliged queer individuals to create an alternative talk, an antidiscourse to subvert traditional gender roles. This is why in the novel when gay characters talk of other guys they refer to them using 'she' pronoun:

> I *know*—well, that's what *she* said.
> But have you seen her since?
> Only briefly, and then I couldn't say anything, because of course you-know-who was in attendance.
> I really like her actually; from what I've seen of her, that is. (*SPL* 66)

Here two gay men are talking about a boy using the feminine pronoun 'she'. This is definitely an insult and a product of heteronormativity. It is an insult not because being a 'she' is a lower rank than being a 'he', but because regarding a male gay as a 'woman' accusing him of effeminacy is a machination of heterosexist ideologies. This is the same with female gay individuals considered 'manly' because they are masculine in the dominant parameters and benchmark. Butler suggests that;

> sexed positions are themselves secured through the repudiation and abjection of homosexuality and the assumption of a normative heterosexuality. What in Lacan would be called "sexed positions," and what some of us might more easily call "gender," appears then to be secured through the depositing of non-heterosexual identifications in the domain of the culturally impossible, the domain of the imaginary, which on occasion contests the symbolic, but which is finally rendered illegitimate through the force of the law. (*Bodies* 111)

Heterosexist ideologies are oppressive and thus leave no room for diversities or differences. They define the other as transient, imaginary, or perhaps as the real since they cannot actually define it. For these ideologies and discourses, therefore, one is either a woman, i.e., a womanly woman, or a man, i.e., a manly man. In-betweenness is not tolerated by these regimes and the punishment is castration. For William, it is only an innocent game:

> It was the typical transsexual talk of the place, which had been confusing to me at first and which had thrown poor James into deep dejection when he innocently overheard a boy he had a crush on talking of his girlfriend. It was all a game, any man in the least attractive being dubbed a 'she' and only males too dire for such a conceit being left an unadorned 'he.' (*SPL* 66)

It might be only a game for campy gay men, yet this game was definitely designed and plotted by the homophobic and heterosexist ideologies and discourses. These systems and discourses feminise the male gay, while at the same time they virilise the female one. Butler problematises the assumption and acquisition of masculine and feminine attributes and argues that these attributes are;

for the former; a descent into feminine castration and abjection and, for the latter, the monstrous ascent into phallicism.... If a man refuses too radically the "having of the phallus," he will be punished with homosexuality, and if a woman refuses too radically her position as castration, she will be punished with homosexuality. (*Bodies* 103)

Heteronormative sexuality bases its notion of the Other on the conventional binary of feminised male homosexuality / masculinised female homosexuality. In this respect, lesbian femme, a masculine gay, or any diversity may easily challenge and subvert the prescriptive and limited understanding of homosexuality in Western epistemology. These unidentified subjectivities pose a threat to the dominant ideologies because they remain outside the symbolic register, queer itself being a challenge to *logos*.

The Swimming-Pool Library is the novel with the most visible examples of the jargon. It is not that the characters in the novel voluntarily want to distance and differentiate themselves from the heterosexist society but, in fact, they use a different jargon to avoid homophobic reactions:

> 'You know that new girl behind the bar?' one square-jawed athlete enquired of his bearded companion.
> 'What, the blonde, you mean—no, she's been there a while.'
> 'No, not her, no, the dark one with big tits.'
> 'I'm not sure I've seen *her*. Nice, is she?'
> It was conversation thrown out with a complex bravado, its artifice defiant as it was transparent. (*SPL* 66)

Metaphors, metonymies and conceits are integral parts of transgender talk because gay people are obliged to refer to the intended signified with different and socially acceptable, or unintelligible, signifiers. Only in this way can they flee from harassment and homophobic attitudes. As the words 'bravado' and 'defiant' also suggest, there comes an expectation for a deconstructive challenge and resistance in transgender talk. However, there is always fear underlying the apparent boldness and courage.

Repressed sexuality shows itself in the use of language and if individuals cannot overcome the barriers they encounter, language becomes the medium to compensate for and replace unfulfilled desires and sexuality. To illustrate, Charles, when he was sixteen years old, after his relationships with Stanbridge and Strong, lived a life full of passionate couplings and orgies. During the day they just looked forward to the night-time. Night and darkness covered their socially unacceptable sex acts. In the diary, Charles writes: "Not that we didn't frig in the day-time too. Our conversation was as salty as we could make it, and there was excitement to be had in seizing brief opportunities for lust in ever more public places"

(*SPL* 113). In contrast to polyandrous happenings at night in the dark, daytime and the light symbolise heteronormativity and the monitoring system. Thus, gay characters in the novel deploy sex and sexuality in their language, for they are yearning for publicity and exposure. A trait of heterotopias "is to create a space of illusion that exposes every real space, all the sites inside of which human life is partitioned, as still more illusory" (Foucault, *Of Other* 27). The space these characters create through language is, therefore, a heterotopia, which solidifies the established gay male subculture and identity.

The Spell is another novel to illustrate the overuse of fun, humour and self-mockery, which culminates in the image of homosexuals as a homogenous group consisting of pathetic and inferior human beings. Humour is another characteristic of camp, but it is not sufficient on its own to subvert heteronormativity. Babuscio analyses the emergence of humour as a camp device and states that it "results from an identification of a strong incongruity between an object, person, or situation and its context…. But in order for an incongruous contrast to be ironic it must, in addition to being comic, affect one as 'painful'" (126). Humour, to put it in other words, must be employed as a strategy to deal with heteronormative identity politics and it must reveal the performativity and theatricality of the stereotypes created, which Hollinghurst deliberately ignores. In his novels, while blaming others for duplicity, sluttishness, and prurience, the characters fail to realise that it is the system that compels them to duplicity. The heteronormative ideologies oblige them to lead double lives; on the one hand, an apparent heterosexual appearance at school, at work, or in any situation where they feel they have to look straight, and on the other hand, their own authentic identities which they can enjoy and expose only in their camp ghettos. They are torn between these two identities, one of which is false. These characters are vigorously struggling to fit in the straitjacket tailored for them by the heteronormative society. They welcome the identity defined on the basis of sexual orientation and lead their lives in their ghettos, the borders of which have been made invisible so that they could feel liberated. However, the liberty in Hollinghurst's work is just an illusion; it imprisons the gay male in a standardised life of sex, drugs, and duplicity, which takes a step further with the marginalisation of the gay male with a language of their own.

The language used by some characters shows the alienation of the homosexual from the heteronormative world. When Alex and Danny go out in Soho, Alex resents Danny's knowing every good-looking person they see. Danny is like a star or a mascot and the talks between him and his acquaintances are campy. Alex feels excluded: "Words like Trade,

Miss Pamela and Guest-list were produced and received with the gratified ennui accorded to a well-established ritual. Anecdotes of excess got the most laughs" (*TS* 74). This is the queer register, a subverted form of the symbolic, and the non-camp cannot get into this register. The camp jargon banishes the non-camp from the discourse.

Apart from the transgender aspect, the language used by the gay male characters is also campy in the Sontagesque sense because it is amoral, coarse, unnatural and full of sexual characteristics. Hollinghurst's gay male characters seem to have no sense of privacy in the novel. The conversation between Alex and Hugh, his friend from university years, demonstrates the lack of privacy:

> Alex chose not to be tryingly truthful. 'The last two weeks have been extraordinary—I feel as if I'm under a beautiful spell'.
> 'The thing about spells,' said Hugh, 'is that you don't know at the time if they're good ones or bad ones. All black magicians learn how to sugar the pill.'
> 'Well I never had your mastery of the occult.'
> 'What's his dick like, by the way?' (*TS* 107)

Once a character states that he is in a new relationship or has slept with someone, the listener immediately asks about the mentioned partner's penis size. Size queens are very common in Hollinghurst's work and asking about one's lover's or partner's penis is quite casual, a question these characters cannot live without. Alex, however, politely refuses to talk about such things, to which Hugh bitterly replies: "It's like money, it's easy not to care when you've got it" (*TS* 107). This is the campy's critique of the non-campy attitude, which may confirm the intended reader's ego, yet further repulse the real reader. The characters' obsession with sexual performance or virility is another important point. This concern reflects the Platonic and Socratic stylistics, too: The juvenile body of the adolescent was the object of desire then, but the boys were supposed to avoid degenerating into softness or effeminisation. What made their body charming to the male gaze was their developing virility, strength, and endurance (Foucault, *Sexuality* 2: 200). The superiority of the love of boys to that of girls can be seen in *The Symposium*:

> The Love who belongs to Common Aphrodite is truly common and engages in his activity as opportunity offers. This is the Love that inferior people experience. In the first place men of this sort love women quite as much as boys, and secondly, their bodies more than their souls, and thirdly, the stupidest people possible, since they have regard only for the act itself and do not care whether it is rightly done or not. Hence their activity is

governed by chance, and as likely to be bad as good. The reason is that the Common Aphrodite, with whom this Love is associated, is far younger than the other Aphrodite, and because of her parentage she has characteristics both of the male and of the female. 'However, the Love who accompanies the heavenly goddess (and who does not descend from the female but only from the male) is the love of boys, and that goddess is older and entirely free from wantonness. Hence those who are inspired by this love incline to the male, preferring what has by nature more vigour and intelligence. Moreover, even among men who love younger members of their own sex it is possible to recognise those who are motivated purely by this heavenly love, in that they do not love boys before the stage when their intelligence begins to develop, which is near the time when they begin to grow a beard. I believe that those who wait until then to embark on a love affair are prepared to spend their whole life with this individual and to live in partnership with him. They will not take him at a time when he is young and inexperienced, and then deceive him, contemptuously leaving him and running off to someone else. (Plato 12-13)

Love in the extract means same-sex desire; the right time to take a boy is associated with the growing beard, which shows that the love affair mentioned is sexual intercourse indeed. In Platonic stylistics, then, there is nothing wrong with loving or desiring men, yet submitting oneself to desire meant effeminateness and Hollinghurst's characters' obsession with penis size is a consequence of the futile efforts to mimic the act of *having* the phallus.

In the novels it is seen that the campy nature of Hollinghurst's gay male characters becomes visible in the transgender and campy language they use. Robertson criticises the general tendency to associate the male gay with femininity: "We also take for granted gay men's camp appropriations of female clothing, styles, and language from women's culture: consider drag and female impersonation, or gay camp slang such as calling one another 'she'" (267). This jargon reveals the heteronormative idea that a gay man, who is not and cannot be manly, must be womanly. This misconception not only demonstrates the traditional subordinate role of the woman, as the secondary gender, but also alienates the gay male from the heterosexual male and reifies the constructed binary. As for the vulgarity of the language they use, which is in accordance with Sontag's definition of camp, their use of language seems to be an attack on the pretentious prudence of bourgeois morality. The characters in Hollinghurst's novels do not have any reservations whatsoever; they can talk about anything to anyone anywhere anytime. Homosexuals, the Other Victorians, cannot deploy themselves in the symbolic order of the bourgeois culture; therefore, they establish an antidiscourse to have their own voice and space. Nevertheless, Hollinghurst's characters' use of language reveals an obsession with sex and the repetitive use of this jargon further stigmatises and alienates the gay male from the domain of the heterosexual and it culminates in the perpetuation of the gay male stereotype with a stable identity and subculture of its own.

As a conclusion, camp cannot be separated from its gay male origin since these two "share the contemporary critical stage, the latter being a central issue for 'queer theory,' one of its partially definitional objects of analysis" (Cleto 12). However, in Hollinghurst's novels, the non-gay is denied access and is not allowed into the camp discourse; it is exclusive. Instead of attempting to subvert heteronormativity, his work further alienates and banishes the gay male from the heterosexist world outside, and similarly the author leaves no room for the heterosexual in the fictional world created. His notion of camp is defined within heteronormative parameters, failing to meet queer-political expectations.

David Ruffolo argues that queer has already achieved its political peak and its "theoretical movements have become limited by its incessant investment in identity politics and its political outlook has in many ways attained dormant status due to its narrowed interest in heteronormativity" (1). Similarly, Hollinghurst invests too much in identity politics and cannot avoid his preoccupation with heteronormativity, the norms of which he has already internalised. Cleto puts forth that "[b]oth camp and queer (and camp as queer) should in fact be assumed as *discursive processes*" (33). However, Hollinghurst does not question camp as a discursive product and instead, as a result of the performative role and identity of the gay male which he has internalised, he endorses the homophobic and heterosexist stereotype of the homosexual in his novels, which may be a reason underlying the popularity of his novels. First, he represents the gay male as if they constituted a homogenous category and banishes the non-gay from this portrayal. In this way, he re-produces gay male identity as a distinct class with its own sub-culture. Next, he identifies the homosexual with all the heteronormative clichés; dandyism, flamboyance, decadence, degeneration, frivolousness, nymphomania, hedonism, and flightiness are all attributed to the Homosexual in his work. Finally drug addiction and AIDS are portrayed as indispensable elements of the gay male identity. In this way, he reconstitutes hetero-cultural misconceptions and biases. As a result, he ends up popularising camp and making it a sensibility; nonetheless, his camp lacks the seriousness present in political camp.

Camp has always been blamed for being a taste and sensibility, which renders it apolitical, apparently. Sontag, for instance, argues that camp "doesn't reverse things. It doesn't argue that the good is bad, or the bad is good. What it does is to offer for art (and life) a different –a supplementary— set of standards" (61). This is exactly what Hollinghurst does in his work; he represents the well-established norms and values of heteronormativity flavoured with the apolitical, dandy, coarse, class-conscious, amoral, hedonistic, unnatural, exaggerated, duplicitous, and extravagant nature of Sontagesque camp. However, the critical and political value of camp needs to be restored, and its theoretico-historical framework should be re-established by underlining the distinction between different kinds of camp. Sontagesque camp is apparently apolitical, yet it is apolitical only from the viewpoint of the stigmatised minority. As for the heteronormative ideology, it is highly political because all the attributes identified with camp, in fact, serve the mainstream discourses and help reify a stable gay male identity and subculture. The meanings and possibilities of camp, its signification for gay individuals and its conceptions by gay individuals have changed in the course of time. However, Pellegrini suggests that camp "responds to the experience of homosexual stigmatization by sending up and theatricalizing the stigma, thereby ameliorating its impact. As a survival strategy this is absolutely necessary" (170). Hollinghurst's four novels are far from responding to the stigma ascribed to the homosexual, theatricalising it or queering the stereotypical attributes of the homosexual; instead, they re-establish the already-well-established campy image of the homosexual and present camp as a gay, or even homosexual, sensibility, which brings the author's employment of camp closer to closet.

Chapter Three

Closet

Camp is a process whereby the queer gains visibility and is positioned in relation to, either within or outside, the society. Therefore, it is directly related to the notion of space, which is a significant concern for Foucault. He refers to the history of space in Western experience and argues that medieval space was configured on a dualistic basis, such as urban / rural, supercelestial / celestial, which reveals the hierarchical structure underlying. However, with Galileo's intervention, the location of an object was no longer considered stable but a point in its indefinite movement. Despite Galileo's effort, contemporary space, Foucault claims, is still not completely desanctified and binary oppositions –like private\public space or family\social space— still predominate in our lives. Foucault focuses on the cluster of relations among sites and emphasises his concern with sites which are "in relation with all the other sites, but in such a way as to suspect, neutralize, or invert the set of relations that they happen to designate, mirror, or reflect" (*Of Other* 24). These spaces, linked with all the others but also contradicting the others, are divided into two by Foucault: First there are utopias with no real location; they depict society in a perfect form or turned upside down. Second there are heterotopias, counter-sites which are outside of all places but at the same time located in reality. For Foucault, the latter is a type of represented utopia which reveals, contests, and inverts the real sites of the culture (*Of Other* 24). Closet is a kind of heterotopia because it exists within societies, yet it is a counter-space as it challenges and subverts heteronormative values. It is real due to the individual experiences and existence; however, in oppressive cultures its existence is denied and it is treated as if it were unreal. Thus, in these contexts closet can be called a hetero-utopia, something which is ignored although it does exist.

Coming out and beginning to camp designate the instant when the queer begins to be represented within the dominant framework by the mainstream parameters. Closet, in contrast to camp, implies secrecy and covertness. Literally, as a noun, closet denotes a small private room, a state of secrecy, or storage space; as an adjective, it means private or confidential; and as a verb it means to hide, to confine, or to isolate. George Chauncey researched and reconstructed the historiography of gay New York, but could not find the term closet before the 1940s. Closet, he argues, emerged in the mid to late 1960s: "Regardless of its precise origins, it is clear that between 1968 and 1972 the term came to signify the concealment and erasure of gays and lesbians specifically in the US. By 1970 the slogan 'Come Out!' was a rallying cry in the nascent gay liberation struggle in New York City" (qtd. in Brown 5-6). The term is quite recent because there was no homosexual 'identity' to closet in the earlier centuries. Only after the homosexual became visible and came out did the challenged heteronormative society, who had never considered itself heterosexual before meeting the Homosexual, want to push them back into the closet.

Same-sex sexual intercourses and relationships have always existed but only from the seventeenth century on the awareness of sexual orientation highly increased and normative discourses began to categorise people on the basis of their sexual object choice. This classification normalised and privileged heterosexuality, while abjecting and stigmatising homosexuality. Coarse axes of categorisation had already been configuring identities based on gender, class, race, and nationality. With the addition of sexual orientation as an identity taxonomic designations rigidified their essentialist nature. Medical, legal, religious, social and psychological discourses all set the norms and regulations on sexuality, and thus defined what was 'normal' and what was not. Marginalising the homosexual culminated in the never-ending hatred called homophobia, which displaced the homosexual from the public sphere and forced them to privatise their lives in order to lessen their undesired visibility. William N. Eskridge employs a diachronic approach and examines the evolution of the closet space in the United States, dividing the process into several periods roughly. The first one covers the years from 1880s to 1946. Since the mention of the closet as a term before the nineteenth century would be anachronistic, beginning the analyses from the Late Victorian times is more common and acceptable. Eskridge begins his study by showing how the Late Victorians transformed the *sexual invert* into *homosexual* and how they created new laws to regulate same-sex relationships and gender-bending. This transformation was of course intentional; the sole purpose was to give a standard definition of homosexuality to create a type. Sedgwick states that any ideology or politics depends for its survival on the definition of homosexual individuals as a distinct minority group and the definition does not dissolve not because of the efforts of those whom the term involves but because of the struggles of those who define themselves against it (83). In the 1900s these attempts to form regulations mostly consisted of family and social pressure, out of the state control. Then, between 1946 and 1961 people turned to law and by the Second World War "legal officials in big cities outside the South were vigorously arresting cruising homosexuals, censoring homoerotic publications, closing down meeting places, and excluding genderbenders from admission to this country and its armed forces. This new legal regime represented society's coercive effort to normalize human relationships around 'heterosexuality'" (18). This was due to the increasing visibility of the homosexual between the two world wars. During that period, many parks, streets, cafés, public lavatories, YMCAs, theatres, subways, diners, bathhouses and bars became places where queer individuals went cruising, felt safe and met other queer people. The appearance of closet spaces brought so-called liberty to queer people, yet it also meant the erasure of homosexuality in all other real public spheres. In the third period, from 1961 to 1981, Eskridge states that the homosexual was monitored, exposed, persecuted, and punished:

> She or he risked arrest and possible police brutalization for dancing with someone of the same sex, crossdressing, propositioning another adult homosexual, possessing a homophile publication, writing about homosexuality without disapproval, displaying pictures of two people of the same sex in intimate positions, operating a lesbian or gay bar, or actually having oral or anal sex with another adult homosexual.... If the homosexual were a professional—teacher, lawyer, doctor, mortician, beautician—she or he could lose the certification needed to practice that profession. If the charged homosexual were a member of the armed forces, she or he might be court-martialed and would likely be dishonourably discharged and lose all veterans' benefits. (98)

These homophobic acts triggered Homophile and Gay Liberation Movements and made queer activists start pursuing the rights of privacy, equality, association, speech and press. As a result, this period turned out to be the one in which GLBT individuals began coming out of their closets and challenging the closet. Closetedness, for Sedgwick, is a performance initiated by the speech act of a silence in relation to discourses surrounding and manipulating it. Likewise, the speech acts which coming out may constitute, she adds, are as strangely specific. These speech acts might not be related to the acquisition of new information (3). In this case, rather than *being* homosexual, *uttering* the phrase of coming out itself gains importance since when one can say 'I am out,' it constitutes a clear-cut break from the previous state of closetedness with this performative work of coming out. From the 1980s on, with this new awareness, many things have changed, but there are still remnants of the closet. Postmodernist thought, gender studies and queer theory have contributed to the changing approach to the homosexual to a great extent, yet homosexuality is still a crime requiring death penalty in some countries and an unacceptable wrongdoing in many others.

Cheshire Calhoun, in *Feminism, the Family, and the Politics of the Closet: Lesbian and Gay Displacement*, claims that what GLBT individuals go through is not oppression but only subordination, on the grounds that homosexuality, unlike gender and race, can be concealed. She states that "unlike social groups whose members are readily identifiable, gays and lesbians evade statistical concentration in a marginalizing place. Thus, sexual orientation does not make the kind of difference to one's material conditions that, by contrast, gender and race do. Lesbian and gay subordination does not materialize" (80). She believes that the homosexual's case is very much like the Anti-Semitism case; one can gain public acceptance as long as he / she manages to conceal his / her identity. Her analysis and comparisons are horrifying because she supports one's closeting his / her identity in order to get accepted by the mainstream people. Sedgwick is another writer who claims that some oppressed minority groups are luckier in that they can conceal their identity. For her, discrimination based on race, gender, age, size or physical handicap is inevitable since the victims are visible and prone to stigmatisation. Other minority groups, on the other hand, have "at least notionally some discretion" (75). Last but not least, Ned Rorem draws a contrast between homosexuality and negritude and states that race cannot be concealed but homosexuality can (qtd. in Higgins 2). Nevertheless, what these writers claim cannot be accepted, for conditional and limited liberty cannot be called 'liberty' at all. Moreover, visibility is a relative and slippery term. It cannot be scientifically proven whether gender, race, or sexual orientation is easier to disguise. If there are numerous hate murders targeting GLBT individuals all over the world, this demonstrates that many queer individuals fall prey to homophobic or transphobic attacks since they fail to disguise their identities. For Summers, homosexuality goes beyond recognition of sexual attraction toward individuals of one's own sex and it reveals "something important about the individual's very being and his relationship to a society that would penalize him for who he is" (14). It is true that some countries and cities grant GLBT individuals equal rights and protection against discrimination and violence; however, these places are actually nothing but the twenty-first-century versions of Panopticon prison, i.e., new GLBT ghettos. Outside these ghettos, queer people are unable to exist, get married, adopt children, get the custody of their children and get visiting rights to their partners / spouses or children. Sedgwick finds it understandable;

> that someone who wanted a job, custody or visiting rights, insurance, protection from violence, from 'therapy,' from distorting stereotype, from insulting scrutiny from simple insult, from forcible interpretation of their bodily product, could deliberately choose to remain in or to reenter the closet in some or all segments of their life. The gay closet is not a feature only of the lives of gay people. But for many gay people it is still the fundamental feature of social life; and there can be few gay people, however courageous and forthright by habit, however fortunate in the support of their immediate communities, in whose lives the closet is not still a shaping presence. (68)

As a result of the never-ending process of coming out, or rather the boundlessness of the closet, in order to get and retain a job, queer individuals are obliged to hide their queerness and pretend to be heterosexual. They have to avoid displaying any affection in public places for fear that they will be harassed or assaulted. They are sometimes denied accommodation or are compelled to move out as a result of homophobic or transphobic neighbours. If they get out of the closet, they will face discrimination, harassment, and even physical attacks including murder. Regarding their families, they are also subjected to therapies and scrutiny of psychologists/psychiatrists, some of whom will look for symptoms of and reasons for their 'improper' manly or womanly attitudes, acts, interests and dressing so as to 'repair' them back to heterosexuality.

The homosexual, allegedly rejecting breeding, poses a threat not only to patriarchy but also to the institutions of family and marriage. Thus, heteronormative registers banish the homosexual from the Discourse. Harold Beaver illustrates how rich the oppressive heterosexist discourses are, stigmatising the homosexual employing a vast spectrum of synonyms; "angel-face, arsebandit, auntie, bent, bessie, bugger, bum-banger, bum boy, chicken, cocksucker, daisie, fag, faggot, fairy, flit, fruit, jasper, mincer, molly, nancy boy, nelly, pansy, patapoof, poofter, cream puff, powder puff, queen, shit-stirrer, sissie, swish, sod, turd, burglar, pervert" (qtd. in Cleto 163). It is not possible to find such rich vocabulary describing the heterosexual since heterosexuality is compulsory and it wears a mask of naturalness. In order to achieve this end, heteronormativity feeds upon the pseudo-symmetrical opposition Heterosexual / Homosexual. After reifying binaries, dominant discourses produce a variety of derogative and / or distinguishing words to depict the repressed, the marginalised and the minority. Thus, one can find more words referring to the homosexual than to the straight, or to the black than to the white, who are considered uncanny by dominant ideologies. The dominant power holder himself does not need any justification or definition. Calhoun argues that the homophobia resulting in the production of the closet

> is ultimately rooted in a particular way of thinking about homosexuality and lesbianism. Homosexuality and lesbianism are equated with sexual acts, especially with sodomy, in a way that heterosexuality is not similarly reduced to a set of sexual acts. As a result, we as a culture think that it is reasonable not to mention homosexuality and lesbianism in the public sphere, either because the acts are too morally abhorrent to bear public mention or, more neutrally, because sex is a private matter that belongs in the bedroom, not in public spaces. Oscar Wilde's famous description of homosexuality as the 'love that dare not speak its name' reflects a long history of referring to sodomy as the 'unmentionable crime'. But even in a more sexually liberalized era, homosexuality continues to be publicly unmentionable because it is equated with private sexual activity. (82)

Reducing homosexuality to sexual acts themselves, while never questioning heterosexuality because of taking its 'naturalness' for granted, is a significant feature of the phallocentric identity politics of the dominant discourses. What is worse, these same-sex sex acts constitute crimes against nature, whereas their heterosexual counterparts do not. Homosexual love is the one which dare not speak its name because in the course of time the flourishing heteronormative discourses stigmatised it with perversion and forbade even its mention, replacing it with silence, for the name itself suggests the act itself. Foucault, explaining how the seventeenth century western culture began to regulate and police sex through creating discourses, states that "[t]here is no binary division to be made between what one says and what one does not say.... There is not one but many silences, and they are an integral part of the strategies that underlie and permeate discourses" (*Sexuality* 1: 27). Brown argues that by saying 'I am gay', a performative speech act, one can get out of the closet, but in fact this coming out will definitely be a never-ending process, for every single new person or atmosphere a gay individual faces will turn out to be a new closet for him/her (37). Another problem queer individuals encounter on coming out is that even after coming out these individuals cannot break off with the heteronormative system. The system moulds individuals within its body and assimilates them for good. According to Meyer, "exiting the closet, all too often the queer discovers herself to be wearing the inappropriate clothes of the heterosexual" (113). For instance, the institution of marriage is a product, a construct of heterosexist ideologies and, as a result, the increase in the allowance and recognition of gay marriages should be problematised instead of being celebrated. The institution is a straitjacket presented to queer individuals as a gift, yet it intends to regulate and police queer sexualities. Thus, instead of rejoicing, one should move queer politics into the heterosexual framework and critique the loopholes in the dominant order. However, not being given the right to get married, the queer is also discriminated and closeted since laws treat married individuals in a different manner than they treat single individuals in almost every field of social regulations such as "taxation, torts, evidence, social welfare, inheritance, adoption, and on and on" (Chambers 306). These social, legal and economic impediments serve heteronormative ends and present heterosexual marriage as the only way to benefit from some of the rights which should be granted to every human being regardless of sexual orientation or marital status.

In addition to its assimilationist policies, the closet is also capitalistic. Since the closet space seems to be the only place for the queer to be accepted and visible, it cannot help falling prey to capitalistic predators and their opportunistic ends. Brown puts forth that the closet is "a material production of heterosexism and is inscribed in urban space. The closet also enables gay desire to be commodified for profit. And in that way the closet is a production not only of heteronormativity in urban space, but simultaneously of capitalist relations" (56). Consequently, gay ghettos emerge as closeted space allowing the visibility of same-sex intimacies and relations, especially in urban settings, to be exploited and commodified for profit not only by heteronormative ideologies but also by capitalism. Queer individuals who prefer to gain visibility and feel a fake sense of freedom in these ghettos actually endorse and serve the heterosexist and capitalistic ends.

Meyer argues that camp transgresses the boundaries established by heteronormative regimes, yet at the same time it does reinforce the dominant order (11). Thus, there is an interaction and a reciprocal relationship between camp praxis and dominant ideologies. Likewise, the closet is both transgressive and oppressive. It is transgressive because in the closet space GLBT individuals make believe they live and act freely. On the other hand, it is oppressive because what allows the existence of these individuals only in specified places is the tyrannical order itself. In other words, there are indeed two agents of closeting; the first one is the dominant heterosexist order and the other is queer individuals themselves. Foucault, regarding power, states that power comes from below and there is no direct confrontation between the ruler and the ruled. Accordingly, it is not fair to put homophobia and being closeted down to the system only. GLBT individuals are, to a certain extent, blameworthy for internalising homophobia and reconstituting the closet by ghettoising themselves. It is true that the dominant ideologies create GLBT ghettos, and exile and relocate these individuals in those specified places. These ghettos, or hetero-utopias, may be in such various forms as a country, a city, a district, a café, a bar, a sauna or a store. The system wants to ensure that it has marginalised all these individuals and that they will not be visible anywhere they like. This is the reason for creating queer space and closeting the queer individuals. However, some GLBT individuals, like Hollinghurst's characters, endorse and reinforce closeting by encouraging discriminatory attitudes and enterprises with their own homophobic, transphobic or even heterophobic attitude. Opening a gay bar may look quite liberalising, but it should not be forgotten that creating a gay space means banishing the non-gay and the transgender and even excluding and alienating gays themselves from the non-gay space. Similarly, a lesbian café excludes all the non-lesbian subcategories such as the straight, the male gay and the transgender, erasing the lesbian existence elsewhere. Today in many parts of the world, there are exclusive queer ghettos reserved for a single category, which ends up triggering different forms of phobia and discrimination. Hollinghurst fictionalises reinforced closeting. By giving voice to the misconceptions of society and reifying a stereotypical homosexual identity, the author fails to help the disavowal of heteronormative discourses stigmatising the homosexual. As a result, his work seems to be the embodiment of Foucault's heterotopia. Foucault likens heterotopias to a mirror; it makes the place one occupies real when one looks in the glass and sees himself / herself connected with the surrounding. However, the image is also unreal and the mirror is a utopia as the reflection is in fact a virtual space, where the onlooker is not (*Of Other* 24). Hollinghurst's fiction is a mirror held up to the English society under Thatcher's administration, focusing on queer communities in particular, yet the image seen is what the dominant heteronormative ideologies and discourses want to see. The author is as if marking his gay characters by pink triangles for the heterosexist society to identify them easily. What he achieves in the end is a reproduction of the queer fantasies of heterosexual individuals; a hetero-utopia.

In Hollinghurst's four novels, which comprise a tetralogy, there are four main manifestations of the closet: First, gay male characters are depicted in a constant search for sexual gratification in gay heterotopias; cinemas, bars, clubs, parks, public lavatories or their home closets. Second, in the contemporary English novel, they still face homophobia and violence, not only in the psychological sense but also in the physical sense. Third, they are imprisoned into and portrayed in relationship chains where one desires and sleeps with any other gay character. Last but not least, they all get cliché gay jobs tailored for them by the biased society or not having to earn a living, they just idle about. This image is an end product of the minoritising view of homosexuality, which takes it for granted that there is a homosexual identity which is fixed and stable and this is valid for all individuals involved in this category. However, this view is in contrast with the universalising view, which argues

> that sexual desire is an unpredictably powerful solvent of stable identities; that apparently heterosexual persons and object choices are strongly marked by same-sex influences and desires, and vice versa for apparently homosexual ones; and that at least male heterosexual identity and modern masculinist culture may require for their maintenance the scapegoating crystallization of a same-sex male desire that is widespread and in the first place internal. (Sedgwick 85)

This incoherence is the author's dilemma underlying his conventionally heteronormative depiction of homosexuality. On the one hand, he attempts to give voice to homosexuality and normalise same-sex male desire; on the other hand, he affirms antihomosexual ideologies by reproducing heteronormative clichés regarding the reified homosexual identity. The inevitable consequence of the reproduction of these stereotypes is that he portrays the homosexual as a distinct minority group consisting of individuals with a stable identity.

3.1 Closeting the Gay Male: Modern Heterotopias

Foucault puts forth that a society "can make an existing heterotopia function in a very different fashion; for each heterotopia has a precise and determined function within a society and the same heterotopias can, according to the synchrony of the culture in which it occurs, have one function or another" (*Of Other* 25). Similarly, in Hollinghurst's fiction, gay male heterotopias have a function both for the closeted individuals and for the closeting society. There are two main types of heterotopias; crisis and deviation. Foucault defines crisis heterotopias as privileged, sacred or forbidden places allocated for people who are in a state of conflict with the society they live in, e.g., adolescents, menstruating women, and pregnant women. This form of heterotopias is a place like the nineteenth century boarding schools or military service, where the first manifestations of sexual virility are experienced or it is like the pre-mid-twentieth century tradition for girls which was called "honeymoon trip," where the young woman's deflowering took place. These spaces, both for men and women, had to be somewhere else than home (*Of Other* 24). The second type of heterotopias is called heterotopias of deviation, which are the modern versions of the former indeed. These spaces, such as rest homes, mental asylums and prisons, are reserved for people who fail to conform to the norms of the society they live in (*Of Other* 25). A cinema is one of these heterotopias in Hollinghurst's novels. The gay cinemas in the novels can be involved in the latter; they are ghettos allocated for the stigmatised non-conformist gay. In *The Swimming-Pool Library*, for example, there is a cinema called Brutus in Soho, in Frith Street, which, for William and many other characters functions as closet. In Brutus, as the name itself implies, customers set their 'beastly' desires free and do 'brutish' things. William admits that "[i]t wasn't so much to see a film as to sit in a dark, anonymous place and do dark, anonymous things" (*SPL* 47). People did not go there to see porn only; what they looked for was random sex and affection perhaps, which they were denied—since it was 'anonymous'—in the heteronormative world outside. The fondness for anonymity stems from the unfortunate fact that homosexual love is the one that dare not speak its name and that is doomed to remain anonymous. The cinema building itself, where these anonymous and polyandrous happenings occur, is depicted like the embodiment of the closet built underground as a ghetto:

> The Brutus Cinema occupied the basement of one of those Soho houses which, above ground-floor level, maintain their beautiful Caroline fenestration, and seemed a kind of emblem of gay life.... One entered from the street by pushing back the dirty red curtain in the doorway beside an unlettered shop window, painted over white but with a stencil of Michelangelo's David stuck in the middle. This tussle with the curtain – one never knew whether to shoulder it aside to the right or the left, and often tangled with another punter coming out—seemed a symbolic act, done in the sight of passers-by, and always gave me a little jab of pride. (*SPL* 48)

The cinema, consisting of a small cellar room hid behind a dirty red curtain disarticulating it from the normalised world of heterosexuals, is emblematic of homophobia and of its end product closet. The curtain is dirty and it gives an insight into how the straight world sees the GLBT individuals, or rather, how they fail to see them, since they are hid behind a curtain and closeted. Another thing about these cinemas is the pictures. William finds the introductory scenes of these pictures the most touching, since men on the street or the beach killing time or doing some kind of work all of a sudden transform into lustful daemons the audience's fantasy world demands of them (*SPL* 50). The transformation might be the same with straight porn industry; however, gay male subjectivity is still defined on the basis of same-sex sexual activities and the conception of relationship between two men is not the same as the one between a man and a woman, for the former is always identified with bestial sex, in sharp contrast with the ancient Greek and Roman notions, which are represented with the stencil of Michelangelo's David in the cinema depicted. The conflict between the pagan and Christian understandings of sexuality is the reason behind this discrepancy:

> Synecdochically represented as it tended to be by statues of nude young men, the Victorian cult of Greece gently, unpointedly, and unexclusively positioned male flesh and muscle as the indicative instances of "the" body, of a body whose surfaces, features, and abilities might be the subject or object of unphobic enjoyment. The Christian tradition, by contrast, had tended both to condense "the flesh" (insofar as it represented or incorporated pleasure) as the *female* body and to surround its attractiveness with an aura of maximum anxiety and prohibition. (Sedgwick 136)

The stencil in the cinema is, therefore, a symbol of the yearning for the sexual liberty and pro-homosexual ideologies in ancient times. The dirty red curtain, on the other hand, is like the censorship of eroticism and nudity in the Middle Ages and the location of the stencil is similar to the removal of statues from outdoor areas to public baths or the castration of statues which were found obscene in the Middle Ages. Summers analyses the abjection of the homosexual and states that the homosexual subjectivity "is frequently accompanied or preceded by feelings of guilt and shame and by a sense of (often quite justified) paranoia" (14). The homosexual's self-definition and self-recognition is based on one's interaction with others and his own other, as in the mirror phase and the emergence of ego. Therefore, this recognition is not only a personal but also a social one. The latter is also a misrecognition since it is based on the illusory abject image of the homosexual as pervert.

Besides the uncanny representation of the gay male, camp cinemas apparently provide freedom and space for gay characters. William notices a man about sixty-five years old in the cinema and remembers seeing him before. He likens the man to a schoolgirl taken to a romantic picture and concludes that he must be looking forward to this weekly outing, for which he must set aside from his pension: "Could he look back to a time when he had behaved like these glowing, thoughtless teenagers, who were now locked together sucking each other's cocks in the hay? Or was this the image of a new society we had made, where every desire could find its gratification?" (*SPL* 51). The dirty cinema seems to be the only place for the old man to try to make up for the years he has lost, just in terms of casual sex, and wail in self-pity. However, one should problematise the fact that these cinemas have become one of the major ghettos where the stigmatised homosexuals are allowed to meet, have random sex, and desperately seek *jouissance*. These people cannot naturally meet someone or fall in love with someone, with whom they can hold hands in public and be visible. That is why they ghettoise themselves in these dirty dark campy anonymous places.

The Line of Beauty is the other novel which perpetuates the theme of man-to-man intimacy in camp cinemas. When still in a relationship, Leo and Nick decide to go to the cinema to see a film with an "enormous length, 170 minutes, each one of which appeared to Nick like a shadowy unit of body heat, of contact and excitement. They would be pressed together in the warm darkness for three hours" (*LB* 144). The movie is not porn in fact, yet Nick's expectations lay bare how the banished gay man perceives being with his partner in the shielding darkness of a cinema. Since cinemas in the author's novels are gay heterotopias of deviation for cruising and sex, it is not hard to realise that even 'heterosexual cinemas' suggest sex to gay characters in the novel. Nick watches the movie feeling Leo's warmth his hand in his lover's open fly.

> They had only made love in parks, or public lavatories, or once in the back of Pete's shop, which Leo had kept a key to, and which felt even more furtive than these cinema handjobs. The thing about the cinema was that they seemed to share in the long common history of happy snoggers and gropers, and Nick liked that. (*LB* 146)

As the quotation makes clear, same-sex sex in cinemas is a ritualised act which has a long historical background. Kissing and fondling male genitals is depicted as a historical tradition passing down from generation to generation. The author's persistent depiction of gays looking for and having sex in cinemas unfortunately affirms the stereotype gay stigmatised and labelled by heteronormative ideologies.

In Hollinghurst's novels, in addition to cinemas, gay bars and clubs, which are Formal Public Sex Contexts, are ghettos commodifying same sex desire, too. These spaces also function as glass closet, or open secret. Sedgwick uses the latter "as a condensed way of describing the phenomenon of the 'glass closet,' the swirls of totalizing knowledge-power that circulate so violently around any but the most openly acknowledged gay male identity" (164). Glass closet is the state of in-betweenness; not being out but not remaining fully in the closet either. It is a way of leading a gay lifestyle without confirming one's own sexual orientation. This is why it is an open secret. Gay bars and clubs are places where both out and closeted gay individuals go; however, once inside everyone can tell they are queer. In *The Swimming-Pool Library*, most characters regularly go to such places without the need to come out to gratify their needs—not only sexual but social and psychological—and socialise. The Shaft is one of these bars. William admits that when he was with Phil, he found himself isolated from the 'normal' gay world, just because he did not go there for a couple of months. He is one of the regulars there:

> I had been an addict of the Shaft. If I was out to dinner I would grow restless towards eleven o'clock.... The Shaft itself I hardly ever left alone, and I had made countless taxi-journeys down the glaring, garbage-stacked wasteland of Oxford Street and along the great still darkness of the Park, a black kid, drunk, chilled in his sweat, lying against me, or secretly touching me. (*SPL* 192)

William goes there to have a good time and find tricks to spend the night with. The bar provides a sense of so-called liberty for him. He can act there freely and sees it as an opportunity to be himself, which he cannot do in the heteronormative world. It is true that power produces discourses stigmatising homosexuality, which, in return, undermine the heteronormative discourse itself; power grants recognition to it by defining and naming it. In this respect, these gay places could be considered loopholes in the symbolic realm and gay space which may be argued to subvert heteronormativity. However, the characters are not aware of the fact that by feeling free only in designated areas restricts freedom and that limited freedom is not freedom at all. Accordingly, the customers enjoy the aphrodisiac atmosphere and do not mind having sex in the lock-ups of the bar.

The Volunteer is another bar ghettoising and commodifying homosexual identity in the novel. It is, for Will, a second-division local gay pub, which he likens to "the waiting room of a station on a branch line where the last train was not expected for quite some time" (*SPL* 17). It is a place Will stops off at and drinks a beer while going home; he is one of the regulars. He is one of those voluntarily ghettoised and commodified gay customers who endorse the dominant order with its capitalistic and opportunistic entrepreneurialism. In addition to the bars, the Corry is an alternative for the gay characters offering a relentless quest for recognition, affection, and sex: "The Corry featured in these days as a lucid interlude –with an institutional structure that time in the flat entirely lacked. I tended to stay late or go to a bar afterwards, not for sex, but for the company of strangers and for talk about sport or music" (*SPL* 31). Will, like many gay characters, lives a life among his house, the club, and bars. The Corry "was a place [he] loved, a gloomy and functional underworld full of life, purpose and sexuality" (*SPL* 9).

Higgins states that homosexuality was extremely common in Roman society and in the Roman world bathhouses and gymnasiums were the arenas for same-sex sex encounters (19). This is why the Corry is chosen as the gay closet; the depiction is a continuation of the traditions of the antiquity and a desire for the sexual liberty lost. However, the club's gloomy and aphrodisiac air and its seclusion from the oppressive dominant ideologies render the club closeted, rather than enabling total freedom. Another club serving as a ghetto to separate the heterosexuals from the other is the Wicks's. It is one of the closet spaces, for Will, where

> people of a certain kind gather together as if to authenticate a caricature of themselves –their freaks and foibles, unremarkable in the individual, being comically evident in the mass. As spoonfuls of soup were raised tremblingly to whiskery lips and hands cupped huge deaf ears to catch murmured and clipped remarks, the lunchers, all in some way distinguished or titled, retired generals, directors of banks, even authors, lost their distinction to me. They were anonymous, a type –and it was impossible to see how they could cope outside in the noise and race of the streets. How much did they know of the derisive life of the city which they ruled and from which they preserved themselves so immaculately and Edwardianly intact? (*SPL* 41-42)

These characters live double lives; outside they lead their lives in a masquerade. Foucault puts this need to masquerade down to the nineteenth century discourse on sex, which was not only infected with old delusions but also with systematic blindnesses to homosexual identity. Evading the truth produced by these discourses was possible only by masking it (*Sexuality* 1: 55). The characters, who mask their sexual orientation outside the closet, are teachers, professors, managers, generals, and so on, yet when they get into the gay space they strip off their roles and statuses, which renders the space carnivalesque. In the heteronormative world some GLBT individuals even get married and have children, sometimes just in order to meet the expectations of the normative society and hide their queerness, whereas in these closeted places they do not have to act and they can be themselves. Charles's uncle is one of these gay male individuals who have to use cover-up girlfriends to conceal their sexual orientation and identity. He pretended and was known to be "a terrific lady's man, and carried on very chivalrously and was seen a lot with the great beauties of the day and *all that*. But really, of course, he was nothing of the kind; and used to tool about with guards" (*SPL* 158). These people can survive only if and as long as they manage to disguise their ex-centric and marginalised subjectivities. Nevertheless, the fact that these gay male individuals can only *be* themselves in disguise and/or in the ghettos specified by the heterosexist society is not liberating at all.

The Folding Star is a novel whose name directly refers to closet since the word 'fold' denotes 'to confine, to close, to enclose and to cover'. The name is an allusion to Milton's *Comus*; it refers to the time when the sheep are all put in the fold, Edward explains to Dawn, in a retrospective conversation scene. Dawn asks: "What about putting the boys all safely in their tent?" (*FS* 254). Their dialogue, in which 'the shepherd' is a metaphor for the agents of heteronormative system and 'the sheep' for gay characters, reveals the closeted lives they lead. Not being given options to choose, the gay male characters in the novel are supposed to lead lives tailored for them by the non-gay society. In fact, closet starts where one divides people into homosexuals and heterosexuals, which, Higgins claims, equals mirroring conventional sexual theories, for it is like dividing mankind into sheep and goats (5). This image may also be a result of the increasing concern and quest of social scientists, starting from the twentieth century, to discover the reason for homosexuality, define the word homosexual, and create a homosexual personality (Higgins 11). The novel, building up the homosexual identity, affirms and re-establishes the minoritising view of the Homosexual.

The major gay heterotopias reinforcing a reified homosexual identity are gay bars in the novel, which proves that there is no distinction between England and Belgium regarding the gay male individual's struggle for recognition and liberalisation. Higgins claims that if one wanted to find a better system to foster homosexual tendencies or acts than the Western system operating for centuries, it would be hard because many social, political and educational institutions have been organised along the division of sex (13). This division promotes or enables homosexuality in such institutions as monasteries, armed forces, and schools, he claims. However, the existence of homosexual acts in single-sex institutions does not mean recognition and acceptance of them by the society. Similarly, the apparent lively and liberal atmosphere in Belgium does not give Edward the freedom and satisfaction he has been yearning for. Edward, full of expectations in the new city, goes from one bar to another in search for sexual gratification. The Cassette, the Golden Calf, Wanne's Bar, or the Bar Biff soon become his second home, where he is doing nothing but chasing oblivion, as he himself admits (*FS* 74). He has been anticipating a sudden change in his life on his arrival in a new city, yet it does not take him long to understand that there will not be any major difference. The Bar Biff, for instance, is a club in the basement of a house. Edward has seen pictures of the place with some cute guys and an overweight barman with his arm round a peroxided fairy, which, he admits, are identical to those in England. He feels familiarity but also a sense of disillusionment:

> Once inside the heavy sound-proofed door with its little wired judas I was in a place so familiar that I would not have been surprised to see my old friends Danny and Simon....There was the same mad delusion of glamour, the same overpriced tawdriness, the same ditsy parochialism and sullen lardy queenery, and underneath it all the same urgency and defiance. We none of us wanted a palace: we liked this humming little hell-hole with its atrophied rules and characters, its ogres and mascots.... And of course young regulars don't all look for novelty: maybe they'd like to score with some strange angelic beauty but they know that heavy truck-driver with brown teeth and a famous dick will give them what they've been waiting for all week. (*FS* 22)

All the attributes and words the author uses show what these gay ghettos are like; heterotopias of deviation. They are commodified ghettos providing the gay male with the liberty they cannot find outside in return for high entry fees and prices. For Allan Bloom, closet space is both internal and marginal to the culture, representing its passions and contradictions, even while marginalised by its orthodoxies. He puts most of the blame on the post-Stonewall gay movements, for they set gay people as a distinct minority group demanding rights just like other minority groups. However, for Bloom, the minoritising modern movements were a recession compared to the glorious past (qtd. in Sedgwick 56). Gay bars are also end products of these movements, which reproduce the conventional binarism heterosexual / homosexual. These places are indeed places like holes serving on Friday and Saturday nights to meet the customers' sexual needs which build up during the week. There are basically two needs to satisfy; the first one is to socialise with gay friends, something hard to achieve in the heteronormative world outside. The second is to find a trick to spend the night with and fulfil sexual needs. Gay bars are heterotopias of deviation and they have a precise and specified function in a society—like a brothel, i.e., the gratification of socially unacceptable desires. Thus, the apparent showiness and indifferent attitudes transform into a struggle and race to find someone in the later hours of the night, in order not to sleep alone. Similarly, Edward, at the end of the night, finds himself trying to choose between Cherif and Ty. When he is fed up with the same people, having tasted most of them, he goes to the other bars for a change.

    A closet is a small confining place off a larger room which is used to hide things, and it is "a spatial force" (Brown 3). Being in the closet is, thus, both for protection and hiding for the gay, which culminates in the alienation and further marginalisation of the closeted individuals. Wanne's bar is itself closeted, with its location among deserted quays and canals, broken-down cottages, and wooden boathouses; being a heterotopia, it is a real space, yet invisible and unreal at the same time. Entering the bar, Edward notices that it is not only the location but also the place itself is the embodiment of the closet, thanks to the "curtain inside the door, and beyond it a narrow brown room with men at the counter listening to a football match" (*FS* 15). Actually Cherif mentions this bar to Edward, who just wants to give it a try; however, his quest results in longing for Cherif, who is not there. The vicious circle the gay characters in the novel go through becomes visible in the depiction of a gay bar in England. When back home for the funeral, Edward meets his old friends Danny and Simon and they go to a bar. Edward envies their steady relationship and resents his being back in the unchanged bar with the same customers, some of whom he has already slept with (*FS* 238).

In the novel, the Town Baths –Formal Public Sex Contexts—are another form of gay heterotopias commodifying people's sexual identities and orientations. They are heterotopias of deviation dating back to Roman bathhouses, which eclipsed even gymnasiums in same-sex encounters. The gay characters in the novel follow in their Roman ancestors' footsteps; while swimming, Edward's trunks keep coming down and Matt, who took him to the baths, puts his hand into Edward's trunks rubbing his crotch, to which Edward reacts and reminds him that they are not in the Bar Biff (*FS* 80). His attitude is pretentious because the reason why he likes the idea of going to the baths is in fact his desire to get naked with Matt. Moreover, he knows that public baths and saunas are also gay ghettos. One day he even comes across Luc, Patrick, and Matt, after Matt has made friends with the boys in France. Edward desperately longs to see Luc naked, since the closet turns him on and triggers his voyeuristic desires. Men's saunas and baths also seem to be places to look for friends in the novel, which again comes from the ancient Greek society where it was common for the mature men to cruise in gyms and bathhouses, and for the young ones to use their charm to impress the older ones. After the funeral in England, Cherif sees Edward in a bar and asks where he has been. Since he has not seen him for a long time, he goes to the men's sauna in order to look for him (*FS* 269). These gay ghettos, surprisingly, have become the second home and address for the gay characters in the novel, as if there were no other means of communication.

The Spell is the story of the magical two-month period in Alex's life, the beginning of which was marked by his visit to Dorset in love with

Justin and return to London in love with Danny. In love with Danny, for two months, he was under a beautiful spell; however, as his friend Hugh tells him, the problem with spells "is that you don't know at the time if they're good ones or bad ones. All black magicians learn how to sugar the pill" (*TS* 107). The novel portrays how gay characters, indeed all of them under spell, never realise their closetedness by the heteronormative society and how they further closet themselves. Like the closet structure in the other novels, the gay characters in this novel are closeted in heterotopias such as bars and clubs, which demonstrates the spatial aspect of the closet. This image supports Summers' view that homosexuality, which used to be a sexual subculture, has transformed into a community "based less on sexual activity than on shared cultural experience" (17). The portrayal of the gay characters sharing similar or the same socio-cultural values and taste implies that gay men form a category different from the non-gay ones and this prescriptive representation of the campy image of the homosexual reinforces homophobic discourses. In fact, the notion of a distinctive homosexual type or personality, a camp subjectivity, which Higgins states has a long pedigree, is nothing but a myth, for it is "impossible to find significant common characteristics…in a group of men who practise homosexual sex" (3).

Gay bars are the major heterotopias in the novel. At the beginning of the novel, Robin's guide in the U.S., an Indian youth, takes him to the town he will stay in. Robin, even before going to his room, gets into the Blue Coyote, a bar his guide recommends. Butler states that "there is a linkage between homosexuality and abjection, indeed, a possible identification *with* an abject homosexuality at the heart of heterosexual identification. This economy of repudiation suggests that heterosexuality and homosexuality are mutually exclusive phenomena" (*Bodies* 111-112). Each pole excludes its other since it sees the other as transient and imaginary. However, the Indian boy takes Robin to a gay bar, which reveals that the non-gay society is aware of the heterotopias of deviation it designates:

> The Blue Coyote had no windows, and so saw nothing of the boulevard-raking sunset, or the gorgeous combustion westward over the mountains…. Any light in the room was husbanded and shielded –by the fake overhanging eaves of the bar and the hooded canopy above the pool table. Even before the door shut behind him, Robin felt at a disadvantage. It was the gloomiest bar he'd ever been in and seemed designed to waken unease in the stumbling newcomer, eyed from the shadows by the dark-adapted regulars. (*TS* 7)

The bar is the embodiment of the closet; it is gloomy and shielded, i.e., concealed, from the heteronormative world outside. Each regular sitting inside is another closet for a stranger like Robin and he feels threatened and underprivileged. In addition to the closety portrayal of the bar, Robin's going there in haste, even before going to his room to unpack, shows how he himself is willing to ghettoise himself in the locations heteronormative society designates and allocates for them. Robin meets Sylvan there and even hearing from Jane and learning that she is pregnant by himself does not excite him; the only thing he wants is sex with Sylvan. Butler refers to the light psychoanalysis sheds on tensions between homosexuality and citizenship / manhood, and highlights the fact that it is a prerequisite to reject, repress or transmute "an always imagined homosexuality" in order to become a subject (*Excitable* 108). However, Robin subverts this process and does not repress his feelings and fails to meet the expectations of the orthodox view.

Another gay bar ghettoising the characters in the novel is the Chepstow Castle, a bar in London, in Danny's, now a twenty-two-year-old gay man, neighbourhood. Alex, in love with Danny, wonders if Danny "ever used that gloomy, velvet-curtained pub, the Chepstow Castle –though of course gay men nowadays were meant to use bars, where there was nowhere to sit down and the drinks cost twice as much" (*TS* 70). Hollinghurst's bars are always closety gloomy ghettos where one cannot even find a seat. However, the crowded atmosphere is not problematised since the objective of people going there is cruising and finding a trick. The two-fold price of drinks shows how the heteronormative system renders gay individuals prey to commodification. The Drop is another gay ghetto to which gay characters are attracted as are fireflies to light. Danny, after getting fired from work because he was caught buying cocaine in the gents, goes straight to the bar. The bar is packed when he arrives and he pushes his way through to the bar and orders a drink. He is served by Heinrich, whom he has had a brief sexual relationship with (*TS* 147). The bar seems to be a place where he can take refuge in case of a crisis which he cannot handle, for he finds relief, excitement, and satisfaction there. He is a gay-bar addict, a night creature who sometimes goes to bars which do not open till three or four in the morning but still in an unbelievable alertness for sex (*TS* 142). However, the depiction of the place is again significant; with the "mysterious dim passageway which started outside the lavatories and went round two corners before ending up by the front door and the cold draught down the stairs from the street above" the bar is another incarnation of a heterotopia. It is dim and gloomy, just like the others in the novel, which suggests that the gay ghetto appeals to the dark faculties of the brain satisfying the libido.

The Line of Beauty, in line with the other three novels, deploys the male gay characters in gay ghettos, all of which turn out to be heterotopias of deviation. As a result, the novel affirms cliché misconceptions and the minoritising view about the homosexual and perpetuates the cultural stereotype of the gay male subjectivity. The major gay ghettos in the novel are, typical of Hollinghurst, gay bars. Chepstow Castle is one of them, where gay characters enjoy their make-believe freedom of same-sex desire. There is a gay bar in *The Spell* which bears the same name, which shows the author's deliberate repetition of the gay scene with a distinct identity. The depiction of the place lays bare the closety atmosphere and nature of the bar: Walking to meet his first date, Leo, Nick

> fixed his thoughts for the hundredth time on the little back bar of the Chepstow Castle, which he had chosen for its shadowy semi-privacy –a space incuriously glanced into by people being served in the public bar.... There was an amber light in there, among the old whisky mirrors and photographs of horse-drawn drays. He saw himself sitting shoulder to shoulder with Leo, their hands joined in secret on the dusty moquette. (*LB* 25)

The space is secluded from the public bar, which is obviously the domain of the heterosexual. The public section of the bar is outside, which shows how normalised and acceptable heterosexuality is, while the shadowy gloomy gay section is inside. Gay section is the part to be closeted and concealed from public eye, for it is a heterotopia of deviation. This is why it is badly illuminated. However, even in this gloomy and closety atmosphere secrecy is highlighted and the stigmatised gay customers are under the judgmental gaze of the heterosexual ones sitting outside.

The characters' inevitable attraction to gay bars and their ineptitude to socialise without gay bars surface in the conversation among Nick, Leo and Pete. This is Pete's first meeting with Nick and when he learns that he has been in London only for six weeks, his tone becomes a bit critical:

> 'I see. You'll still be doing the rounds, then. Or are you just shopping local? You've done the Volunteer.' Leo saw Nick hesitating, and said, 'I wouldn't want him going to that old flea-box. At least not till he's sixty, like everyone else in there.' 'I'm exploring a bit,' said Nick. 'I don't know, where do the young things go these days?' 'Well, there's the Shaftesbury,' Nick said, naming a pub that Polly Tompkins had described as the scene of frequent conquests. 'You're not so much of a pubber, though, are you?' Leo said. 'He wants to get down the Lift,' said Pete, 'if he's a bit of a chocoholic.' (*LB* 97)

Escaping from the boredom and loneliness in Barwick, Nick closets himself in London, a huge gay ghetto itself. Pete indicates that there are two options for a newcomer; they can go to various gay bars and make 'friends' or they can remain within their own neighbourhood or class meeting people only in their own circles. In either case, though, the queer cannot get out of the closet. The closet itself is a heterotopia; it is not an accessible public place. Either the entry is compulsory or there are rites to submit to. Once inside, it is impossible to leave it for good.

The gay bars in Hollinghurst's work are ghettos, yet they are the only places where the characters feel safe. On his first date, Nick actually sits with Leo outside the bar and finally they find a bench. However, once out of the gay ghetto and among heterosexual people, Nick "found himself wondering how they looked and sounded to the people around them . . . It was all getting noisier as the evening went on, with a vague sense of heterosexual threat. Nick guessed Leo's other dates would have met him in a gay pub, but he had flunked that further challenge. Now he regretted the freedom he would have had there" (*LB* 29). The characters cannot help having the sense of paranoid, a kind of fear of the normative heterosexual. They can feel free and be themselves only out of the criminalising stigmatising and pathologising heteronormative gaze. The Y and Heaven are such places serving as a shelter for the queer, yet they are also cruising places, and thus lead to arguments, like the one between Nick and Wani: "'You didn't say where you were last night.' 'Oh, I went to Heaven,' said Nick, with mild apprehension at telling an innocent truth. 'I wondered,' said Wani, without looking round. 'Did you fuck anyone?' 'Of course I didn't fuck anyone. I was with Howard and Simon.' 'I suppose that follows,' said Wani" (*LB* 188). Wani's utterance reveals the nature of gay ghettos; the sole purpose of going there for the characters is to find a trick and gratify their sexual needs. Gay characters in a relationship do not go there with their boyfriends, yet some of them do so without their boyfriends. In this way, the characters in fact ghettoise themselves in these bars for the sake of sex.

Apart from the bars, the gay characters also take refuge in a nudist yard, another Formal Public Sex Context in the novel. The place is allocated for the lecherous hedonistic gay loiterers and it possesses the aphrodisiac air which is often found in the author's gay space depictions:

> Nick went ahead on the path and held the gate open for Wani, so that for several seconds the outside world had a view of naked flesh before the gate, with its "Men Only" sign, swung shut behind them. It was a small compound, a concrete yard, with benches round the walls under a narrow strip of roof. It was like a courtyard of the classical world reduced to pipes

and corrugated iron. There was something distantly classical, too, in the protracted nakedness, and something English, school-like and comfortless in the concrete and tin and the pond-water smell. (*LB* 159)

The gate isolates this gay h(e)aven reminiscent of the classical antiquity from the oppressive patriarchal world outside. The author refers to the classical era because homosexuality was not stigmatised then and it was even considered superior to heterosexual relationships, which were regarded as natural, procreative, and thus bestial. The remoteness of the image is due to the stigmatising and normalising heteronormative discourses ongoing in modern times, which are, as Foucault points out, in sharp contrast to the discourses before the seventeenth century. In this yard, gay men get naked, swim, sunbathe, cruise and have sex freely, which shows the extent to which Hollinghurst is under the influence of the function of gymnasiums and bathhouses in the ancient Greek and Roman homosexual subculture. However, freedom in confined spaces is not freedom; in contrast, it means the ghettoisation, effacement and relegation of the queer.

In Hollinghurst's novels, just like cinemas and bars, public conveniences in parks and bars are also frequently used as heterotopias allocated for the abjected queer. This image is related to the reified urban homosexual subculture which has always been restricted to certain districts since antiquity. Casper, the German forensic scientist writing in the 1860s, claims that in all big towns in Europe cruising and same-sex sex acts go on in secrecy and there is no inhabited place where it does not happen. Moreover, he adds that writers have for a long time specified;

> "certain peculiarities in the walk, look, demeanour and voice" by which such men "may be recognised." He reported that one informant, who seems to have been exaggerating just a little bit, told the curious doctor that "We discover each other at once, at a single glance, and by exercising a little caution, I have never been deceived".... It takes one, as the old saying goes, to know one. Cruising is a venerable tradition, and the city offers anonymity and opportunity. (qtd. in Higgins 13-14)

This notion, in line with the minoritising view of homosexuality, is nothing but another effort to closet the gay male in the space designated by the non-gay. It is common in Hollinghurst's novels to find gay characters cruising in such places and cottaging. To illustrate, William met Charles in a public toilet, while he was loitering and following an Arab boy. Since there were not any decent and acceptable means of meeting other homosexuals in the past, desperate gays looking for something memorable went to parks and public toilets. In this way, the stigmatising, criminalising and psychologising dominant discourses paved the way for the exile of the homosexual.

In *The Folding Star*, public lavatories are depicted by the author as cruising places where gay men ghettoise themselves, which shows that closet is not only a metaphor but has spatiality. Edward, when he goes to the station to meet his friend Edie, has to wait there for a while and he describes his mood while waiting: "It was one of those vacant interludes, when pleasant boredom mixes with anticipation, and six or seven minutes of anonymous sex in the mopped and deserted Gents is what you would like best" (*FS* 153). It is weird to see that Hollinghurst still portrays cottaging as something attractive and common. Cottaging for Edward is not only theoretical; he puts it into practice when he finds an occasion. For example, in the Bar Biff, when the young boy he likes and stares at goes to the lavatory, he follows him. However, the boy pees in a lock-up stall and he cannot do anything (*FS* 23). In this way, gay characters in the novel voluntarily closet themselves in gay ghettos without noticing that they do ghettoise themselves.

The function of the gents is exactly one of the principles of heterotopias of deviation; it has a specific service in a society. Moreover, a public lavatory is a juxtaposition of several spaces; it provides public with two basic needs; excretion for the non-gay and sex for the gay. This is why, in *The Spell*, Danny, while working for a company as a security officer, goes to the gents frequently to masturbate, sometimes up to three times a shift. Once when he is there for the same purpose, another man working there comes in and goes into a cubicle. "Danny couldn't check on him, as the partitions came prudishly down to the floor –there was no opening for the quick bold contacts you could have in American rest-rooms. Still, he heard the knock of the seat-lid being closed, and just made out the rustle of paper and the hurried chopping noise of a plastic card on the china cistern; then a pause and a couple of sniffs; and then the chopping and the sniffing repeated" (*TS* 144). The process of chopping cocaine and snorting a line is almost ritualised and gay characters' alertness in public toilets is another striking point in Hollinghurst's narrative. After listening to the man in the next cubicle, Danny begins the transaction and offers him money in return for some cocaine, as a result of which his boss fires him. Then he goes to another gay bar and chops and snorts cocaine in the gents there. These homophobic depictions create the impression that gay characters will perform any stunt for sex and/or drugs.

Public lavatories in gay bars are ghettos within ghettos and they are frequent cruising places in Hollinghurst's work. Butler sees performativity as "that reiterative power of discourse to produce the phenomena that it regulates and constrains" (*Bodies* 2). Thus, the repetition of the same heterotopias is of great significance to heteronormativity in the process of reifying, deploying, and subjectifying homosexuality. In the Blue Coyote, where young Robin met Sylvan years ago, Robin admits that the gents is bleaker and more functional than the bar itself, adding that when he went to "the lavs at Parker's Piece or in the Market Square, eyebrows raised as if at the exploits of someone else, he always seemed to find gratification at once, from a man who clearly was a loiterer, and had probably been loitering for hours" (*TS* 10-11). The bar area seems to be allocated to cruise and meet people, whereas consummation takes place in the lavatories in Hollinghurst's novels. Closeting gay characters in this vicious circle is itself a sign of homophobia and unfortunately it affirms heteronormative myths about the Homosexual. The use of sex and public lavatories together should be problematised because the public lav is a negative reinforcing stimulus and it reinforces the traditionally unnatural and stigmatised deployment of same-sex sex acts. The depiction of sex scenes in an unhygienic atmosphere like a cubicle in public lavatories is humiliating, which has to do with the power assumed by medical discourse since it emerged as;

> the supreme authority in matters of hygienic necessity, taking up the old fears of venereal affliction and combining them with the new themes of asepsis, and the great evolutionist myths with the recent institutions of public health; it claimed to ensure the physical vigor and the moral cleanliness of the social body; it promised to eliminate defective individuals, degenerate and bastardized populations. (Foucault, *Sexuality* 1: 54)

The medical discourse stigmatised the gay individual as the degenerate, defective, and unclean. As a result, the gay male, victim and vector of AIDS, was deployed as a threat to public health and hygiene. Another problematic scene in line with homophobic medical discourse is when Alex is in a gay bar with Danny; he loses track of him there after a while and wonders where he is. He goes to the lavatories and notices that people were very "busy here, men in pairs queuing for the lock-ups" (*TS* 86). The people queuing up to have sex in the cubicles with the men they pick is far from being realistic and hard to be found even in heterosexist myths about the homosexual. Sedgwick, in her analysis of *Dorian Gray*, compares the dead body of Dorian to his portrait and suggests that at the end of the novel the old, ugly, dead man on the floor is "the moralizing gloss" on his beautiful portrait (131). The sharp contrast between the two shows that the beautiful portrait is only an illusion, a utopia, whereas in the world outside a homosexual is regarded as the horribly ugly and sinful dead man on the floor. The discrepancy also reveals Oscar Wilde's own castration by Victorian society and Hollinghurst's repetitive use of these heteronormative myths uncovers the author's own castration in the twenty-first century.

Cottaging, therefore, is a very common theme and there are so many scenes in Hollinghurst's novels where readers find men cruising, having sex and cocaine there. As Justin puts it, when he finds out that Alex and Danny will spend time in Robin's country house in Dorset: "It's called Love in a Cottage, darling. Make the most of it, because it doesn't last long" (*TS* 170). Here, by using the word 'cottage', he refers to the country house in the literal sense. However, the capitalised word suggests that the cottage refers to the act of cottaging, which does not last long. The use of the word love, again capitalised, is also important in that it reveals how the characters cannot tell apart between sex and love. Justin is a cottaging addict himself. During his trial separation from Robin, he goes to Soho and makes most of his freedom, going from bar to bar and sleeping with various men. One day he goes into the gents at Oxford Circus, this time from need, where he sees that the skinny black guy he sucked off years ago is standing in exactly the same place and gives Justin the same sneaky look (*TS* 193). Hollinghurst depicts the desperate and miserable gay men seeking pleasure in public conveniences and the black guy Justin sees is in the same place and gives him the same look, which reveals the vicious circle and the circular plot structures these characters are confined in. In this way, the author re-presents the minoritising view of the homosexual and endorses the post-Stonewall attempts to create a distinct gay identity with rights granted to other minority groups, as if it were a category. Kim Duff agrees that Hollinghurst's fiction represents minoritising view of homosexuality because he "pursues the kinds of problematic, and often reductive, representations of gay and transgendered identities in 1980s Conservative Britain" (181). The campy group of individuals the author depicts forms a minority group with a distinct identity and subculture to be exploited. The gay heterotopias springing up actually mean the commodification of same-sex desire and the tolerance to the existence of such heterotopias of deviation is a consequence or requirement of "a new kind of consumerism and national identity borne of Thatcherite neoliberal and privatizing policies" (Nunn qtd in Duff 188).

In *The Line of Beauty*, gay male characters have sex in public lavatories, common ghettos reiterated frequently in the author's work. For example, in the nudist yard Nick and Wani meet Leslie and his partner Andy. Leslie says that his boyfriend is devoted to him, but after a while Nick sees Andy coming out of a cubicle with a "mischief in his eyes" and out of the same cubicle comes a grey-haired man (*LB* 168). Once again

Hollinghurst depicts couples cheating on each other and having sex with others in lavatories. Lavatories are also blind-date and cruising places for the characters. Once Nick goes to the Shaftesbury, when Wani is abroad, and comes across Joe, a man he remembers from the Y and from the showers: "Then he went downstairs to the Gents, and found, when he peeped sideways along the reeking trough, that the man had followed him; so they stood there for a bit, in a tense delay whilst other people came and went, until the man nodded towards the empty lock-up" (*LB* 369). The consummation of their brief 'love' does not take place in the end and they go to Joe's place in Soho. The incident shows that there is a well-established ritual among gay men; after they meet and make a pass at someone, the only thing they are expected to do is to walk into the toilets and wait for the other. As soon as they find an empty lock-up, they can consummate their 'love'. Having sex in bathrooms and lavatories is so common in the novel that even when Wani and Nick rent Tristão, they go to Nick's bathroom, snort cocaine, and have sex there (*LB* 336). Hollinghurst seems to be obsessed with associating public conveniences with gay sex; however, portraying gays constantly loitering and having sex in these places means ghettoising and closeting them in heterotopias.

Besides certain cinemas, bars, and cottages, queer individuals are also closeted in their own houses, hotel rooms, or homeland by Hollinghurst. In *The Swimming-Pool Library*, Will and Arthur's relationship is a totally closeted one; they spend almost all their time, when together, at home. Home is the only space where they can be lovers. Talking about their relationship, Will says that their first week was "a week spent in bed, or trailing naked from bedroom to bathroom to kitchen; sleeping at irregular times, getting drunk, watching movies on the video. I was engrossed in him.... Perhaps he felt stifled in the flat. After hours of languid vacancy he would spring up and run from room to room" (*SPL* 13). There is no life outside home for a gay couple and they are imprisoned there eternally leading a self-enclosed life. Arthur's feeling stifled is also significant; it shows the suppression and the need for concealment he suffers from. Especially after Arthur kills his brother's mate and begins to live with Will, Will feels closetedness more and more. He identifies his life in his flat with the feelings of love and guilt: "At home it was always very hot; the central heating throbbed away as if we feared exposure, and often, though high up and not overlooked, we kept the curtains drawn in the daytime, only a mild bloom of pinkish light penetrating into the rooms from outside" (*SPL* 28). The fear of exposure and the function of the drawn curtains are significant as they show the extent to which the couple isolate themselves from the oppressive and hazardous life outside and that they can feel secure only at home. They barely talk and just take refuge in the warmth of the darkened flat. In this sense, their house also turns out to be a heterotopia for them since it is real, though outside all other spaces constituted by heterosexist ideologies.

Charles's house is also depicted like a heterotopia alienated from the heteronormative world outside: It is closed to traffic and no longer marked in the London maps. It has an air of privacy and exclusion, too. Charles admits the closeted nature of his house: "We don't get any sun here –only in the attic. Those houses block it out. We're very cut off here, of course" (*SPL* 73). The house, closed to traffic and not getting any sunshine, symbolises closetedness, which stems from homophobia. The heteronormative society persecutes Charles, puts him into prison only because of his identity, and then imprisons him in such ghettos as clubs, bars, and his house. William, when first invited to Charles's house, feels obliged to pay extreme attention to his clothes and manners:

> I'd put a suit on, smarter perhaps than I needed to be, but I enjoyed its protective conformity. I so rarely dressed up, and not having to wear a suit for work I seldom took any of mine off their hangers. My father had had me kitted out with morning suits and evening dress as I grew up and I had always relished the handsomeness of dark, formal clothes.... Entering the smoking-room I felt like an intruder in a film, who has coshed an orderly and, disguised in his coat, enters a top-secret establishment, in this case a home for people kept artificially alive. (*SPL* 34)

The meticulous manner in his clothing reveals how he perceives Charles's house and the social atmosphere there. Surprisingly, he finds wearing a suit protective. This might be significant in that feeling secure in a suit shows that he does not feel so when he is in his everyday clothes. This is another indication of the level of oppression gay male individuals are subjected to. Clothes of course do not refer only to clothes in a literal sense; on the contrary, they refer to the visibility of the homosexual and show that they cannot be themselves.

Another ghettoised house belongs to Sandy. He appears in Charles's diary as a special friend who Charles wanted to have to himself, yet failed to do so. Sandy was apparently absorbed in Otto Henderson, an artist. Charles, in his notes, depicts Sandy's house in Soho as a closet, which he identifies with lasciviousness:

> I was at Sandy's studio in the afternoon when without a word he & Otto tore off their clothes & clambered on to the roof.... there was something so prurient about the nudity when I compared it to days on tour when all our party wd stop at a river, & the men strip off their shirts & drawers to wash

them & spread them on the boulders to dry. I nursed those little idylls to myself, & thought of sitting among the bushes with my pipe while the men dived & splashed, or roamed through the muddy shallows. Then we were many miles from civilisation. (*SPL* 151)

Sandy uses the roof as a place where he can sunbathe naked with his friends, get drunk, and act freely. The space the roof provides is a temporal heterotopia. Unlike heterotopias of indefinitely accumulating time such as museums and libraries, these heterotopias are not oriented toward the eternal, but they are linked to slices in time –heterochronies- in their temporary, transitory and precarious aspect. Foucault's examples for these heterotopias are Polynesian vacation villages which offer primitive and eternal nudity to city-dwellers (*Of Other* 26). The roof, similarly, gives the gay men who live in Soho a chance to experience freedom, in a limited sense though. Charles, however, feels uneasy because of the aphrodisiac air, perhaps just because of his jealousy. He, then, compares his present life, in 1925, to the old days when he went on tours in the countryside with his friends, which he finds relatively innocent. However, there is no difference at all between the days in his past and present; those days, he says, he lived away from civilisation, and likewise, now he lives in Soho but still away from civilisation. Civilisations are based on heteronormative and patriarchal grounds, which always cast the odd one out. This is why Sandy lives in Soho, but at the same time 'he' does not. For Lacan, the subject pronoun 'I' does not have a stable referent and he claims 'I' is not 'me' (qtd. in Homer 45). The referent of 'I' could be the subject—constituted in the symbolic order, the ego or the unconscious. That is why in Sandy's case, 'he,' the one living in Soho, cannot be 'him.' 'He' does not exist so far as he is not visible outside and he is closeted in his flat and roof.

In the title of the novel, the use of the words of 'swimming pool' and 'library' together to refer to the space William and his friends used for their polyandrous same-sex sex acts is "a notion fitting to the double lives [they] led" (*SPL* 141). A pool is a real place, yet a library is a heterotopia of indefinitely accumulating time where time never ceases to build up (Foucault, *Of Other* 26). In Hollinghurst's work, the characters feel free only in the designated heterotopias like gay bars, cinemas, parks and public lavs, and their flats. Heterotopias are not

> freely accessible like a public place. Either the entry is compulsory, as in the case of entering a barracks or a prison, or else the individual has to submit to rites and purifications.... There are others, on the contrary, that seem to be pure and simple openings, but that generally hide curious exclusions. Everyone can enter into these heterotopic sites, but in fact that

is only an illusion: we think we enter where we are, by the very fact that we enter, excluded. (Foucault, *Of Other* 26)

The designated places in the novel are in fact public places and they are accessible for anyone. However, one cannot simply go there and get into the closet itself; it would only be an illusion. For the ones within the closet, the entrance was compulsory and they had to submit to some rites to get accepted. Thus, the outsider is bound to be excluded, yet even in this exclusive atmosphere, Hollinghurst's characters still face homophobia and violence in the heteronormative society due to homosexual panic and the consequent gay-bashing.

In *The Folding Star*, gay characters' hometowns or homelands, where their families live, turn out to be their closet. It is, therefore, families rather than places that give the characters the impulse to run away. Edward, the protagonist, is an Englishman from Rough Common, a small town in the south of London. He moves to Belgium for a temporary job but when his mother asks for an explanation, he fails to give a plausible one. However, looking for a room in Belgium, he dismisses some alternatives because they are "too pinned and stifled with rules and considerations for someone who ha[s] finally left home" (*FS* 13). The sense of relief and freedom he feels away from home and family shows that all those years he lived in the closet and was desperate to leave. After settling in Belgium, he realises that the life out of the closet he has been seeking so far is available there: "For most men, it is important that they hold a tourist visa in their pocket that guarantees an exit…. Most travellers are drawn to foreign countries because they hold out the fantasy that possibilities exist in that country that they cannot realize in their own domestic land" (Bernstein 721). For Edward, accordingly, Belgium functions as the foreign exotic country where he can do anything and everything he cannot back home. He goes to a gay bar and finds kids, even some under eighteen, snorting cokes. He states that it is acceptable in Belgium, unlike in his homeland, and puts it down to "the classical, commonplace good sense of Europe" (*FS* 22). England, representing the castrating symbolic register, is contrasted to the uncanny represented by Belgium, which also has implications of the pre-symbolic. When Edward unexpectedly returns home after two friends of his, Colin and Dawn, die in a car crash, to attend their funeral, he realises much better why he left home: "In a few minutes I would lose the surprise, the disconcerting and exact sameness of everything in the house I had lived in all my life. My mother was out, it was dusk, and this was the silence that had been around us all the time…. I hadn't meant to be back so soon in my room with its wall of second-hand books, its air of determined privacy and make-believe" (*FS* 196). The highlighted privacy and silence imply the closeted life Edward led in his hometown. When a gay individual in a homophobic environment comes out, both sides may get injured due to the double-edged weapon and a child's coming out may plunge the mother into the closet in her conservative community (Sedgwick 80). That is why Edward cannot come out but instead he flees from his hometown. He has a traditional family and he is so tired of his life in England that he does not even miss it. Willie, one of his obsessions, is now married to Alison and they have a baby, Ralphie. Edward still has a crush on Willie and he tries to kiss him, but gets rejected once again. Comparing such societies as China, Japan, India, Rome, and the Arabo-Moslem to the Western societies, Foucault contrasts their *ars erotica* to *scientia sexualis* the Western epistemology practises. The latter, for him, has been producing discourses on sex to create and tell the truth for centuries (*Sexuality* 1: 58). The desire for the lack of *ars erotica* disturbs Edward and it underlies his yearning for the escape from England. He knows that he cannot change anything there; he has a tedious life, a traditional family, and friends, which render England the closet he wants to get out of.

The reasons underlying Edward's desire to flee are the same as those for Luc in Belgium. After his getting expelled from school, because of the obscure event with the sailors on the ship, Luc wants to improve his English to leave for England. He talks about it to Edward:

> "'So you've had to go back to England?'
> 'I'm afraid so.'
> 'Then you prefer it here?'
> 'I suppose I must do,' I said, thinking how I had been sick to return, and how odd these personal questions were from him, who had never shown so much curiosity before. But he turned aside again to a bleak comment of his own.
> 'I would prefer to be there. I am looking forward to going to the University of Dorset, if I can get permission." (*FS* 275-276)

Just as Rough Common is a closet for Edward, his homeland signifies the same for Luc. That is why Edward is teaching him English. Luc does not find it nice to be in his hometown where he has lived all his life and where his family have lived for centuries. Anne-Marie Fortier asserts that the queer diaspora is related to the feelings of exile and estrangement experienced by queer subjects and that these feelings deploy them away from the heterosexual family, nation and homeland (188). That is why both Edward and Luc believe that freedom is somewhere away from the heteronormative home.

Paul Echevin, Marcel's father, cannot be said to be a heterosexual, but his life is also closeted and he seems to be a patriarchal figure now. Edward sees his study in the Orst Museum and he likens it to a cupboard, which is reached through a brick tunnel. Then he sees Paul's portrait photograph on the wall; "a lean-faced man of fifty, with a short, pointed silvery beard, sitting with cheek tilted towards the jewelled knob of a cane: the fastidious ironic look of the heterosexual bachelor, half dandy and half clergyman, and an air of steely enigma" (*FS* 37). His portrait represents the mainstream life style of a Belgian father. Belgium is not of much difference from England indeed; the existence of the closet does not depend on the country one lives in. In contrast, it depends on who you live with. Sedgwick argues that

> a lot of the energy of attention and demarcation that has swirled around issues of homosexuality since the end of the nineteenth century, in Europe and the United States, has been impelled by the distinctively indicative relation of homosexuality to wider mappings of secrecy and disclosure, and of the private and the public, that were and are critically problematical for the gender, sexual, and economic structures of the heterosexist culture at large. (71)

Homosexuality, for centuries, has been related and relegated to secrecy and privacy since it has been regarded as something to feel ashamed of. This is the reason why Edward, as soon as he arrives in Belgium, finds a new closet for himself, while he is actually trying to escape from it: "The room I chose was so hidden away that it gave me the sensation of having entered, with dreamlike suddenness, into the secret inner life of the city" (*FS* 13). He has chosen a room away from public attention and scrutiny in order to regain his freedom and live as he wants to. However, soon he discovers that in Belgium he is not safer than he was in England. When he meets Rose in a bar, he feels the risks and danger he is exposed to, and he realises that the man is a con trying to fool him, a fresh fool who knows nothing about himself. He went there as he thought that the city was famous for its music and pictures, so this new awareness puzzles him: "I couldn't quite admit to myself the uncertainty I felt already at its deadness, its air of a locked museum" (*FS* 7). This new recognition shows him that Belgium is not what he dreamt of; it is not a place where he can get rid of the closet he suffered from in England. The closet haunts him no matter where he goes because *scientia sexualis* is practised by individuals as well as by social institutions like family, not only by countries.

Before Edward rents a room, he stays in a hotel, where he has booked a room before coming. He sees it advertised in the English gay press; its name is *Mykonos*. Mykonos is a Greek island commodifying GLBT identities and attracting many gay tourists every year; therefore, the name of the hotel is quite significant. Those days he meets Cherif in the Town Museum, where Cherif always cruises men, and takes him to his hotel room. He feels the receptionist might know Cherif because he may have brought his tricks there before. The room, a safer closet, turns Cherif on: "The moment I had locked the door he was on to me, chewing and stuffing my mouth and knocking my glasses up skew-whiff over the top of my head. He was an animal" (*FS* 10). The hotel is like a gay ghetto where people bring their tricks or even customers, and Cherif's soaring libido once inside the room shows how sharply the closet differs from the world outside. After leaving the hotel, Edward rents a room far from public eye. While describing the room, Edward in fact defines the closet itself word for word:

> All down one side of the room ran usually deep cupboards, each with an enamel number, and a door that shut with a boom....The facing wall was a partition, rough with nail-holes and nail-heads hammered in, that made me wonder what had been stored here, what work had been done here, and when it had come to an end. It seemed an encouraging setting for my own projects, the bits of writing I was going to take up again. (*FS* 13-14)

The room is the embodiment of the closet and the consummation part is to be carried out by Edward with his projects. He states that he means writing but he will never start writing and his projects will consist of bodies he has had in that room. His room will be like the garden his room overlooks; a garden to which no door leads. He wants to get down there, yet decides to leave it unvisited for ever, for he thought the "beauty of it lay not so much in itself as in its solitude; like any high-walled place" (*FS* 14). The essential feature of the closet is that one can never get out of it completely; each new occasion or circumstance builds new walls for the gay individual to climb. However, the gay man oppressed and stigmatised by the normative society also feels safer among high walls around himself. This is why the enclosed garden attracts Edward but then he decides to leave it untapped. His room is his secret garden; he feels different and much better when he comes in: "I was in my room and closed the door. It felt warm and remote there, like a room left behind when everyone has gone to church" (*FS* 47). Being free from the churchgoers and being alone at home when they are absent shows Edward's attitude towards traditions which constantly attempt to normalise and transform him into someone who is not him at all.

Matt's house bears similar characteristics to Edward's room as it functions as a closet for him, where he carries out his underground business and leads a hedonistic life out of public eye:

> The house he was at the back of belonged to an elderly and reclusive woman, deaf and cat-loving. Matt, it appeared, was not allowed to use her front door or to go into her part of the building at all; so access to his rooms was through the back yard and a glassed-in porch full of half-dead plants. It was odd that we both lived hidden away behind old people whom we never saw; comforting too, as if it allowed us to be children again, free and disadvantaged. (*FS* 100)

Using the back yard and not being allowed to use the front door symbolises the banishment of the queer from the heterosexual's world. Their not seeing the old people renting them their rooms shows that traditions do not accept ex-centric figures, and likewise, these individuals ignore the heteronormative culture with its old-fashioned traditions. That is why Matt and Edward feel like children, disadvantaged but free. This is how the system works; it imprisons the queer in the closet but lets them feel free within the borders of the closet, which brings mutual benefits, apparently.

The Spell also depicts gay male characters closeted in their houses. For instance, Robin's house and life in the country, in Dorset, symbolises closet in contrast to the campy life in London. When Alex arrives in the country, Justin says: "This is the country…. You can tell because of all the traffic, and the pubs are full of fascists. Apparently there's another homo moving into the village. We're terribly over-excited" (*TS* 17). Justin is bored to death in the country since he is fond of gay ghettos and every single change, no matter how tiny, is noteworthy in the monotony of the country life. This is why he is excited to have learnt that another gay man is moving into the village. He accuses the local people of being fascists because they tend to be oppressive and monolithic, denying the existence of the queer and pretending to be consisting of rigidly uniform heterosexual individuals. The closety atmosphere in the country makes gay individuals feel lonely. Justin "longed for crowds and the purposeful confusion of the city; he wanted shops where you could get what you wanted, and deafening bars so full of men seeking pleasure and oblivion that you could hardly move through them. It was deadly still here" (*TS* 43). He looks back on his life in London and misses the gay ghettos teeming with new men and new hopes. It is true that with the oppressive heteronormative air, the country life is a closet for the queer, formed by the power and discourses external to the queer individual. However, once in the gay scene allocated by the same sources and agents of power, the queer individual deliberately closets himself in a gay ghetto. Justin, a self-ghettoising gay, especially when Robin goes out of town, goes almost hysterical and makes a pass at other men, accusing Robin of leaving him locked up there, just like a slave or a mistress (*TS* 93). He feels as if he had the right to cheat on his lover, who left him alone in the loathsome country. He finds it difficult to understand how anyone could prefer living in the country, "with its cows and sheep, both literal and figurative" (*TS* 193). When he temporarily breaks up with Robin, he goes to Soho and loiters from bar to bar having sex with numerous men, some of whom are rent boys. When the trial separation period is over, he comes back to Robin and admits that he is "a city girl" (*TS* 204). Alex, on the other hand, loves the country life, and disagrees with Justin: "Well, we think it's marvellous being in the country" (*TS* 170). Alex uses the first person plural pronoun 'we', including Danny as his boyfriend; however, Danny, another 'city girl', at that time is rolling a joint, for he cannot stand country life or a monandrous life without drugs.

In addition to cinemas, bars, and public conveniences, certain parks, bushes, and woods are also accepted and designated –by dominant ideologies— as gay loitering and cruising closets. A heterotopia juxtaposes several spaces in a single real place, just as the theatre or cinema does. A stage or screen brings together a whole series of places incompatible with one another (Foucault, *Of Other* 25). Likewise, parks and public lavatories function in the novel as the juxtaposition of diverse meanings. Whereas they are public facilities for non-gay societies, they serve as a heterotopia of deviation for gay communities to gratify sexual needs. In *The Swimming-Pool Library*, Will's six-year-old nephew Rupert knows about such places: "I went for a walk. A really long walk, actually, up that very steep path, you know—where homosexuals go" (*SPL* 58). Rupert knows that his uncle has gay friends, though Will does not tell him he himself is gay, and he definitely has got gaydar. Rupert is not homophobic, yet it sounds weird for a child at his age to be aware of not only gay individuals but also gay closet. His awareness implies that the society stigmatises and confines gay individuals to certain paths and parks so obviously that even children know these places. However, this acceptance does not mean legal recognition or safety for the homosexual. Charles was imprisoned, though the actual reason looks ambiguous, because of cottaging. He spent six months there and after leaving the prison, he sees long and logical dreams of being back there, variations of his arrest. In one of them, he discovers that the cottages he is looking for have long been closed or demolished and replaced with a highly respectable shop. His dreams show "how all closures, all endings, give warning of closures, greater yet, to come" (*SPL* 250).

In *The Folding Star*, the use of parks and public lavatories as gay heterotopias is reiterated by Hollinghurst, functioning as gay ghettos specified and stigmatised by the heteronormative society. The repetition of the same spaces is an influence and consequence of the transformation of the pre-modern concept of sodomy into the modern concept of homosexuality and of the minoritising view and taxonomic identity discourses trying to establish a fixed homosexual type. Hermitage is the main park where polyandrous intercourses are observed in the novel. It is a heterotopia juxtaposing a park as a public place and stigmatised same-sex encounters. Matt is the one taking Edward there for the first time; as soon as they climb the walls, Matt disappears, and Edward is alone in the dark gardens where he cannot see a sign of life at first. After walking for a while, he hears some music and finally sees someone with a torch, like an usher in a cinema. He sees couples having sex in the dark and meets some people, his excitement and desire increasing every minute:

> Each yew-niche was a place of available secrecy, and I loitered round the circle, finding out what was going on. From some came steady little rhythms, or muttered encouragements, or deep, delayed intakes of breath, as pleasure turned serious. From some came girlish giggles and whispering....You never knew what to expect. You never knew what they expected. You hadn't had the advantage of being at college together, or persuading yourself you fancied him over drinks and supper, or knowing each other's name, or anything. The absolute black ignorance was the beauty of it, and the bore. (*FS* 56-57)

Secrecy and darkness are emphasised in the description of the place, which shows the closet aspect of the park. It is anonymity what gives the event an aphrodisiac air and mystery. Darkness also functions as the Lacanian Real for the characters: It is a part of social reality, yet it resists symbolisation. Its origin remains beyond symbols and it is pre-symbolic in this sense; a space without light and away from the scrutiny and gaze of heteronormativity. However, it also brings its own threats and risks, since these people do not have the advantages of heterosexuals. In the novel, it is implied that heterosexual individuals enjoy the opportunity of meeting outside, getting to know each other, and start flirting if there is mutual fondness. However, closeted gay people live in a world of threats with people they do not know and they cannot easily trust. This ignorance is the beauty of it for some, yet it also brings one despair and loneliness.

Paul knows Hermitage, too. He has been there once and met a twenty-five-year old boy, Willem. He was still very young and did not know what to do, so he just followed Willem into the trees. It was an ideal place to meet him; he used his visits to old Edgar Orst as a cover to go there, and Willem came from a nearby village. Their relationship, Paul tells Edward, went on for a couple of months and though he was hesitant at first, they did everything later on (*FS* 425). A similar place is seen in Rough Common, too. Edward remembers that years ago his brother Charlie was home and he said the queers went up by the wood at night for cruising. This revelation intrigued and fascinated young Edward. Soon he was there to come across Dawn: "'I should have known I'd meet you up here,' he said, with a hint of routine school jeering, and a hint of flattery too . . . . 'I'm always up here,' I said, to encounter any suggestion it was his place, not mine" (*FS* 224). Charlie, representing heteronormative society, knows and designates a ghetto for the non-heterosexual, which the non-heterosexual Edward adopts immediately. Being closeted, on the other hand, gives the gay characters in the novel pleasure. While talking to Willie about the secret he shared with some other boys at school, Edward likens themselves to night-sighted animals:

> You need to do it when you're a lad and you feel like part of a secret society, and an old, country thing, standing still and seeing night-sighted animals busying about.... After a while you are [night sighted] I can't remember the individual nights, isn't it awful, the whole phase of my life has somehow rendered down to a few scenes. (*FS* 243)

He describes the pleasure he had as levitation, which reveals that these gay characters do not mind being closeted at all so long as they can gratify their sexual needs. This ironic situation indicates that it is not only the heteronormative society but also gay male individuals themselves closeting the Homosexual. Higgins states that sometimes self-styled homosexuals feel superior to others just because they are homosexual and he puts it down to the nineteenth century, when a homosexual tradition was established under the influence of Johann Winckelmann, the German art historian who appropriated and celebrated a distinct homosexual aesthetic shaping the growth of a homosexual identity (4). In the extract above, Edward likens themselves to animals with night vision and, just like night-sighted animals, they go hunting at night. Day light symbolising the dominant sexual ideology is disturbing and oppressive for them. After the funeral in England, once again a park and darkness are chosen by the author as the setting for Edward's cruising and sex scene. Towards midnight, he is rambling home from somebody's house, another trick probably, when he decides to walk in a park. He finds a bench and sits next to a guy. After the exchange of a couple of sentences about the weather, they start to kiss and have sex there in darkness and fog (*FS* 264).

Parks, bushes, and woods as gay heterotopias appear in *The Spell*, too. The male gay characters in the novel often go cruising and have sex in such places, which reveals the author's –perhaps unconscious yet homophobic—tendency to closet. During Danny's birthday party, in Robin's country house, there are many guests most of whom Robin, as the host, does not know. Robin walks with Lars across their garden and all of a sudden an Arab-looking boy runs into them, "coming back from doing who knew what under the trees" (*TS* 130). Outdoor sex might be far from appealing to some gay individuals, yet the author time and again portrays prurient male gays having sex in such places as parks and woods. Another incident, confirming the representation of gay men seeking fun in such places, is the one involving Alex after Danny dumps him. One day, he gets a bit drunk and goes to the Heath to see if he can meet someone. He sees a nice man with short grey hair and begins to follow him in the bushes:

> There were a number of men mooching about in the bushes. He couldn't see the man he had followed…. He walked on, had a look at his watch, wondered if he should just go home after all, and then within a few seconds he had stumbled into a large and still relatively leafy bush with a dark, thickset man, and was kneeling in the sex-litter and soft loam with the stranger's stiffening cock in his mouth. The man chewed gum and looked around, apparently indifferent to the exquisite thing that was being done for him. Occasionally he said 'Yeah', like someone on the phone. Then he pulled his hips back quickly, and nudged out a little load over Alex's cheek and nose. (*TS* 247)

Apparently there are a lot of loiterers, each looking for moments of pleasure, but the pleasure, something exquisite for some, is a bore to others. People seem to be going there daily, find someone, actually anyone will do, ejaculate, and go back home; it is like having routine sex, the sole aim being to gratify biological needs, which does not bear any special meaning for the participants. A garden, for Foucault, is one of the oldest examples of heterotopias merging and juxtaposing contradictory sites (*Of Other* 25). Just like other heterotopias, gardens have different functions in different heterochronies. Whereas a garden was a sacred space for the Persians, in Hollinghurst's novel it serves as a space for homosexual encounters. Gardens, bushes, and parks are repetitive heterotopias the author employs to strengthen the identity ascribed to the homosexual.

Parks, gardens and woods also appear frequently in *The Line of Beauty* as places where gay characters meet and have sex. On their first date, Nick and Leo, not living alone and unable to host each other, go to Kensington

Park Gardens and enter the garden where only the key holders are allowed. They walk towards the gardener's hut, which they find locked, and instead of the hut they have sex in the shadowy area beside the hut (*LB* 34). Darkness once again helps the couple keep out of public eye and the bush becomes their closet. In many Anglo-American novels and stories forests and bushes symbolise the evil, conflicting desires and dark motives. Similarly, in Hollinghurst's work, the use of such places is significant because gay characters can express their hidden impulses and achieve self-fulfilment only in these dark places. Whereas visibility and daylight stand for heteronormativity and heterosexual relationships, darkness seems to be representing the unacceptable, unspoken, and thus invisible.

Last but not least, Hollinghurst employs the pool in *The Swimming-Pool Library*, which is the metaphoric closet in the novel, representing the space where marginalised individuals achieve self-realisation and act as they desire, which subverts and challenges the external heterosexist world, instead of doing what the society demands. For William, the place enabled the space he needed to lead his double life:

> A quarter of a mile from the school buildings, down a chestnut-lined drive, the small open-air bath and its whitewashed, skylit changing-room saw all my earliest excesses. On high summer nights when it was light enough at midnight to read outside, three or four of us would slip away from the dorms and go with an exaggerated refinement of stealth to the pool. In the changing-room serious, hot No 6 were smoked, and soap lathered in the cold, starlit water, eased the violence of cocks up young bums. Fox-eyed, silent but for our breathing and the thrilling, gross little rhythms of sex – which made us gulp and grope for more—we learnt our stuff. (*SPL* 140)

The space, though functioning as camp, is a consequence of homophobia and it turns out to be a heterotopia for the gay characters in the novel; a heterotopia of deviation as the gay characters can exist there as they are, unlike in the heteronormative world where they are obliged to wear masks and pretend to be what they are not. Analysing the closet's exhaustive and exacting ontological demands, which rule that one cannot exist unless they are someone who they are not, Brown argues that "the closet is a *spatial* metaphor: a way of talking about power that makes sense because of a geographic epistemology that is largely taken for granted" (1). The homosexual poses an ontological threat and challenge to the epistemological world where his existence is denied. The symbolic register feels safe when it ghettoises the uncanny felt in the homosexual individual in the closet. Hollinghurst's gay male characters resemble the termite colony in the documentary which Will sees the Brutus Cinema attendant watching. The cinema actually serves porn enthusiasts, but when Will goes there one day, he finds the attendant watching a documentary which

> contained some virtuoso footage shot inside a termite colony. First we saw the long, questing snout of the ant-eater outside, and then its brutal, razor-sharp claws cutting their way in. Back inside, perched by a fiber-optic miracle at a junction of tunnels which looked like the triforium of some Gaudi church, we saw the freakishly extensile tongue of the ant-eater come flicking towards us, cleaning the fleeing termites off the wall. (*SPL* 48)

Ants live underground to avoid visibility and to protect themselves against predators. However, the ant-eater, just like the heteronormative discourses, puts its nose into their space, invading their privacy to sweep them away. What makes homosexuals a distinct community—like that of ants—is not a shared sensibility like camp, but the inevitable sense of alienation, oppression and otherness they suffer from (Summers 15). Gay characters in *The Swimming-Pool Library* are, like ants, imprisoned in ghettos and they are still persecuted in various ways and by various tools.

3.2 Homo-phobia: Fear of the Same

The second aspect of the closet is direct homophobia, such as physical attacks and violence. One reason for this is homosexual panic, a term coined by Edward J Kempf in 1920, which refers to the psychosis suffered because of unsolicited same-sex sexual advances. Another reason is homosexual panic defense, which is forensically employed by or in favour of gay-bashers. Sedgwick suggests that this defense stems from the distinction between anti-gay crime and other bias-related antiminority crime, and she adds that the irrational fear of homosexual advances is in fact a consequence of individuals' –latent homosexuals'- insecurity about their own masculinity or heterosexuality (20). Homosexual panic and the awareness of the possibility of using it as a justification of violence form the grounds on which gay-bashers are allowed to do anything.

In *The Swimming-Pool Library*, Charles falls prey to gay-bashing; his diary shows that he was harassed in his first week in college. He was a teenager and not used to getting naked in public and he had never seen a mature boy naked before. Thus, he was staring at other boys' penises, particularly Strong's, and this must have been taken as a sign. After that, other boys, especially Stanbridge, begin to harass him verbally and physically. They call him names like 'tweake'*,* which do not make sense to him at all. The rough mocking, harassment, and torture continue until one night Stanbridge finalises it in the dormitory:

> He came over to my bed & put his hand down under the blankets. I shrank away, but he reached for me, and felt me fiercely. He was a wiry, humourless, red-headed boy. Then he got into the bed too, though he was fully clothed, & still had his shoes on.... He made me bite on a handkerchief while he buggered me. I cannot remember much about it except that I cried and cried, in a soundless, wretched way, & the hot pain of it, & an agonised guilt, as if it had all been my fault, about blood on the sheets –though no one ever said anything about it. Later it became obvious to me that other men in the dormitory had known about it. I was deeply aware that it was not a thing that could be appealed against. Also after that the teasing stopped, & I was shown a companionable respect. (*SPL* 110-111)

As soon as the boys discover that he is gay and different from them, they start calling him names and bullying him. A non-manly man, after all, is a 'woman' for the heteronormative mind and a woman is considered subject to a man. This is why the boys feel free to do anything to Charles, and Stanbridge even rapes him in the dormitory. The portrayal of the rape scene is touching and reveals the extent to which the incident was traumatic for Charles. Surprisingly, after the rape, they accept him into their community and stop teasing. Foucault suggests that power masters not only discourses but also silences, and that repression at the level of language begins with the seventeenth century, when the need to control sex emerged: "Without even having to pronounce the word, modern prudishness was able to ensure that one did not speak of sex, merely through the interplay of prohibitions that referred back to one another: instances of muteness which, by dint of saying nothing, imposed silence. Censorship" (*Sexuality* 1: 17). After the rape, the boys do not talk about the event or ask about the blood on Charles's sheets. Sex, especially if same-sex, cannot be mentioned. The silence replacing teasing is a kind of 'don't ask don't tell' policy, *lex non scripta*, regulating the relationships in this male community and in heteronormative societies.

After a while, Strong gets closer to Charles and the two start hanging out together, which attracts the attention of the other boys. Their relationship is glass closet, an open secret, and the other boys' homophobic reaction marks the beginning of Charles's need to re-enter the closet. Charles feels as if their secret were revealed, though he himself does not know the secret as he is not aware of his actual feelings for Strong. They go for a walk, wander arm-in-arm, and in fact fall for each other further every day. People tease the couple: "'You look a bit stiff, Strong' & somebody else said, 'You two look fairly tweaked.' There was a general impression that we had made love to each other, which was pruriently celebrated by the other boys, as if on the morning after a wedding" (*SPL* 112). Hollinghurst's use of vocabulary is significant in that it implies and refers to the nuptial act, and thus, the traditional binary Man \ Woman. The word 'stiff', used for Strong, shows that the boys think Strong tops Charles and they feminise Charles. Sedgwick states that anal sex was the main signifying act of same-sex male intercourse before the visibility of oral sex between men increased and that oral sex is more difficult to define in bipolar terms like active / passive and male / female (237). However, these binary terms must not be taken as identities. In ancient Greece a man's femininity meant his submission to pleasure and there was no equation between being bottom and femininity or between being top and virility. Therefore, the parallelism drawn between Strong's being top during the sexual intercourse with Charles and his manliness is arbitrary and misleading. It does nothing but re-establish and strengthen the bipolar terms 'manly / womanly'.

Charles feels obliged to re-closet himself when he meets Webster, the first black man in his life. Charles takes up swimming only because the man he likes swims. One day, after a race, Charles lounges beside him and putting his arm round his shoulders says: "'That was damned close' but thinking inside 'I love you, I love you, I love you'" (*SPL* 114). This seems to be a significant aspect of the closet; one cannot voice his love for a same-sex person easily as there are social, legal, religious, medical, and even psychological barriers to overcome to be able to express and accept same-sex love. For this reason, unrequited love may be a very common trauma for a gay individual. Another aspect of the closet is what the other people say and think, which influences the first aspect in return. The others' opinion, i.e., homophobia, is seen in Charles's relationship with Webster, too, when "other men commented on [their] being together, & called [Webster] cruel, unthinking names" (*SPL* 114). However, Charles did not even bother to argue with them or need to justify his being with Webster.

Another incident of homophobia in which Charles is involved is sighted when a number of American soldiers come to Winchester during the last year of the World War. One day Charles goes to a bar with his friends, where a tall black soldier comes over and asks them where he could get a girl for the night. As he cannot get an answer and most probably understands they are gay, he humiliates and swears at them. Later, in the pissoir of the pub, the black soldier follows Charles and starts talking to him, which excites him indeed:

> He was looking at me, grinning. My eyes darted about & I just made out that he was stroking his penis. He took his hands away from it & reached towards me, leaving his brutal, aching sex massive and erect. I fled from

that pissoir & joined my half-drunken friends for the walk back to College, the awkward, well-tried climb back in, my head ringing with the unutterable shock of it. It had been too sudden an offering of what I too deeply desired. I never saw the soldier again. A thousand, thousand times I've wished I had. (*SPL* 115)

Charles wanted him but he could not do anything because he was shocked. The apparent homophobic attitude of the soldier suddenly turns out to be reaction formation arising from the latent same-sex desire he wants to repress. It is "entirely within the experience of gay people to find that a homophobic figure in power has, if anything, a disproportionate likelihood of being gay and closeted" (Sedgwick 81). To be configured in the symbolic and to gain full humanness, the initial step is to repress same-sex desire or latent homosexuality and this is why homosexual tendencies are often denied or concealed. Another implication of the scene is that the soldier wanted to have Charles just for the sake of sex and this is more worrying for the deployment of the homosexual; for the straight the homosexual is a sex toy, a toy boy, who is always considered suitable. This misconception results from the conventional sex-based definition of the homo-sexual.

In addition to these incidents in Charles's past, William suffers from homophobic assaults at present. After a long time without Arthur, he is worried about him and fears that he might be dead, so he decides to go to his neighbourhood and make a visit. The neighbourhood Arthur and his family live in is a poor and dangerous slum area. He goes to their building but decides to give up at the last minute, and while he is walking back, he comes across some skinheads. The guys want to mug him but they also begin to insult him calling him such names as "poof, shit-hole wanker, and nigger-fucker" (*SPL* 172-173). They beat him badly and the attack results in a lost tooth, a purple cheek, a swollen lopsided mouth, a broken cut nose, and a narrowed eye. All his life Will has lived in his closet and never been exposed to homophobic attacks or harassment before. This is why the incident leads him to contemplate about and acquire an insight into the life in the world outside the closet:

> The pavements were normal, the passers-by had preoccupied, harmless expressions. Yet to me it was a glaring world, treacherous with lurking alarm. A universal violence had been disclosed to me, and I saw it everywhere –in the sudden scatter across the pavement of some quite small boys, in the brief mocking notice of me taken by a couple of telephone engineers in a parked van, in the dark glasses and cigarette-browned fingers of a man –German? Dutch?—who stopped us to ask directions. I

understood for the first time the vulnerability of the old, unfortified by good luck or inexperience. (*SPL* 176-177)

William, mugged, beaten badly, and insulted, acquires a new awareness; now he has encountered homophobia and realises how comfortable he has been in the closet. For the first time he understands that [3]*il n'y a pas de hors-coffre*. The closet he lives in is a direct result of homophobia, yet he has lived there all his life without noticing it. In fact, even his using the words love and sex interchangeably is a sign of the invisible power and oppression originating from heteronormative discourses. For instance, in the showers, upon James's noticing his erection, Will says, "Of course I've got an erection. I'm in love" (*SPL* 117). Since a gay male individual's identity is defined based on his sexual orientation and object of desire, sex itself seems to overweigh in a same-sex relationship. However, since this is not socially acceptable for the normative society, the gay characters in Hollinghurst's novels, just like the ones in real life, unintentionally blur the boundary between the two terms and replace the latter with the former, rendering their relationship more socially-acceptable through sublimation. These novels in fact follow the footprints of the minority gay canon, the beginning of which can be traced back to 1891, argues Sedgwick. It is the year, she explains, in which discourses of homosexuality in medicine, psychiatry, language and law flourished, and *A la Recherche du Temps Perdu*, *Death in Venice*, *Billy Budd*, and *Dorian Gray* became foundational texts of modern gay culture which "mobilized and promulgated the most potent images and categories for (what is now visible as) the canon of homophobic mastery" (49). In other words, these novels established the terms and definitions for the modern homosexual identity as a stable one, and they endorsed the minoritising view of homosexuality as a homogeneous group of individuals with distinct manners, looks, and style.

William's grandfather is a symbol and agent of the minoritising view in the novel, for he was involved in Charles's arrest. His homophobia is disclosed in his talk to Will and James when they go to the opera. During the interval, they have a chat about the opera, *Billy Bud*, but the two boys cannot express their feelings straightforwardly. James, for example, says he is enjoying it, yet Will knows that the real topics

> he would want to talk about would be the suppressed or (in his usual term) deflected sexuality of the opera. We must all have recognised it, though it would have had an importance, even an eloquence, to James and me that would have been quite lost on my grandfather. He had spent all his adult

---

[3] There is no outside-the-closet

life in circles where good manners, lofty savoir-faire and plain callousness conspired to avoid any recognition that homosexuality even existed. The three of us in our hot little box were trapped with this intensely British problem: the opera that was, but wasn't, gay, the two young gay friends on good behaviour, the mandarin patriarch giving nothing of his feelings away. (*SPL* 120)

Billy Bud is an opera from a libretto written by E. M. Forster and Eric Crozier, based on a short novel by Herman Melville. The three main characters, all of whom are male, are gay but when the libretto was written homosexual acts were still regarded as crime, and thus homosexuality is only implied. It is the story of a young charming man, Billy, falsely accused and victimised by a villain who is in love with him; Captain Vere, also in love with Billy, cannot save Billy's life and signs his death sentence. The opera is not openly gay but definitely reveals homoerotic feelings. Thus, the grandfather's avoiding any gay interpretations means imposing silence and it is definitely a homophobic attitude. He is within the dominant ideology favouring *lofty savoir-faire* and callousness which requires deflecting sexuality, especially if it is same-sex.

The Folding Star depicts homophobia and violence which lead the characters to surrender and get back into their closet. One of the major issues related to external oppression is the dilemma and trauma Edward goes through. He has liked Luc since he first saw his photo, even before coming to Belgium. However, after meeting him in person, he has fallen for him further day by day. He decides to give one of his poetry books to Luc, so that they could study poetry, he thinks; "without his knowing how their phrases ran through my past, the melancholy secrecy of reading. It struck me I should buy him other books as well, they would be presents, too musty to be recognised as such, with invisible inscriptions" (*FS* 46). Edward loves Luc, but he is employed as a teacher by Luc's family and this conflict brings him despair, as well as inciting his desire. The closet in this respect is twofold: First, it would be a relationship between a middle-aged teacher and a teenage-pupil; and second, it would be a same-sex relationship. Therefore, such a relationship would never be accepted by the society. Alan Bray suggests that until the Restoration, homophobia in England was religion-based, but by the end of the eighteenth century, with the emerging male homosexual role and culture, "a much sharper-eyed and acutely psychologized secular homophobia" had replaced the former (qtd. in Sedgwick 184). This is what makes things more difficult for Edward. Therefore, he can only imply his love through poems and his invisible messages between the lines of those poems: "'I love you.' He looked down at his exercise book and aligned his red, black and blue felt-tip pens with its upper edge. I pumped off a few more rounds of silent 'I love you's" (*FS* 59). It is difficult for him to voice his love also because he knows his love is unrequited and thinks Luc is in love with Sibylle.

Paul is another closeted mystery character in terms of his sexual orientation. He is married with a son and he seems to be a traditionally protective father figure. However, he had an affair with Willem when he was young and it was his first love. This might be the reason why he does not express a strong disapproval of Edward's being in love with Luc. However, Paul never came out of the closet and kept his affair a secret all his life: "I've never told anyone about my first affair, because it would have caused distress and served no purpose.... Oh, in my case it was a summer's passion, when I was seventeen too, as it happens –with an older man" (*FS* 420-421). Like many gay or bisexual men, he preferred to get married and have a family, instead of facing the heteronormative oppression all his life. His preference reveals what happens in a gay man's life; dominant discourse stigmatises, criminalises, psychologises, psychiatrises and marginalises him. Thus, the gay male sometimes takes refuge in a heterosexual family unit rather than struggling with the normalising society. Telling Edward about his meeting Willem that night in the woods at Hermitage, Paul does not try to hide his actual feelings:

> Well, they were the first shocks of sexual reality for me –a man's large hands, a man's rough chin and cheeks, as well as all the rest. I was not a little confused, my dear Edward, and terribly aware of doing wrong. But I found I was excited by the risk. And then afterwards what inflamed me, as much as the guy's big prick and everything, was his gentleness, like being cradled and protected by some great giant. (*FS* 423)

Paul tries to put his desire down to his adolescence and lack of experience. However, summer and adolescence passions cannot be considered excuses for having same-sex sex acts. He went to Hermitage intentionally and did everything with the man he met there. Moreover, he fell in love with Willem and his relationship with him continued for a couple of months. It is obvious that he was sexually attracted to his own sex. His feelings about the dentist he met in Munich also show that he is gay or has latent homosexual feelings. He meets the man at a party at the big Symbolist show and having heard of Paul's Orst connections, the man says he has bought a painting which has the EO monogram on. They go to his flat to see the painting but the dentist appears without his jacket and tie in the doorway of his dimly lit bedroom. Paul has to get into the bedroom to see it. Later on Paul admits he had to be flirtatious to convince him to lend the painting to the museum, which Maurice finds a ghastly experience.

However, Paul's answer is significant: "He was quite a handsome dentist" (*FS* 94-95). He does not have any homophobic attitudes or opinions and though he does not state explicitly, he might have had sex with the man when he went to his flat. However, he has a family and a status in the society, so he seems to be partly concealing facts. He works for a museum, which, for Foucault, is a heterotopia of indefinitely accumulating time, and which connects and juxtaposes different heterochronies. He is not homophobic, yet he is now within the mainstream ideology, just like a library, juxtaposing different heterochronies. For instance, he knew everything about Edward's obsession with Luc, but Edward thinks Paul "simply, kindly held back from touching on a situation which he could only see as futile and perhaps improper" (*FS* 296). This is a typically homophobic attitude of apparently-liberal but conservative-in-essence systems; they pretend not to see homosexuality, by way of which they do not grant it recognition. Another example proving Paul's location in the mainstream thought is the guide he has prepared for the museum. Orst had syphilis, a venereal disease, but when Edward asks why he has not mentioned it in the guide, Paul acknowledges that he is of the school disapproving of publicising artists' private lives (*FS* 289). In other words, he prefers to closet some facts if they are socially unacceptable and related to heterosexuals, which increases the likelihood of his closeting his own sexual orientation.

Luc's unreturned love and the pain he suffers because of his unfulfilled desire are also related to the closet they live in. Desire has been manipulated and re-constituted by heteronormativity, and just like homosexuality, desire today does not signify what it used to. Aristophanes's account of sexual attraction is quite significant in that it deploys desire as the pursuit of the whole. In his account, originally there were three sexes, men, women, and hermaphrodites, but these human beings were a rounded whole, with double backs, flanks, faces, genitals, four hands, and four legs. As a consequence of their *hubris*, one day they attacked gods and Zeus punished them cutting each of them in two:

> Those men who are halves of a being of the common sex, which was called, as I told you, hermaphrodite, are lovers of women, and most adulterers come from this class, as also do women who are mad about men and sexually promiscuous. Women who are halves of a female whole direct their attention towards women and pay little attention to men; Lesbians belong to this category. But those who are halves of a male whole pursue males, and being slices, so to speak, of the male, love men throughout their boyhood, and take pleasure in physical contact with men. Such boys and lads are the best of their generation, because they are the

most manly…. When they grow to be men, they become lovers of boys. (qtd. in Higgins 22-23)

This was the Greek world depicted in *The Symposium*; a notion of sexuality and desire totally different from modernity. Whereas it was something to be proud of, it has become an embarrassing situation to be closeted in the course of history. It is hard to come out of the closet and express one's love to a person of the same sex, especially if one fears losing the beloved. Butler analyses this fear referring to Freud's "On the Mechanism of Paranoia," in which he associates the suppression of homosexual drives to the configuration of a social being, and "On Narcissism," in which Freud explains the constitution of the social feeling:

> The "ego-ideal," he writes, has a social side: "it is also the common ideal of a family, a class or a nation. It not only binds the narcissistic libido, but also a considerable amount of the person's homosexual libido, which in this way becomes turned back into the ego. The dissatisfaction due to the non-fulfillment of the ideal liberates homosexual libido, which is transformed into sense of guilt (dread of the community). (*Excitable* 109)

The individual is supposed to disavow same-sex desires in order to be configured as a subject and recognised as a 'full' man in the symbolic; otherwise, there is the fear of castration, which, in this case, refers to losing the love and respect of other people. The same fear prevents Luc from coming out and declaring his love in the novel. Since same-sex love is traditionally ignored and its existence is not accepted, gay individuals are regarded as friends and most of the time they are not given a chance by the beloved, who never question their heterosexual position. Heterosexuality is taken for granted and it is never questioned; it is an obligatory and acquired identity. This is the reason for Luc's unbearable pain: "It's that very bad thing, where you are in love with somebody and think about them all the time but they are also your dear friend and you see them all the time too. But they are not in love with you. And every time you see them you feel more in love" (*FS* 335). Edward thinks the one he is in love with is Sibylle, but later on he learns that it is Patrick. Towards the end of the novel, Luc runs away from home and Edward finds out that what Luc is trying to escape from is his feelings for Patrick and the cost he suffers from. Patrick, like Paul, had same-sex sex acts in the past, with Luc, yet he states that he cannot do such things any longer. He is, therefore, another transformed heterosexual who leaves homosexuality behind to gain access to the symbolic, and thus, he does not want to talk about his latent homosexual feelings any more.

Foucault mentions the diversity of the nature of sexuality referring to the sexualities ascribed to different ages, particular tastes and practices, different roles and relationships, and even those attributed to specific spaces such as home, school, or prison, and he suggests that all these diversities are related to the procedures of power. He argues that these "polymorphous conducts were actually extracted from people's bodies and from their pleasures; or rather, they were solidified in them; they were drawn out, revealed, isolated, intensified, incorporated, by multifarious power devices" (*Sexuality* 1: 47-48). In this way, power intrudes, invades, and possesses bodies and pleasures whereby it produces truths and stigmatises identities and practices which do not conform to the constructed truths.

The stigma attached to the nonconformist bodies of the gay male becomes visible in various minor scenes in the novel. For instance, at Wanne's bar, Edward asks the barman if he knows Cherif. The barman says that Cherif or any of 'his type' is not welcome there (*FS* 16). This is definitely a homophobic attitude banishing the gay from the non-gay space.

Luc's school case is another example to lay bare homophobia and the tendency to closet the gay male. After he was found on a ship out at the port with some Norwegian sailors in the early hours of the morning, he was required to leave school. Instead of investigating the case and supporting their son, the parents try to keep the event out of the newspapers and help their son escape to England, which is also an instance of closeting the gay. The privileged status of the non-gay is also a factor in the configuration of the closet. There is even a defense strategy – homosexual panic defense—which is frequently used to avoid conviction or to lighten sentencing of gay-bashers. This defense justifies antigay violence by implying that the responsibility of the accused diminishes due to a pathological psychological condition. Sedgwick argues that the wide acceptance of this defense in the world reveals the misconception that all gay men may be charged with making advances to strangers and that hate crimes targeting homosexuals are more typical and public than other disadvantaged groups (19). This is the fear underlying the parents' not being able to support their son and not taking legal action against the school.

The external pressure makes the gay male conceal his identity and lead a double life. Leading a life between gay ghettos seeking sex and teaching at two dignified households, Edward feels disoriented at times and complains about his "own sense of dislocation, out of breath after running between one world and another, a smoky bar with a juke-box and the silent elegance of an unknown house" (*FS* 35). The closet he lives in is a heterotopia; it juxtaposes several sites which are in themselves incompatible. He is a relentless predator at night cruising for sex here and there like a nymphomaniac, whereas during daytime he is the decent English teacher. He is indeed torn between two different worlds; a socially accepted real space and a heterotopia of deviation. He looks back on his school days, when he was in a relationship with Dawn, and regrets that other boys, i.e., the straight ones, had girlfriends and they did not hesitate to share every single detail with their friends (*FS* 255). There is no privacy when straight boys talk about their experiences with their girlfriends, but the process works differently for gay men, who are bound to be excommunicated if they attempt to come out of their closet. The self-recognition and the acceptance of homosexual identity is "a gradual and frequently torturous process" and it is the "culmination of intense introspection and evaluation" because of the feeling of in-betweenness (Summers 14). The same disturbing process, the incompatibility between the two lives, forced Gerard, a young musician Edward meets at the bar, to marry a girl when he was seventeen. He states that "she was a strong, demanding girl and had almost convinced him that he was straight. But after a year or so he found his thoughts were turning all the time to other men, as they had done before he met her" (*FS* 50). The couple got divorced soon, yet the extent to which normalising heteronormative discourses can spread is frightening. It is a tragedy, not only for the gay but also for the straight marrying the latent homosexual, when the marriage is an arranged one used as a cover.

In *The Spell*, despite living in gay heterotopias of deviation, Hollinghurst's gay male characters still face external oppression and homophobic attitudes. Homophobia is most visible in the country. On Danny's birthday, the Halls drop in for a drink with a present for Danny. Robin is pleased to see them since "they were among the few people in the village who remained friendly and hospitable after Simon's death. Not that they could be said to revel lubriciously in the reported details of gay life. On occasion they were merrily caustic" (*TS* 117). Simon died of AIDS and the village people's changing attitude right after his death is definitely homophobic. Moreover, the ones who remain friendly in fact do not approve of homosexuality and at times can be very harsh. While leaving before the party begins, Margery Hall says "I don't know who they're going to find to dance with" (*TS* 121). Robin cannot be certain whether she is just joking or not. The incident shows that even the friendly Halls intend to 'normalise' the gay; they cannot accept them as they are. Heteronormativity, represented by the village people including the Halls, is monolithic and cannot tolerate diversity. These village people seem to be aware of the reason for Simon's death, and thus, of Robin's and his friends' sexual identity; however, they still try to configure them in relation to the opposite sex. After the party, Justin talks to Alex about the people and explains how their attitude has changed:

> 'I should warn you that we're hideously unpopular down there.'
> 'Since the party?'
> 'They weren't mad about us before, but they loathe us now. There were formal complaints. PC Bertram Burglar came round and gave us a wigging.'
> 'Did he darling?' Alex was sorry to have missed that.
> 'It was only noise, wasn't it?'
> 'It was homosexual noise. That's what they don't like.' (*TS* 156)

It is obvious that the village people are homophobic and they can tolerate difference so long as it is invisible. Becoming visible is the point where homosexuality starts challenging the heterosexuals' own identities, which they relentlessly and futilely try to differentiate from the other. Justin admits that Mrs. Dodget is still with them, and the Halls, who are themselves outcasts yet "only play Gregorian chant" (*TS* 156). Gregorian chant is a liturgical chant of the Roman Catholic Church; it is unaccompanied and monophonic. The properties and definition of the chant hold a mirror to the homogenous and homogenising structure of heteronormative societies. Even outcasts themselves keep invisible and do not stand out in the normative crowds. The pretentiously conservative attitude reappears when the Halls pay another visit to Robin and Justin. Margery finds Danny too silent and Justin puts it down to the country air, adding that Danny would rather have a cloud of LSD. Margery and Adrian Hall say they do not believe Danny would do such a thing. When Adrian asks if Danny sees such drug business in London, Danny thinks "it would be absurd to lie. 'Oh yeah,' he said warmly. He could be nice to them, he guessed, but he hated the silly compromises that were forced on you when you entered the remote moral atmosphere of closety old bores" (*TS* 232). Even the few friendly people in the village are old-fashioned and prejudiced; this makes life harder for campy gays in the country. The country turns out to be another closet for them.

Danny is aware of the sharp distinction between life in London and that in Dorset. That is why he hates to be called darling by Alex in public. He believes that Alex "was so conditioned to a world in which everyone was gay that he found it hard to bear in mind, down here, a hundred miles from London, that almost everyone wasn't" (*TS* 213). His tendency or feeling obliged to closet his identity in the country exposes how the closety life style there differs from the heterotopia in London. A role of heterotopias is "to create a space that is other, another real space, as perfect, as meticulous, as well arranged as ours is messy, ill constructed, and jumbled," which Foucault calls heterotopias of compensation (*Of Other* 27). Gay characters want to see all the other sites like London, a heterotopia of deviation, and perhaps better. Nevertheless, a heterotopia of compensation for the homosexual is a utopia; it was real only in the golden age of antiquity and it is impossible to re-establish any civilisation similar to the ancient Romans' or Greeks'.

Due to the difference between the urban and rural subcultures, Alex finds it difficult to closet his identity, as seen in the dinner party scene in Wandsworth. He found the atmosphere too straight and the people, though contemporaries, much older: "He wanted to tell them about his new impromptu life, so remote from these pleasant predictable evenings, and he noted their nostalgia and worry when the talk touched on what their teenage children did, but he kept it to himself" (*TS* 157). Alex is out in London and also among gay people in the country; however, since each new encounter leads to a new closet, he has to readapt himself to the environment and their expectations. Thus, he cannot express his feelings or opinions at the dinner party; he is invited to dinner as apparently-straight Alex. Otherwise, he would not be a guest. Mrs Badgett, another outcast, perhaps only because she went rock'n'roll dancing every week when she was young, criticises the village people, too: "They're a lot of stuffy old buggers in this village. When did they last go out dancing, I wonder? They've got no idea of how to have fun, most of them" (*TS* 159). In the country, most people are biased and they marginalise anything different; the gay male is not an exception.

Facing homophobia whenever they attempt to come out, the gay male characters give up trying after a while. Simon, for instance, is able to say he loves Robin in the presence of his sister and father for the first time only hours before he dies (*TS* 34). This is the obligatory silence of same-sex love. Alex's grandmother also symbolises heteronormativity in the novel. She gives him a chain, which Alex gives to Danny. The chain was left to Alex by her grandmother and she thought Alex would give it to his future wife (*TS* 214). Such icons passed down to following generations are actually intended to ensure the maintenance of ritualised heteronormative traditions. The chain is nothing but an indicator of a grandmother's worries about a single grandson and her wish to marry him off before her death. The external oppression is quite influential on the gay individual indeed and sometimes he ends up closeting and even denying his sexual orientation. For instance, Gordon, one of Danny's sex partners, talks to Robin during the birthday party and tells him he has spoken to Arthur Conan Doyle through a friend of his, a medium. He seems to be under the influence of the mysterious event, since Doyle gave him some information about his future and his earlier lives in the past:

> 'He also told me that I'm not really gay. I just happen to be attracted to certain men. It's a spiritual thing, in fact, a spiritual magnetism; usually we've known each other in another life. Arthur said what I really have to find is a wife, he was strict about that.' And here Gordon too looked round the room with a tinge of anxiety. 'It's the woman's destiny to support the man,' he said. (*TS* 140)

Doyle represents the literary canon and Western epistemology in a macrocosmic context. Under the influence of the apparition, or the alleged conversation, Gordon is convinced that people live as homosexual in some parts of their lives, but they are not homosexual. This is very close to the notion of homosexuality before it was stigmatised, criminalised, and psychiatrised; it was considered an act, not an identity, i.e., doing, rather than being; thus, Gordon's leading a homosexual life without defining himself as gay is an open secret, a glass closet. Moreover, his attitude towards homosexuality, while sleeping with men, is self-contradictory and his inner conflicts result from the oppression he suffers from.

Oppression begins where the gay subject becomes visible; nevertheless, remaining invisible is another source of trauma for him. Alex, for example, hates the obligation of secrecy and being imprisoned in a glass closet. When he goes to a bakery to buy a cake for Danny's birthday, the baker proudly says that it is a lovely wedding cake and wants to know whether Alex is the lucky man: "'I do feel quite lucky,' Alex said. He had the eerily restful country feeling that his homosexuality was completely invisible to these people" (*TS* 113). The words Hollinghurst chooses to describe Alex's feelings are noteworthy; the tranquillity and the safety arising from the covered gay male identity in the country is indeed a temporary heterotopia and aware of the temporality, gay men always feel frightened and strange anticipating homophobia sooner or later. Even in the bakery scene, the baker's question aims to put Alex into the heterosexual frame and being considered outside the frame all the time is traumatic for him.

In *The Line of Beauty*, the gay characters are victimised and persecuted by homophobic dominant ideologies and the novel depicts the late twentieth century, when the homosexual, unlike the heterosexual, banished from public visibility, did not have any means to meet and make friends with other gays apart from going to gay ghettos or giving ads in some magazines. Nick meets Leo through Leo's lonely hearts advertisement; "Black guy, late 20s, v.good-looking, interests cinema, music, politics, seeks intelligent like-minded guy 18-40" (*LB* 8). The homosexual does not have the privileges the heterosexual individuals are granted. They cannot meet someone, fall in love and declare their love to the beloved. Because same-sex love is a crime, a sin, or just a socially unacceptable situation, the beloved considers himself heterosexual from birth and does not even expect to be the object of desire for his own sex. Thus, the homosexual's desire is bound to remain invisible and unexpected for those regarding themselves as intrinsically straight.

Halperin takes coming out of the closet and the increasing visibility as freedom in the sense of resistance, but not in the sense of liberation (30). The increasing visibility and partial acceptance of gay bars, clubs, saunas, marriages and various related rights are actually exclusive and restrictive. Even gay marriages, if it is a right, should be taken as a reconstruction of Western heteronormative epistemology since it prioritises coupling and excludes single gay individuals. For Ingraham, marriage is "the primary requirement for social and economic benefits and access" (77). If one, gay or straight, does not take his place in the system, he cannot have access to any social, economic, or legal rights. These apparently liberating facilities and rights are nothing but agents of modern oppression and strategies of modern homophobia; and they feed and broaden the gap between homosexuality and heterosexuality. The closet in urban space is a production of heteronormativity and capitalism; therefore, the places where the closet materialises are "produced not merely for the stimulation and satisfaction of desire, but also for potential profit" (Brown 60). In this way, same-sex relations are successfully commodified by the dominant ideologies and heteronormative cultural representations are endorsed.

Family is one of the major agents of homophobia in the novel. Power is not visible at the level of the government; family unit, at the bottom of the chain, is the place where obligatory heterosexuality is taught and homosexuality is forbidden. Nick does not live with his own family, so the Feddens' attitude towards homosexuality should be analysed to gain an insight into the closet Nick lives in. Gerald and Rachel pretend to be open-minded about homosexuality, like the government policy during those years, yet they are essentially conservative. Once Leo calls Nick and Gerald answers the phone, giving Nick a stern and disappointed look, "as if to say that the brute reality of gay life, of actual phone calls between shirtlifters, was rather more than he had ever imagined being asked to deal with" (*LB* 108-109). As a matter of fact, the facts of gay life remain a taboo with Gerald and he cannot reconcile with them. In the changing world he is in a pretentious acceptance of the situation, yet he does not approve of it wholeheartedly. Catherine is the one who makes Nick come out in the household, for she tells her parents Nick is dating Leo. "It was annoying to have her frankness applied to his tender plans, and a treacherous reward for his silence about her affairs. He coloured, and felt a further crackle of social static pass through the room. Everyone seemed to be humming, doubtful, encouraging, embarrassed, he couldn't tell" (*LB* 24). Nick can never feel certain about whether the Feddens are homophobic or gay-friendly, perhaps partly because of the paranoia the ambivalent policies of the government created.

Nick cannot share his happiness, despair, or any other feelings, neither with the Feddens nor with his own family. The homosexual does not have a voice; he can never enjoy the freedom and 'normalcy' the heterosexual possesses. Nick, though Rachel and Gerald know that he is gay, always fears that someone will understand he is gay. The couple know that Nick is gay, but they never talk about it, or his boyfriend, straightforwardly. They are in a blissful ignorance of the unpleasant situation, which they do not accept but just bear. Catherine, for instance, has boyfriends and she can freely talk about them to her parents, which makes Nick wish that "he was in a position to speak about Leo as freely as she spoke about Russell" (*LB* 52). Nick is quite restrained and guarded when he is with the Feddens, especially after the Hector Maltby case. Maltby, a married junior minister in the Foreign Office, was caught with a rent boy in his car and had to resign from his post immediately. When Toby brings up this subject, Nick, thinking of his own closetedness, blushes and feels the apprehension in the household:

> 'Well, I don't see why he had to resign,' Catherine said. 'Who cares if he likes a blow-job now and then?' Gerald smoothed this over but he was clearly shocked. 'No, no, he had to go. There was really no alternative'…. Gerald frowned, and pulled a bottle from the cardboard crate. 'You have the oddest idea of what might do people good,' he said, musingly but indignantly. 'Now I thought we might have the Podier St-Eustache with dinner.' 'Mm, lovely,' Rachel murmured. 'The thing is, darling, quite simply, that it's vulgar and unsafe,' she said, in one of her sudden hard formulations. (*LB* 23)

What makes the minister resign or what Rachel refers to when she says 'vulgar' and 'unsafe' is homosexuality. It would not be the case if the minister was caught with a female hustler; however, homosexuality cannot be tolerated, especially by the Conservatives.

The homophobic attitude forces Nick to retreat into his closet and this is why he cannot come to terms with his relation with Leo. Heteronormativity is so well-established that most gay individuals have difficulty reconciling with their identities. It is difficult for them to accept the idea of a male couple. When Nick comes across Toby and his girlfriend Sophie in the street, Sophie asks him about Leo, but her query distresses Nick, who "just hadn't got used to it yet, to the idea of anything so secret, so steeped in his own fears and fantasies" (*LB* 113-114). Heterosexual relationships, for they are normalised, are not directly associated with fantasies or sexuality itself, yet homosexuality is considered just a same-sex desire and a fantasy. This is the reason why Nick feels marginalised and stigmatised, though Sophie's attitude was not in the least homophobic.

Leo's mother is also homophobic. When Nick goes to Leo's house in the suburbs, he sees that Mrs Charles is a pious woman whose house is full of religious souvenirs. She expects Nick to be a regular churchgoer, too. Upon learning that Nick has already met Pete, she feels surprised: "It's a small little world... He was a great help to my son. He helped him with getting through college, and with the job on the council. And he didn't stand to get nothing from it –leastways not in this world. I always say to Leo he's his fairy godfather" (*LB* 137). The world is really small for the characters closeted into gay ghettos and rendered invisible elsewhere. Because Leo cannot come out and tell his mother that he is gay, Mrs Charles thinks Pete is just a good friend to her son. After Leo dies, Leo's sister Rosemary comes to see Nick with her girlfriend Gemma and reveals her mother's nature and critiques her desire to take his son to the altar:

> 'Well, he's been to the altar now,' said Rosemary with a harsh little laugh, as though it was her mother's fault. 'Almost, anyway.' . . . 'She doesn't accept he was gay. It's a *mortal sin*, you see,' said Rosemary, and now the Jamaican stress was satirical. 'And her son was no sinner.' 'Yes, I've never understood about sin,' said Nick, in a tone they didn't catch. 'Oh, the mortal ones are the worst,' said Gemma. 'So she doesn't think AIDS is a punishment, at least.' 'No, it can be,' said Rosemary. 'But Leo got it off a toilet seat at the office, which is full of godless socialists, of course.' (*LB* 355-356)

Mrs Charles cannot accept the fact that both her children are gay and it seems that she has tried hard to marry them off. She puts her son's death down to a so-called contagious disease which her son got off a toilet seat. Her case shows the likely consequences of the double-edged weapon of coming out. Her son was in a glass closet in fact, but this even is sufficient for her to feel in the closet in relation to the homophobic world outside.

Another family closeting their son is the Ouradis. Wani leads a double life in fact just because he is not and cannot be the one his family expects him to be. When in an open relationship with Nick, his life is clearly divided into two halves;

> A couple of nights a week Wani spent uncomplainingly at his parents' house in Lowndes Square. Nick had been ironical about this at first, and piqued that he seemed to feel no regret at passing up a night they could have spent together. The family instinct was weak in him –or if it flared it involved some family other than his own. But he soon learned that to Wani it was as natural as sex and as irrefutable in its demands. On other nights of the week he might be in and out of the lavatories of smart restaurants with his wrap of coke, and roar home in WHO 6 for a punishing session of sexual make-believe; but on the family nights he went off to Knightsbridge in a mood of unquestioning compliance, almost of relief, to have dinner with his mother and father, any number of travelling relations, and, as a rule, his fiancée. (*LB* 178)

Wani, a drug and sex addict, lives a life full of hypocrisy. He plays the decent heterosexual son who dotes on his parents, though he does not feel any commitment to them. What forces him to lead this life based on lies is the heteronormative structure in his family. In fact Wani's mother knows that his son is gay but she cannot tell the heterosexist patriarchal father. Instead, she gives Martine –the cover fiancée—an allowance to play her role. The father is not told about the situation since marrying his son off is "his last illusion" (*LB* 383). The gay male subject facing homophobia in the heteronormative world often needs to pretend to be heterosexual to fit in. Not everyone can come out and even if they do, it takes time to come to terms with the self and to stand up against the society.

Maurice and Sally Tippers, friends to the Feddens, also attempt to closet the homosexual employing the stigmatising and homophobic discourses produced by the mainstream ideologies. They visit the Feddens right after Pat's death and the topic is inevitably his death and AIDS. Sally seems to find his death, since he slept around, quite predictable. Nick, asked questions by Sally related to Pat, wonders if she knows he himself is gay. He cannot decide whether he should put her coldness down to her homophobic attitude or accept that she is just blind to his own sexual orientation:

> There would be the social strain of coming out to such people in such a place, and the wider matter of AIDS concerning them all, more or less. He said, 'I think I heard you say your mother had a long final illness.' 'That was utterly different,' Sir Maurice put in curtly. 'It was a blessed relief,' said Sally, 'when she finally went.' 'She hadn't brought it on herself,' said

Sir Maurice. 'No, that's true,' Sally sighed. 'I mean, they're going to have to learn, aren't they, the...homosexuals.' (*LB* 295)

The Tippers identify AIDS with homosexuality and show the syndrome as the fulfilment of divine justice; the tragic end the homosexual brings on himself. The homosexual's death from AIDS is horrible and infernal, whereas that of the heterosexual is blessed and heavenly. The Feddens also pay attention not to use the word AIDS as if it were synonymous with sleeping around. Sedgwick critiques the arbitrary identification between AIDS and homosexuality:

> One of the many dangerous ways that AIDS discourse seems to ratify and amplify preinscribed homophobic mythologies is in its pseudo-evolutionary presentation of male homosexuality as a stage doomed to extinction…. The lineaments of openly genocidal malice behind this fantasy appear only occasionally in the respectable media…. A better, if still deodorized, whiff of that malice comes from the famous pronouncement of Pat Robertson: "AIDS is God's way of weeding his garden." (128-129)

The heteronormative discourses ascribing AIDS to homosexuality ignore the great number of cases stemming from direct heterosexual transmission because identification of a deadly syndrome with this minority group will be another point in antigay movements and gay-bashing. When Maurice first asked how Pat died, "Gerald made a sort of panting noise, and Rachel said quietly, 'It was pneumonia, I'm afraid. But he hadn't been well, poor old Pat'" (*LB* 292). They do not want to admit the fact that Pat, for he was an old friend of Rachel's, liked anonymous sex and they try to conceal the reason why he died.

The Feddens' masked homophobia comes out when newspapers find out and write about Gerald's affair with her assistant Penny, Wani's illness and the gay sex link to Gerald's house. Nick feels sorry for the shame he brings on the family. To make things worse, Barry comes to visit Gerald and insults Nick calling him names, for he believes wholeheartedly that Nick is the only reason for all this trouble. Barry also blames Gerald for hosting a gay for more than four years:

> 'I mean, what's the little pansy doing here? Why have you got a little ponce hanging round your house the whole fucking time?'…. I know the type. Never says anything—always nursing his little criticisms. I remember sitting next to him after dinner here, years ago, and thinking, you don't fit in here, do you, you little cocksucker, you're out of your depth. And I'll tell you something else: he knew that. I could see he wished he was upstairs with the women.' . . . 'They hate us, you know, they can't breed

themselves, they're parasites on generous fools who can. Crawling to you, crawling to the fucking Ouradis. I'm not remotely surprised he led your poor lovely daughter astray like this, exploited her, there's no other word for it. A typical homo trick, of course. (*LB* 416-417)

His speech shows how much he has missed and how mistaken he is. He does not know what has been going on in the household, and thus, puts all the blame on Nick. He does not know about Catherine's life, her suicidal attempts, or her boyfriends. As for Gerald's disclosed cheating on Rachel, he remains silent. This is the heteronormative tendency to cover up wrongdoings as long as they are within the heteronormative and patriarchal framework; however, once an individual is regarded as ex-centric, he is easily stigmatised as the scapegoat. Gerald agrees with Barry on every accusation he has made and insults Nick saying "it's an old homo trick. You can't have a real family, so you attach yourself to someone else's. and I suppose after a while you just couldn't bear it, you must have been very envious I think of everything we have, and coming from your background too perhaps…and you've wreaked some pretty awful revenge on us as a result" (*LB* 420). He never questions his own position in the chain of scandals. Surprisingly, Rachel does not react and Penny is determined not to leave Gerald claiming they are in love. The events and the characters' reactions show that mistakes or crimes are easy to whitewash so long as they fit in gender roles. Gerald's adultery is ignored by his friends and family, whereas Nick, whose only 'wrongdoing' is his being gay, is banished from the Feddens' pretentiously conservative life.

3.3 Closetedness in Polyandrous Happenings

The third form of closet in the novels is the gay relationship chains, which is seen in love/sex triangles, or rather polygons. In Hollinghurst's work, gay characters sleep with one another and they do not mind having an affair with the partner of a friend. Their notion of a relationship resembles the competition between Basil Hallward and Lord Henry Wotton for Dorian Gray's love. The plot of *Dorian Gray* "seems to replicate the discursive eclipse in this period of the Classically based, *pederastic* assumption that male-male bonds of any duration must be structured around some diacritical difference –old/young, for example, or active/passive—whose binarizing cultural power would be at least comparable to that of gender" (Sedgwick 160). Moreover, in Ancient Greece the young beloved was always free to choose another lover since he did not belong to anyone. As for the mature lover, he was not supposed to love the young boy forever; his love for the boy was until the boy grew up. This is the traditional precarious nature of same-sex relationships depicted since the antiquity. This image illustrates how gay individuals internalise closetedness and they closet themselves into these conventional vicious circles.

The Swimming-Pool Library follows the pattern in classical texts. Bill, for example, is referred to as the 'pillar' of the club and he knows everyone. It is not surprising, thus, to find him in love with Phil. However, Will desires Phil only because Bill fancies the boy (*SPL* 24). This attitude is in accordance with the ancient Greek stylistics Foucault mentions in *The History of Sexuality*; the competition for the young beloved. Will finally has Phil and they start dating. However, after a while, Will begins to be jealous of his beloved because he does not have any authority over the boy; the young beloved is always free to choose. When Will is invited to Staines's house, for instance, he takes Phil with him. Bobby is another guest in Staines's place and when Staines offers to show Will around, Will hesitates: "We were going in, and I dithered on the sill as to whether I could leave my darling Phil with Bobby. Phil looked resigned –or perhaps actually didn't mind: I had been surprised and shamed by his tolerance of people to whom I took an unhesitating dislike" (*SPL* 159). As he himself is not reliable, being ready to make a pass at anyone especially those in a relationship for they are more valuable, he cannot trust people and hesitates to leave his boyfriend with another man. This attitude of Will's is almost paranoia and it shows how gay characters in Hollinghurst's work turn into a consumer society commodifying sex. On the other hand, Phil has many other suitors at the club and Will time and again suffers from twists of jealousy:

> The men at the Corry came in for particular attention. 'I really dig that Pete / Alan / Nigel / Guy', he would quietly celebrate as we dressed after a shower, or emerged on to the evening stress again. The wonderfully handsome, virile and heterosexual Maurice seemed to excite him in particular. 'What a pity he's *straight*, man,' Phil would say, with charming and earnest shakings of the head…. In the pool one evening I'd introduced him to James, who had clearly fallen parasitically for him at once; but I saw no danger there. There were more reckless propositioners, like the laid-black Ecuadorian Carlos with his foot-long Negroni sausage of a dick…. I had heard him, forgetful or careless of this, say to Phil: 'Hey, you got a really hot ass, boy.' (*SPL* 142)

The depiction of the pool bears resemblance to the antiquity and reveals the author's own personal fantasies of a long-departed golden age. Higgins refers to *The Symposium* and contrasts the image of the ancient world as a homosexual paradise to ours:

Homosexual love is presented as superior to heterosexual passion, and all the speakers in the dialogue are chiefly interested in young men. Greek society at that time supported institutions and practices which fostered relationships between older and younger men as an important element in what modern social scientists would call "the socialisation of the young citizen." Physical beauty and athletic prowess were highly prized, and many men regularly visited the gymnasium to spy out the talent. Younger men, in the manner of the starlet, used their beauty to capture the affections of powerful and influential older men. (18)

Precariousness and the underlying competition were major, perhaps indispensable, elements of love affairs in the Classical world and it is not surprising that the gay characters in the novel follow the traditional types. Because of the very nature of their relationship, i.e., precarity, Will neither trusts his boyfriend nor the other gay men around. He behaves as if Phil may cheat on him any time. This small group of gays go through circular plot structures in their ghettos because they have been closeted into polyandrous and endogamic happenings by the patriarchal system. They are not allowed to socialise or become visible wherever they like; thus, they acquire this habit of going to the same heterotopias of deviation and as a result they end up with the same men.

The gay characters in *The Folding Star* are also closeted in relationship chains, functioning as heterotopias of deviation. This is a result of the ghettoisation of the gay male subjectivity; since they are imprisoned in certain places, they end up falling for or sleeping with one another. This minoritising view of the homosexual results from the nineteenth century strategies which formed four major concerns: the sexualisation of children, the hysterization of women, the regulation of populations, and the specification of the perverted (Foucault, *Sexuality* 1: 114). The gay male, regarded as pervert, had to be distinguished from the normalised monogamous heterosexual and this is why the gay characters in the novel are depicted as polyamorous prurient men. Hollinghurst, as a gay writer, cannot avoid the influence of heteronormative discourses and the stigmas attached to the homosexual. For example, the night Edward meets Ty, Cherif is also in the bar and Edward cannot decide which one of them he should take home, while he claims to be in love with Luc. Talking about Matt's porn and fetish objects business, Edward reveals his own thoughts about love: "Love was blindly introduced and as a prefix was fully interchangeable with fuck: love-poles were destined as a rule for love-holes, and at the end it was geysers of white-hot love-juice that (paradoxically) cooled the lovers down" (*FS* 132). This is how Hollinghurst's gay characters view love, and ironically how they fail to tell apart between love and sex. This is another consequence of homophobia and closet. Since gay individuals are marginalised and stigmatised, they do not have the chance to experience all the steps in the process of a heterosexual relationship. Sedgwick expresses her astonishment at the fact that

> of the very many dimensions along which the genital activity of one person can be differentiated from that of another (dimensions that include preference for certain acts, certain zones or sensations, certain physical types, a certain frequency, certain symbolic investments, certain relations of age or power, a certain species, a certain number of participants, etc. etc. etc.), precisely one, the gender of object choice, emerged from the turn of the century, and has remained, as *the* dimension denoted by the now ubiquitous category of "sexual orientation." (8)

Among so many sexual taxonomies, somehow the homosexual got identified with decadence and perversion, and only homosexuality got transformed into an identity by heteronormative discourses. Edward, while in love with Luc –i.e., desiring Luc, has sex not only with Cherif and Ty but with many others like Frits and Matt. He even desires Martin Altidore and Patrick. Similarly, Matt has Cherif and Luc, while he is after Patrick. People in a way exploit one another and lead a life in this world of deceit and lust, which shows how they are closeted by the society and how they endorse and expand the borders of the closet. Moreover, attachment, loyalty, or long-term affairs in gay relationships are not allowed by heteronormativity lest they would blur the reified binary Heterosexual \ Homosexual. They are attributes attached to the straight only and granting them to the non-straight would weaken the constructed distinction.

The Spell is also repetitive regarding the depiction of gay relationship chains, which are also forms of heterotopia, into which the characters imprison themselves unintentionally. Danny and Justin seem to be sleeping with the most men in the novel. Alex, George, Hector, Aubrey, Terry, Gordon, Heinrich the barman, Lars, Luis and Edgar are some of the characters only Danny sleeps with. As for Danny's affair with Alex, they are in a relationship for a while, though "Alex felt the incongruity of chasing after Robin's son. He wasn't sure if he was taking a devious revenge on Robin for stealing Justin" (*TS* 70). However, Danny does not waste time thinking about such ethical issues. He is in his early twenties and despite his young age he is quite experienced with men. Even when he is with Alex, he is not in love with him. His lack of interest becomes clear in the restaurant scene:

> They had a table in the window, and Danny sat breaking up bread and looking out past Alex's shoulder at the parade of pleasure-seekers outside.

At first he said 'Yes...yes' with distracted regularity while Alex was telling him sweetly self-deprecating stories about the office: he had never had any special arts of courtship, being very nice was his only technique. He watched Danny's cool grey eyes slide from right to left, passing briefly over the obstacle of himself. (*TS* 74-75)

Danny, just like most of the young lustful queens in Hollinghurst's novels, is too young to settle down and what he is looking for is not a relationship indeed. When Terry asks what he sees in Alex, Danny says he has not got a type, for his "utopian policy was to have everyone once" (*TS* 222). Another trick for him, George was the one who introduced him to the world of drugs. They were together for a while, but then remained friends. In the novel, like George and Danny, quite a few sex partners remain friends and carry on seeing, sometimes even sleeping with, each other. This form of relationship between friendship and sex creates the image of love and sex as a game. Sex does not have any special meaning, so after sex partners do not mind seeing each other as friends. In this way the circle of acquaintances, consisting of ex-lovers or ex-tricks transforming into friends, steadily expands, adding new members each and every day.

In accordance with the other novels, in *The Line of Beauty*, the author depicts the gay characters sleeping around and forming sex chains in their small world—a heterotopia, which is another way of closeting the gay. Nick has had a crush on Toby and obviously still desires him, yet as soon as he meets Gerald, he notices his firm body, brown legs, muscled buttocks, and his sexual potential (*LB* 21). Likewise, he feels attracted to Gerald's friend Badger. He sees them after they play tennis and calls them "two big hot boys" (*LB* 105). Meanwhile, Nick is in a relationship and in 'love' with Leo, of course. He transforms his desire for other men into passion for his boyfriends. For instance, when he notices the sexual potential in Gerald, he puts it down to his excitement before meeting Leo. Similarly, the "love he ha[s] felt for Toby ten minutes before migrate[s] into a sudden hungry imagining of Leo" (*LB* 65). Those days he also has a crush on Tristão, arranges a meeting after Toby's birthday party, yet he manages to rent him only after he starts his relationship with Wani. In this new phase in his life, Nick picks people for threesomes or sometimes gets a rent boy, for Wani is really into it (*LB* 307). By forming these chains, gay characters shrink their already-small world and closet themselves further. As a result, they use phrases like "Don't I see you at Bang last week?" (*LB* 163) and "Didn't I see you in the Volunteer last week?" (*LB* 165). They all seem to know one another, at least by sight, and this familiarity makes their confined heterotopias even more compact.

3.4 Closet and Occupation: Stereotyping the Gay Male Subject

The last medium of closeting fictional gay characters is attributing to them particular jobs, or no job at all, which is a minor theme in Hollinghurst's novels. Sedgwick, analysing the incoherence and conflict between minoritising and universalising views, states that "[t]o be gay in this system is to come under the radically overlapping aegises of a universalizing discourse of acts and a minoritizing discourse of persons" (86). A minoritising view suggests that homosexuality is of primary significance to a certain group of actual homosexuals, who have 'stable' homosexual identities. A universalising view, in contrast, argues that homosexuality is a concern for individuals across a wide range of sexualities.

Hollinghurst's attribution of specific kinds of employment or total unemployment and parasitic life to his characters in *The Swimming-Pool Library* is in line with the minoritising view and he fails to reach the universalising discourse of acts. William, to start with, is idle and he is not looking for a job:

> I wasn't in work—oh, not a tale of hardship, or a victim of recession, not even, I hope, a part of a statistic. I had put myself out of work deliberately, or at least knowingly. I was beckoned on by having too much money, I belonged to that tiny proportion of the populace that indeed owns almost everything. I'd surrendered to the prospect of doing nothing though it kept me busy enough. (*SPL* 3)

He leads a hedonistic life seeking pleasure only and he is well aware of the fact that he is in the privileged class. He studied history at Oxford and now he spends his time, remaining from his pursuit of sex, going to galleries and looking at pictures. He admits that he is spoilt and that he has too much money. Writing Charles's biography, or rather accepting to write it, is the only thing he does in the novel. Hollinghurst's depiction of the gay male as campy élite is problematic; it not only portrays them as idle, spoilt, and parasitic, but also closets them to a particular image, strengthening dominant anti-gay discourses and myths. James critiques his friend's attitude: "It's too pathetic. I know you think you're too grand to do any work, but you've got to commit yourself to something. Otherwise you'll end up an old-young queen who's done nothing worthwhile. Famous last words of the third Viscount Beckwith: 'Fuck me again'" (*SPL* 87). It seems that, in this depiction, narcissistic gay characters think the world of themselves and just idle about. In addition to this image, the gay male is also closeted in a certain group of jobs and fields such as fashion, design, cinema, theatre, singing, photography and so on. All of these attributed jobs are more or less related to fine arts, which is traditionally identified with the Woman. In the novel, this myth is confirmed by Hollinghurst. Ronald, for example, is a photographer, a job associated with taste and style. As Charles states, all his "society is pretty bloody interesting" (*SPL* 41). The need to depict the homosexual as marginal to grab attention unfortunately culminates in closeting them. For instance, there are books on the greatest homosexuals in history, which Higgins does not find politically correct and likens to the "proletarianisation of 'homosexual history'" (15). Repeating the heteronormative clichés like most gays are artists does nothing but reinforce homophobia and closet. These characters are closeted in cliché gay jobs, dealing with arts most frequently, and in this way the scope of the closet expands and heteronormative myths about the homosexual are affirmed. In this way, the homosexual becomes a personage, a type, with the author's minoritising approach and the novel itself becomes a hetero-utopia.

The Folding Star is another example of Hollinghurst's closeting his gay characters by way of assigning them cliché gay jobs or parasitic lives without a job at all. Gore Vidal, a writer fighting against the use of the word homosexual as a noun, argues that there is no such thing as a homosexual or heterosexual identity, nor can there be a gay sensibility. For him, homosexual "is just an adjective that describes a sexual act between members of the same sex, an act as normal, whatever that may mean, or natural—clearer meaning—as that between two members of the opposite sex" (qtd. in Higgins). They all are constructs produced by the minoritising view and heteronormative discourses. The repetitive "stereotypical associations of homosexuality with effeminateness or, at certain periods, with hypermasculinity are time-bound, culturally reinforced social constructs," just like other stigmas—such as AIDS—attached to queer characters and the author cannot avoid this conventional image (Summers 15). The first example in the novel is Rose, the con Edward meets in the bar. He is interested in Edward's money and when Edward admits he is not rich, Rose is put off: "I offered him a cigarette, but he shook his head contemptuously. 'I've got to get hold of some money,' he said, looking away from me, pretending to accept my plea of poverty. I saw it was all over, I hadn't worked out for him" (*FS* 8). When he sees that Edward is not wealthy, he does not even tell him his name; Edward calls him Rose because of the four letters –R,O,S,E— tattooed on his fingers. Another example is Ty, the model who, Edward thinks "was obsessed by his career and seemed to feel destined for success in London, and that I would somehow be able to bring this about" (*FS* 23). These characters hope to live off other people, offering their flesh in return. The theme of male prostitution is also an extension of the Roman traditions. The Roman state "taxed male prostitutes, who also enjoyed an official holiday each year, allowing them to take a short rest from their labours" (Higgins 19). Hollinghurst's novel has affinities with the classical literature in his portrayal of the homosexual subculture. Dawn is also a parasitic character; after the relationship he had with the editor of a magazine, he lost his job, too. Then he was idling about and Edward notices "his giddy footing and fucking around, of the various older, richer men who needed to look after him. It was 1983. When we met again he was different, flamboyant, high on sexual deceits. Then it started to go adrift –a lover of his died with incomprehensible swiftness. Suddenly he didn't have any money" (*FS* 213). He was a gigolo satisfying his boyfriends and using their money in return for his services.

   Some characters even turn into criminals. Matt, for instance, steals people's items and sells them as fetish objects. He also deals in porn movies and so on. The two guys in the showers are also criminals. The dark one was hot and Edward liked him a lot. The skinny one with long fair hair was his accomplice; while the dark one, Mark, was talking to Edward and distracting him, his partner was stealing Edward's wallet. Luckily, he caught the boy and did not report them, especially because Mark promised to do anything Edward liked on condition that he not report. Edward realised that Mark "was a better criminal than his accomplice" (*FS* 84). It is a world of make-believe; gay characters are closeted and they also closet themselves in this world. Hollinghurst's frequent depiction and use of such characters also means closeting the gay male subjectivity in a certain image and affirming heteronormative myths about it. However, writers and theorists still try to resolve the conceptual incoherence between minoritising and universalising views, and claim that 'homosexual' is not a category. Sedgwick underlines the constructed nature of the taxonomy: "For surely, if paradoxically, it is the paranoid insistence with which the definitional barriers between 'the homosexual' (minority) and 'the heterosexual' (majority) are fortified…that most saps one's ability to believe in 'the homosexual' as an unproblematically discrete category of persons" (83-84). The more heteronormativity tries to stabilise homosexuality as a category, the more it lays bare its own constructed naturalness and loopholes; however, Hollinghurst insistently depicts the gay male as a distinct category of being with a distinct culture of its own, which closets the homosexual subject and serves the mainstream ends.

The Spell is also rich in gay characters who engage in jobs traditionally attributed to the homosexual or who do not work at all. Justin, to start with, is a parasitic character idling about and living off other men. Alex, when invited to Robin and Justin's house, buys some gifts for Justin, but Justin only shows some surprise, for "he was still unable to say thank you, which was a perverse flaw in someone who lived so much by taking" (*TS* 22). Justin, at the age of thirty-four, does not have a steady job and claims that he has worked as an actor. However, in the novel, he is not doing anything apart from idling about and seducing men. On his visit to the country, Alex looks back on his relationship with Justin and remembers "the things his friends had said about Justin, with funereal relish, after he had gone –how he was a cheat and a bore and a drunk and an ungrateful slut, and actually they'd always thought so" (*TS* 26). What is more painful for Alex is his knowing that his friends were right and that duplicity is Justin's nature. He is a kept boy who lives off the backs of his boyfriends and the author feminises him throughout the novel, not only in his sexual but also social life. Defining same-sex desire and homosexuality on a gender basis is antilogical, yet it is a common representative of the minoritising view of the universalising majority. Even by 1902, the new German gay rights movement was in a dilemma and could not know if a man desiring men should be regarded as feminised—as in the proto-modern English molly-house culture, or virilised—as in the Greek pederastic model (Sedgwick 134). Hollinghurst's fiction is based on the former; couples are depicted like straight couples, one 'masculine' and one 'feminine', i.e., the giver and the taker, respectively.

Danny thinks that he is different from Justin and he wants to stand on his own feet, yet his self-analysis is nothing but a dramatic irony. He does not have a steady job and he is a lustful junkie who, Justin thinks, is "rudderless, doing bits of work here and there, sharing a house that smelt of smoke and semen with various other young pill-poppers and no-hopers" (*TS* 44). He is young and does not want to settle down in any sense. He gets bored easily and constantly needs a change. This is why, towards the end of the novel, he makes up his mind to leave for the United States to live with his mother, who will help him get a job there.

Another character affirming the minoritising view of homosexuality is Dave, who deals in porn stuff and drugs. Danny takes Alex to his shop when they want to buy cocaine. When they walk into the shop, Alex sees Dave sitting "among the shiny flesh-colours of shrink-wrapped pornography and rubber sex-aids like a big black deity in a garish little shrine" (*TS* 79). He sells a wide variety of porn videos and magazines in addition to drugs. George is another character with a cliché gay job; he deals in antiques. Finally, Robin is an architect with a PhD degree. In conclusion, Hollinghurst's gay characters are either doing nothing and living as a group of stock characters parasitic upon their partners or they are doing jobs attributed to the élite homosexual, such as dealing with antiques, arts, literature, and so on.

The Line of Beauty affirms the minoritising view of homosexuality by portraying gay characters idling around, leading utterly vagabond parasitic lives, or dealing with illegal stuff. Nick is a well-educated young man pursuing his graduate studies; however, the life he lives is that of a junkie wanderer. He lives with the Feddens and sometimes with Wani. He does not have a proper job and a steady income, yet he pretends to be working for Wani in their Ogee office to publish a magazine. This is the cover he uses to his family and the Feddens; in fact he is Wani's marionette responsible for seeing drug dealers and arranging orgies, in return for which he gets paid. Wani's father, Bertrand, calls Nick 'the aesthete' of the magazine and hopes they will make money soon. Nick reacts to this expectation:

> 'I'm the aesthete, remember! I don't know about money side of things.' He tried to smile out through his blush, but he saw that Bertrand's little challenges were designed to show him up in a very passive light. Bertrand said, 'You're the writing man—' which again was something allowed for, an item in a budget, but under scrutiny and probably dispensable. Nick felt writing men were important, and though he had nothing to show for it as yet he said again, 'That's me.' (*LB* 195)

This is Nick's make-believe world of extreme self-esteem and self-delusions. He does not work and does not even write a single word for the so-called magazine, yet he feels very important. He is the prurient, dandyish, junkie, hedonistic male gay stock character Hollinghurst frequently employs in his novels.

Another stock character is Ricky, the boy Wani and Nick meet at the nudists' yard. He is an idle man who seems to be living off other people. Nick invites him to their place and asks him to pretend to be married or to have a girlfriend at least. "Ricky shrugged and shook his head. 'I've got a girlfriend.' 'Have you?' Nick stopped for a second with his chin tucked in, while Ricky stared at him and then winked. 'Quick on the uptake, aren't I?'" (*LB* 169). He is just like an actor, one gifted by birth, and accepts the invitation without any hesitation. He volunteers to take his part in Wani's fantasy world, where he seduces the 'straight', who sometimes is not straight at all. For Hollinghurst's gay characters, there is a clear cut boundary between the homosexual and the heterosexual. However, Ricky's case shows that just like gender, sexual orientation and identities are performative, too. Homosexuality can be performed and reconstructed by the heterosexual and similarly heterosexuality can be reconstructed by the homosexual. The so-called binary between the two is in fact constructed and Ricky's case blurs the boundary. However, it affirms the heteronormative misconception that the homosexual is indiscriminate in the choice of sexual partners and can do anything and everything for pleasure.

As a conclusion, in all four novels, Hollinghurst depicts two agents of closeting; the dominant heterosexist order, i.e., the external factor, and the gay male characters themselves, i.e., the internal factor. As for the gay heterotopias, such as bars, cinemas, and parks, they are products of the dominant heterosexist system designed in order to keep the homosexual out of their way and render them invisible. Going to these places, of course, means the gay men's endorsing the heterosexist and capitalistic plots against themselves. Homophobia, aiming to push the gay back into his closet, is another form of closeting the homosexual in the novels, stemming from external power relations and homosexual panic. As for the gay jargon used by some characters, it is a direct result of homophobic reactions and attacks. Gay characters' sleeping around and forming sex chains appears to be an internal form of ghettoisation, yet it is actually a consequence of the homosexual's being detained and confined in such marginalised places. Finally, the author's preoccupation with the intellectual and wealthy or idle, criminal, and parasitic gay characters exemplifies the heteronormative notion and conceptualisation of the gay male subjectivity. Thus, the blame cannot be put on the system only but also on gay individuals, to a certain extent, who internalise homophobia and reconstitute the closet by ghettoising themselves. However, Hollinghurst's repeated use of the same or similar attributes in his depictions of gay life paves the way for the minoritising view of homosexuality. Furthermore, there is no queer person or persona in the texts and the texts are not interplays between the minoritising and universalising understandings of homosexuality. As a result, Hollinghurst's fiction is constituted of a distinct minority group consisting of types with similar tastes, lives, and personalities. The novels do not pose any questions or challenges to heteronormativity; in fact, they depict characters longing for and trying to re-establish the golden days of antiquity in a modern hostile environment. This hostility stems from male homosexual panic, which, Sedgwick suggests, has to do with paranoid

Gothic[4], "in which homophobia found its embodiment and a genre of its own…through a more active, polylogic engagement of 'private' with 'public' discourses, as in the wildly dichotomous play around solipsism and intersubjectivity of a male paranoid plot like that of *Frankenstein*" (186-187). She especially highlights the importance of intense homosocial desire in this genre. Gothic genre involves such elements as setting in a dark gloomy castle, horror, stock characters, and desire. Hollinghurst's fiction bears resemblances to paranoid Gothic, too. He employs dark gloomy gardens, rooms, bars or cinemas as heterotopias of deviation in his depiction of the closet. His characters are inflicted with the precarious nature of gay relationships, which is the fear and suspense element in his work. His characters are stock characters and many of them are just types, as in gothic novels. Finally, Hollinghurst's fiction has got not only intense homosocial but also homo-sexual desire. In this respect, homophobia and the minoritising view of homosexuality also find their embodiment in his work.

---

[4] By "paranoid Gothic" Sedgwick refers to Romantic novels in which a male hero is in a close and usually murderous relation to another male character, who may be his double and to whom he seems to be mentally transparent.

CHAPTER FOUR

CONCLUSIONS

This book is an attempt to analyse camp and closet in Alan Hollinghurst's four novels with the intention of discovering whether the author employs a queer narrative style subverting heteronormativity or his fiction is just an extension of the dominant heteronormative discourses in England in the 1980s. Hollinghurst has been chosen for this monograph not only because he is a gay male writer writing about gay issues but also because he is a well-educated contemporary writer who studied gay fiction and his own work could give an insight into the development of gay fiction. His novels, though they do not depict the twenty-first century queer identity, portray the late-twentieth-century atmosphere in England and demonstrate how the governing ideology closeted the homosexual, while recognising their visibility at the same time.

In the second chapter, the author's deployment of camp has been put under scrutiny in order to find out whether his use of camp intends to parody heteronormative values or it fails to go beyond the clichés ascribed to the homosexual. Hollinghurst, in all four of his novels, employs camp as an exclusive characteristic of the homosexual; he depicts an illusory world belonging to the homosexual only and the non homosexual has no room there. Moreover, his gay characters are hedonistic, dandy, nymphomaniac and flighty junkies who sometimes lead parasitic lives living off other men. This representation reinforces the conventional portrayal of the homosexual as essentially different from the heterosexual and confirms the misrepresented stereotypical gay male subjectivity. Finally, camp shows itself in the transgender jargon, which is used by the male gay characters in the novels. It is full of humour, self-mockery and fun, which distances camp from its serious and political origin and renders it an anti-serious and apolitical sensibility—i.e., Sontagesque camp. Ross Chambers considers the author's work within the tradition of 'loiterature,' a genre that, she claims, is concerned with the ordinary and the trivial. In these works, the narrator or the protagonist, who is mostly a man, is depicted "as an engaging, entertaining ne'er-do-well, a descendant of the ancient *parasitus* and the early modern picaresque hero—a social misfit who...has time on his hands and uses it to explore the sensations of the present, moment by moment, to recall the experience of the past (he is a man of memory), and to write" (207). The concern with the trivial and the loitering hedonistic gay male narrator is also in accordance with the apolitical nature of the Sontagesque camp, which adds to the reification of the gay male stereotype in Hollinghurst's novels.

As for the closet, in Hollinghurst's fiction there are four main indicants: First, the male gay characters are imprisoned in a relentless search for sexual gratification in gay heterotopias; cinemas, bars, clubs, parks, public lavatories, or their home closets. Second, they still face homophobia and violence, in both psychological and physical senses. Third, they are portrayed in relationship chains where one sleeps around and can never achieve satisfaction. Finally, they all deal with cliché gay jobs tailored for them by the prejudiced heterosexist society or they simply do not have to earn a living as they just idle about and live off other men.

Hollinghurst's novels are reflections of the conflicts and ambiguities which gay individuals experienced in England in the 1980s. The 1980s was a period of oscillations, contradictions and attempts to find a midway. The move toward privatisation and free-market economy gave the gay community power and recognition to some extent. Homosexuality was decriminalised in this period and there were even gay ministers in the cabinet, which proved that Thatcher's administration was not homophobic. Nevertheless, the addition of Section 28, which involved the prohibition of the promotion of homosexuality, disappointed and confused gay individuals harming their trust in the government.

The confusing and ironic attitude towards homosexuality underlies in all four novels of Alan Hollinghurst. He is, after all, a gay novelist who experienced the life in London in the 1980s and his first novel *The Swimming Pool Library* was published in the year when Thatcher's government enacted Clause 28. Despite the law, Thatcher was not totally homophobic. The government's move toward the privatisation of formerly state-owned enterprise was an opportunity for wealthy individuals, including the stigmatised or marginalised homosexual people as well as the racial, ethnic or any other minority groups. Duff uses Wani, in *The Line of Beauty*, as an example to reveal the irony of the situation, who, as an immigrant, was given access to become a member of the Conservative upper class especially thanks to his closeting his sexual orientation by using a cover fiancée. In fact, "material wealth allows Wani and his family to overcome the kinds of ethnic roadblocks that Stuart Hall wrestles with, while Nick's obvious homosexual identity relegates him to be the perpetual 'guest' despite being from an 'English' family from the country"

(186). Through his fiction, Hollinghurst reveals the socio-political contradictions of the period, which is quite similar to what Oscar Wilde did under the rule of another matriarch. Wilde depicts the other Victorians with all their extremities, yet this portrayal of the existence of campy life does not question or subvert the bourgeois values and heteronormativity. Likewise, Hollinghurst represents the late-twentieth-century camp and closet in England, especially under the rule of Thatcher and Blair. However, his depiction represents only one leg of the conventional homosexual / heterosexual binary and it excludes the heterosexual world. Moreover, it does not queer, challenge, or subvert heteronormative values; instead, his fiction represents minoritising view of homosexuality as he employs the problematic and reductive representations of gay subjectivities in 1980s Conservative Britain. The campy group of characters portrayed by the author forms a minority group with a distinct identity and subculture to be exploited. The gay heterotopias springing up are nothing but the commodification of same-sex desire and the tolerance to the existence of such heterotopias of deviation is a consequence of the new understanding of consumerism and national identity resulting from the neoliberal and privatising policies which were introduced by Thatcher's government. The two-faced approach and attitude to the homosexual is in line with Thatcher's own ambiguous and confusing attitude; the conflict or contradiction between her private self, which was apparently not homophobic, and her public persona, which was under constant gaze and was supposed to be homophobic in Conservative England. Hollinghurst's fiction is an embodiment of the contradictions of the period and of Thatcher herself; this is why one can find not only camp but also closet in his four novels.

As a result of the consumerism and privatisation in England in the 1980s, sociopolitical contradictions emerged related to the status and deployment of the marginalised minorities. The deployment of homosexuality is also related to the transforming ideas of public and private ownership, and public and private space. With privatisation, public places turned into privately owned places serving public, culminating in private public –or public private—spaces. However, with the privatisation of British identity and spaces, homosexual identity was also privatised and was closeted in privatised heterotopias of deviation, which frequently appear in Hollinghurst's novels in form of Formal Public Sex Contexts such as gay bars, cinemas and clubs or Informal ones such as parks, gardens and public conveniences, which serve the campy white upper class homosexual mainly.

David analyses the outrageous consumerism sweeping through the 1980s and argues that in the early 80s gay individuals prospered as much as their straight equivalents. For him, it was an era of "boom and buoyant property prices — of well-paid 'service industry' jobs in estate agency, retailing, the music business; of holidays in Sitges or Playa del Inglés arranged by the gay tour company Uranian Travel; of 'tasteful' dats furnished from Peter Jones and the Habitat catalogue. Style was all; details were important" (253). This is the social, political and economic atmosphere which constitutes the background in Hollinghurst's four novels and the atmosphere creates the obligation to camp for gay individuals. To exist and gain public acceptance, the homosexual had to use their social or economic status. When Labour Party and Blair came to power in England in 1990, Hollinghurst continued employing the 1980 London as his setting because he was disappointed and disillusioned with the new political term. Therefore, "writing during Blair's cabinet in 2004, Hollinghurst takes aim at the ways Thatcherite policies of privatization, immigration, social reform, centralization, and issues around gay rights still haunt British culture" (Duff 195).

Foucault implies the ironic interaction between camp and closet, though he does not name it, by suggesting that discourse produces and transmits power but it exposes and undermines it at the same time:

> There is no question that the appearance in nineteenth-century psychiatry, jurisprudence, and literature of a whole series of discourses on the species and subspecies of homosexuality, inversion, pederasty, and "psychic hermaphrodism" made possible a strong advance of social controls into this area of "perversity"; but it also made possible the formation of a "reverse" discourse: homosexuality began to speak in its own behalf, to demand that its legitimacy or "naturality" be acknowledged, often in the same vocabulary, using the same categories by which it was medically disqualified. There is not, on the one side, a discourse of power, and opposite it, another discourse that runs counter to it. (*Sexuality* 1: 101)

Foucault's analysis of the overlapping spaces of anti-gay and pro-gay discourses is significant in the analysis of camp and closet in Hollinghurst's work. It provides an insight into the contradictory status of the homosexual during Thatcher's administration. Homosexuality was, on the one hand, decriminalised and gay individuals were allowed to have social, economic, and/or political power. On the other hand, under the same government, gay individuals were threatened and marginalised as seen in the acceptance of Section 28.

As a consequence of the affinities between the period he lived in and his four novels, both camp and closet are observed in the four novels written by Hollinghurst, who could not keep away from the socio-political atmosphere of the era. Brookes includes Hollinghurst on his list of the first generation of post-Stonewall gay novelists and contrasts these writers to the post-AIDS period gay fiction writers, who do not confine themselves to gay-themed fiction and the experiences of gay characters only (191). These writers extend the boundaries of gay fiction and do not limit themselves to heteronormative clichés about homosexuality. However, Hollinghurst, though still a productive author, cannot go beyond the established norms and representations of the campy, closeted, and self-closeting homosexual. His fiction is within the domain of the *logos*, and thus, it follows the restrictive and prescriptive notion of a heteronormative centre, which a gay male author writing about the gay experience with an alleged gay perspective is expected to challenge and undermine. It is not a concern of Hollinghurst's to investigate into how meanings, origins and truths are produced. Instead of questioning and posing a challenge to the Truth, he seems to prefer being in the true without attempting to problematise or redefine it. For this reason, he may be considered totally political in terms of phallogocentrism, whereas he remains apolitical regarding queer movement and expectations. His novels, in other words, satisfy and affirm the dominant logocentric discourses and this may be a factor underlying his being awarded the Somerset Maugham Award for *The Swimming Pool Library* in 1989, the James Tait Black Memorial Prize for fiction with *The Folding Star* in 1994, and the Man Booker Prize for *The Line of Beauty* in 2004. Rather than subverting the minoritising view of the gay male and problematising such identity categories as homosexual, bisexual, top and bottom, he disregards the existence of the dominant ideology, along with its end product heteronormativity, and creates a hetero-utopia, which is far from being realistic. Due to the hetero-utopia he cretaes, his narrative dehistoricises and universalises the minoritising view of the gay male subject. Moreover, he depicts phallogocentric relations among his male gay characters, which culminates in his remaining imprisoned in the binary trap, and his narrative fails to address specificity and subjectivity, which are ontological issues pertaining to the reified gay male identity and subculture. By looking at these features of Hollinghurst's use of camp and closet, this monograph comes to the conclusion that Hollinghurst does not write with a queer approach or narrative style but remains within the heteronormative framework. However, his work is significant among the first generation post-Stonewall novelists as it is almost a declaration of the end of coming-out novels of the mid-twentieth century which were no more than the gay versions of the bildungsroman. In his dissertation, Hollinghurst studied

Hartley, Forster and Firbank, who wrote when they were not allowed to write about homosexuality. Alderson states that "[d]espite obvious differences, these figures are very much the literary and ideological antecedents of Hollinghurst's work, informing his perspective on history, sexual identification and subcultural life" (30). The only distinction between the work of these novelists and Hollinghurst's fiction is quite similar to the one between homophile movements and gay liberation movements; whereas the former was based on the principle of similarity since it aimed to present an acceptable image of the homosexual within the heteronormative framework, the latter antagonised and disturbed the society highlighting the difference. In Hollinghurst's work, the gay male characters' self-recognition, coming to terms with their sexual orientation and identity, and their coming-out processes are not major themes. Instead, the characters enjoy the freedom granted mainly in the designated gay heterotopias and sometimes outside their closets, which may give the heterosexist reader a piece of *jouissance*. Thus, Hollinghurst's fiction does not have a queer approach and it cannot be regarded as a part of queer movement, yet it could be taken as a result and celebration of gay liberation movements in that it depicts and recognises the existence of a distinct gay male identity with a distinct subculture; and even though it does not subvert sexual identity categories, it does invert the traditional heterosexual / homosexual binary, naturalising and foregrounding the formerly shadowy leg.

BIBLIOGRAPHY

Primary Sources

Hollinghurst, Alan. *The Folding Star*. New York : Bloomsbury, 2005.
—. *The Line of Beauty: A Novel*. New York : Bloomsbury, 2005.
—. *The Spell*. London: Chatto & Windus, 1998.
—. *The Swimming-Pool Library*. London : Penguin Books, 1988.

Secondary Sources

Adam, Barry D. "From Liberation to Transgression and Beyond: Gay, Lesbian, and Queer Studies at the Turn of the 21st Century." *Handbook of Lesbian and Gay Studies*. Richardson, Diane and Steven Seidman, eds. London: Thousand Oaks, 2002.
Alderson, David. "Desire as Nostalgia: The Novels of Alan Hollinghurst." *Territories of Desire in Queer Culture: Refiguring Contemporary Boundaries*. David Alderson and Linda Anderson, eds. Manchester: Manchester UP, 2000.
Babuscio, Jack. "The Cinema of Camp (*aka* Camp and the gay Sensibility)." *Camp: Queer Aesthetics and the Performing Subject*. Fabio Cleto, ed. Edinburgh: Edinburgh UP, 1999.
Barnard, Ian. *Queer Race: Cultural Interventions in the Racial Politics of Queer Theory*. New York : Peter Lang, 2004.
Barry, Peter. "Lesbian/gay criticism." *Beginning Theory: An Introduction to Literary and Cultural Theory*. Manchester: Manchester UP, 2002.
Barthes, Roland. *Mythologies*. New York: The Noonday Press, 1991.
—. *S/Z*. Richard Miller, trans. Oxford: Blackwell, 2002.
Bernstein, Jeanne Wolff. "Love, Desire, Jouissance: Two out of Three Ain't Bad." *Psychoanalytic Dialogues*. 16(6) pp711-724, 2006. The Analytic Press, Inc.
Bersani, Leo. *Homos*. Cambridge: Harvard UP, 1996.
Boggis, Terry. "Affording Our Families." *Queer Families Queer Politics: Challenging Culture and the State*. Bernstein, Mary and Renate Reimann, eds. New York: Columbia UP, 2001.

Booth, Mark. "Campe-*toi!*: On the Origins and Definitions of Camp." Camp: *Queer Aesthetics and the Performing Subject*. Fabio Cleto, ed. Edinburgh: Edinburgh UP, 1999.
Bristow, Joseph. "Gay, lesbian, bisexual, queer and transgender criticism." *The Cambridge History of Literary Criticism: Twentieth-Century Historical, Philosophical and Psychological Perspectives*. Knellwolf, Christa and Christopher Norris, eds. Cambridge: Cambridge UP, 2001.
Britton, Andrew. "For Interpretation: Notes against Camp." Camp: *Queer Aesthetics and the Performing Subject*. Fabio Cleto, ed. Edinburgh: Edinburgh UP, 1999.
Brookes, Les. *Gay Male Fiction Since Stonewall: Ideology, Conflict, and Aesthetics*. New York: Routledge, 2009.
Brown, Michael P. Closet *Space: Geographies of Metaphor from the Body to the Globe*. London: Routledge, 2000.
Bruhm, Steven. *Reflecting Narcissus: A Queer Aesthetic*. Minneapolis: The University of Minnesota Press, 2001.
Butler, Judith. *Bodies that Matter: On the Discursive Limits of 'Sex'*. New York: Routledge, 1993.
—. *Excitable Speech: A politics of the Performative*. London: Routledge, 1997.
—. *Gender Trouble: Feminism and the Subversion of Identity*. London: Routledge, 2002.
—. "From Interiority to Gender Performatives." Cleto, Fabio, ed. Camp: *Queer Aesthetics and the Performing Subject: A Reader*. Edinburgh: Edinburgh University Press, 1999.
Calhoun, Cheshire. *Feminism, the Family, and the Politics of the* Closet: *Lesbian and Gay Displacement*. New York: Oxford U.P., 2000.
Capote, Truman. "Camp." *Encyclopedia of Gay and Lesbian popular Culture*. Luca Prono, ed. Westport: Greenwood, 2008.
Case, Sue-Ellen. "Toward a Butch-Femme Aesthetic." Camp: *Queer Aesthetics and the Performing Subject*. Fabio Cleto, ed. Edinburgh: Edinburgh UP, 1999.
Chambers, David L. "What if? The Legal Consequences of Marriage and the Legal Needs of Lesbian and Gay Male Couples." *Queer Families Queer Politics: Challenging Culture and the State*. Bernstein, Mary and Renate Reimann, eds. New York: Columbia UP, 2001.
Chambers, Ross. "Messing Around: Gayness and Loiterature in Alan Hollinghurst's *The Swimming-Pool Library*." *Textuality and Sexuality: Reading Theories and Practices*. Judith Still and Michael Worton, eds. Manchester: Manchester UP, 1993.

Cleto, Fabio, ed. Camp: *Queer Aesthetics and the Performing Subject: A Reader.* Edinburgh: Edinburgh University Press, 2008.

Cocks, H.G. *Nameless Offences: Speaking of Male Homosexual Desire in Nineteenth-Century England.* London: I.B.Tauris Publishers, 2003.

Cohan, Steven. *Hollywood Musicals, the Film Reader.* New York: Routledge, 2007.

Colebrook, Claire. "On the Very Possibility of Queer Theory." *Deleuze and Queer Theory.* Nigianni, Chrysanthi and Merl Storr, eds. Edinburgh: Edinburgh UP, 2009.

Coleman, Brian. "Thatcher the Gay Icon." 25 June 2007. www.newstatesman.com/blogs/brian-coleman/2007/06/lady-thatcher-gay-tory. Web. 02 Dec. 2011.

Core, Philip. "From Camp: The Lie That Tells the Truth." Camp: *Queer Aesthetics and the Performing Subject.* Fabio Cleto, ed. Edinburgh: Edinburgh UP, 1999.

David, Hugh. *On Queer Street: A Social History of British Homosexuality 1895-1995.* London: HarperCollins Publishers, 1997.

Dollimore, Jonathan. *Sexual Dissidence: Augustine to Wilde, Freud to Foucault.* Oxford: Oxford UP, 1991.

Dollimore, Jonathan. "Post/modern: On the Gay Sensibility, or the Pervert's Revenge on Authenticity." Cleto, Fabio, ed. Camp: *Queer Aesthetics and the Performing Subject: A Reader.* Edinburgh: Edinburgh University Press, 1999.

Duff, Kim. "Let's Dance: The Line of Beauty and the Revenant Figure of Thatcher." *Thatcher & After Margaret Thatcher and Her Afterlife in Contemporary Culture.* Hadley, Louisa and Elizabeth Ho, eds. London: Palgrave Macmillan, 2010.

Doty, Alexander. "There's Something Queer Here." *Out in Culture.* Creekmur, Corey K. and Alexander Doty, eds. London: Duke UP, 1995.

Dyer, Richard. "It's Being So Camp As Keeps Us Going." Cleto, Fabio, ed. Camp: *Queer Aesthetics and the Performing Subject: A Reader.* Edinburgh: Edinburgh University Press, 1999.

Eadie, William F. "In Plain Sight: Gay and Lesbian Communication and Culture." *Intercultural Communication: A Reader.* Larry A. Samovar, et al. Boston: Wadsworth Cengage Learning, 2009.

Edwards, Tim. *Erotics & Politics: Gay Male Sexuality, Masculinity and Feminism.* London: Routledge, 1994.

Escoffier, Jeffrey. *American Homo: Community and Perversity.* Berkeley: University of California Press, 1998.

Eskridge, William, N. *Gaylaw: Challenging the Apartheid of the* Closet. Massachusetts: Harvard UP, 2002.
Finch, Mark. "Sex and Address in *Dynasty*." Camp: *Queer Aesthetics and the Performing Subject*. Fabio Cleto, ed. Edinburgh: Edinburgh UP, 1999.
Flinn, Caryl. "The Deaths of Camp." Cleto, Fabio, ed. Camp: *Queer Aesthetics and the Performing Subject: A Reader.* Edinburgh: Edinburgh University Press, 1999.
Fortier, Anne-Marie. "Queer Diaspora." *Handbook of Lesbian and Gay Studies*. Richardson, Diane and Steven Seidman, eds. London; Thousand Oaks, 2002.
Foucault, Michel. *The History of Sexuality: Volume I: An Introduction.* New York: Vintage, 1990.
—. *The Use of Pleasure: The History of Sexuality: Volume II.* New York: Vintage, 1990.
—. *The Care of the Self: The History of Sexuality Volume III.* London: Penguin, 1990.
—. "Of Other Spaces." www.jstor.org/stable/464648, Spring 1986. Web. 12.10.2011.
Hall, Donald E. *Transitions: Queer Theories.* New York: Palgrave Macmillan, 2003.
Halperin, David. M. *Saint Foucault: Towards a Gay Hagiography.* Oxford: Oxford UP, 1995.
Higgins, Patrick. *A Queer Reader: 2500 Years of Male Homosexuality.* New York: The New Press, 1998.
Hollinghurst, Alan. Interview by Stephen Moss. *I Don't Make Moral Judgements*. The Guardian 21 Oct 2004. Print.
Homer, Sean. *Jacques Lacan*. New York: Routledge, 2005.
Ingraham, Chrys. "Heterosexuality: It's Just Not Natural." *Handbook of Lesbian and Gay Studies*. Diane Richardson and Steven Seidman, eds. London; Thousand Oaks, 2002.
Isherwood, Christopher. *The World in the Evening*. London: Methuen, 1954.
Jenness, Valerie and Kimberly D. Richman. "Anti-Gay and Lesbian Violence and Its Discontents." Richardson, Diane and Steven Seidman, eds. *Handbook of Lesbian and Gay Studies*. London; Thousand Oaks, 2002.
Jagose, Annamarie. *Queer Theory: An Introduction*. New York : New York UP, 1996.

Kanazawa, Satoshi. "Why Intelligent People Use More Drugs: Intelligent People Don't Always Do the Right Thing." Psychologytoday.com, 31 Oct, 2010. Web. 11 Aug 2011.

Lacan, Jacques. *Écrits*. Bruce Fink, trans. New York: W. W. Norton & Company, 2006.

Mellard, James M. *Using Lacan, Reading Fiction*. Urbana: Illinois, 1991.

Merriam-Webster's Collegiate Dictionary. Springfield: Merriam-Webster, 2008.

Meyer, Moe, ed. *The Politics and Poetics of* Camp. London: Routledge, 1994.

Miceli, Melinda S. "Gay, Lesbian and Bisexual Youth." *Handbook of Lesbian and Gay Studies*. Diane Richardson and Steven Seidman, eds. London; Thousand Oaks, 2002.

Moon, Dawne. "Religious Views of Homosexuality." *Handbook of Lesbian and Gay Studies*. Diane Richardson and Steven Seidman, eds. London; Thousand Oaks, 2002.

Morrill, Cynthia. "Revamping the Gay Sensibility: Queer Camp and Dyke Noir." *The Politics and Poetics of* Camp. Moe Meyer, ed. London: Routledge, 1994.

Nardi, Peter M. "The Mainstreaming of Lesbian and Gay Studies." *Handbook of Lesbian and Gay Studies*. Diane Richardson and Steven Seidman, eds. London; Thousand Oaks, 2002.

Pellegrini, Ann. "After Sontag: Future Notes on Camp." *A Companion to Lesbian, Gay, Bisexual, Transgender, and Queer Studies*. Haggerty, George E. And Molly McGarry, eds. Oxford, Blackwell, 2007.

Piggford, George. "'Who's That Girl?' Annie Lennox, Woolf's *Orlando*, and Female Camp Androgyny." Cleto, Fabio, ed. *Camp: Queer Aesthetics and the Performing Subject: A Reader*. Edinburgh: Edinburgh University Press, 1999.

Plato. *The Symposium*. M. C. Howatson, trans. Cambridge: Cambridge UP, 2008.

Restuccia, Frances L. "Graham Greene's Lacanian Encore : *The End of the Affair*." *Religion and the Arts*. 7:4 2003 pp369-387. Brill Academic Publishers, Inc., Boston.

Richardson, Diane and Steven Seidman, eds. *Handbook of Lesbian and Gay Studies*. London; Thousand Oaks, 2002.

Ringer, R. Jeffrey. "Constituting Nonmonogamies." *Queer Families Queer Politics: Challenging Culture and the State*. Bernstein, Mary and Renate Reimann, eds. New York: Columbia UP, 2001.

Robertson, Pamela. "What Makes the Feminist Camp?" Cleto, Fabio, ed. *Camp: Queer Aesthetics and the Performing Subject: A Reader.* Edinburgh: Edinburgh University Press, 1999.

Rosenfeld, Herbert A. Steiner, John, ed. "A Clinical Approach to the Psychoanalytic Theory of the Life and Death Instincts: An Investigation into the Aggressive Aspects of Narcissism." *Rosenfeld in Retrospect.* East Sussex: Routledge, 2008.

Ross, Andrew. "Uses of Camp." Cleto, Fabio, ed. *Camp: Queer Aesthetics and the Performing Subject: A Reader.* Edinburgh: Edinburgh University Press, 1999.

Ruffolo, David V. *Post-Queer Politics: Queer Interventions.* Surrey: Ashgate, 2009.

Sedgwick, Eve Kosofsky. *Epistemology of the Closet.* California: California UP, 1990.

Sontag, Susan. "Notes on 'Camp.'" *Camp: Queer Aesthetics and the Performing Subject.* Fabio Cleto, ed. Edinburgh: Edinburgh UP, 1999.

Sullivan, Nikki. *A Critical Introduction to Queer Theory.* New York: NYUP, 2003.

Summers, Claude J. *Gay Fictions: Wilde to Stonewall: Studies in a Male Homosexual Literary Tradition.* NewYork: Continuum, 1990.

Tourage, Mahdi. *Rūmī and the Hermeneutics of Eroticism.* Leiden: Brille, 2007.

Turner, William B. *A Genealogy of Queer Theory.* Philadelphia : Temple UP, 2000.

Walters, Suzanna Danuta. "Take My Domestic Partner, Please: Gays and Marriage in the Era of the Visible." *Queer Families Queer Politics: Challenging Culture and the State.* Bernstein, Mary and Renate Reimann, eds. New York: Columbia UP, 2001.

Waugh, Patricia. *Literary Theory and Criticism: An Oxford Guide.* Oxford: Oxford UP, 2006.

Wilchins, Riki. *Queer Theory, Gender Theory: An Instant Primer.* LA: Alyson Pub, 2004.